Spanish for Employers

William C. Harvey, M.S.

BARRON'S

All inquiries should be addressed to:
Barron's Educational Series, Inc.
250 Wireless Boulevard
Hauppauge, NY 11788
www.barronseduc.com

ISBN-13: 978-0-7641-4078-5 (book only)
ISBN-10: 0-7641-4078-7 (book only)
ISBN-13: 978-0-7641-9540-2 (book and CD package)
ISBN-10: 0-7641-9540-9 (book and CD package)

Library of Congress Catalog Card Number: 2008938823

PRINTED IN THE UNITED STATES OF AMERICA

9 8 7 6 5 4 3 2 1

Contents

Before You Begin

A NOTE FROM THE AUTHOR

Spanish for Employers teaches English-speaking employers how to understand and speak to their Spanish-speaking employees. This book provides readers with all the Spanish vocabulary and phrases that are needed to interview, train, counsel, and discharge employees, as well as converse socially about life and everyday activities. To accelerate the process, all Spanish language skills are taught gradually, and reinforced systematically through practice and review.

Pronunciation in English follows every Spanish word, and the most frequently used terminology is strategically placed for quick reference and review. At the end of the book, you will find a variety of support material along with an English-to-Spanish glossary.

Please note that the book focuses on formal ways of communication (the **usted** form). Although the familiar way of addressing anyone with the Spanish **tú** may at times seem friendly and informal, all too often it can be interpreted as overbearing.

TEACHING SEGMENTS

This book provides readers with the following teaching segments, which are scattered throughout the text:

Extra Info!
(Information, tips, and suggestions)

The Culture!
(Insights on Hispanic cultural awareness)

Action Words!
(Spanish infinitives and commands)

Verbs!
(Basic Spanish verb tenses)

Let's Practice
(Review practice exercises)

Chapter One

Basic Skills
Las habilidades básicas
(lahs ah-bee-lee-'dah-dehs 'bah-see-kahs)

Pronunciation
La pronunciación *(lah proh-noon-see-ah-see-'ohn)*

You only need to remember <u>five</u> sounds in order to speak well enough to be understood. These are the vowels, and unlike their English equivalents, each one is pronounced the way it is written. Read each letter aloud, and follow the corresponding pronunciation guide.

a (*ah*) as in *yacht*
e (*eh*) as in *met*
i (*ee*) as in *keep*
o (*oh*) as in *open*
u (*oo*) as in *tool*

Here's how you pronounce the rest of the letters:

Spanish letter	English sound
c (after *e* or *i*)	s as in *sit* (**cilantro**)
g (after *e* or *i*)	h as in *hop* (**general**)
h	silent, like k in *knife* (**hombre**)
j	h as in *hat* (**José**)
ll	y as in *yes* (**tortilla**)
ñ	ny as in *canyon* (**señorita**)
qu	k as in *kit* (**tequila**)
rr	the "rolled" r sound (**carro**)
z	s as in *son* (**zapato**)

Although some dialects may vary slightly, the rest of the letters in Spanish are similar to their equivalents in English:

b	**bueno**
d	**dinero**
f	**fiesta**
l	**loco**
m	**mucho**
n	**nada**
p	**pronto**
r	**tres**
s	**sí**
t	**taco**
v	**avispa**
x	**México**

Extra Info!
¡Más información! *(mahs een-fohr-mah-see-'ohn)*

Any part of a word with an accent mark (´) needs to be pronounced LOUDER and with more emphasis (e.g., María). If there's no accent mark, say the last part of the word louder and with more emphasis (e.g., Bea**triz**). For words ending in a vowel, or in **n** or **s**, the next to the last part of the word is stressed (e.g., Ar**tu**ro). Remember also, that in some cases, the letter **u** doesn't make the *oo* sound (e.g., guitarra [*gee-táhr-rah*], guerra [*géhr-rah*]).

Let's Practice
¡Vamos a practicar! *('vah-mohs ah prahk-tee-'kahr)*

Every time you see a number inside a circle, check the Answer Keys beginning on page 274.

Read the following words aloud, and then guess at their meanings:

televisión	mañana	vertical	burro
problema	favorito	amigo	excelente

Common Expressions
Las expresiones comunes
(lahs ex-preh-see-'oh-nehs koh-'moo-nehs)

Use these common expressions to practice Spanish pronunciation. Notice how they are grouped for easy practice around the workplace:

Please.	**Por favor.** *(pohr fah-'vohr)*
Thank you very much.	**Muchas gracias.** *('moo-chahs 'grah-see-ahs)*
You're welcome.	**De nada.** *(deh 'nah-dah)*
Hi!	**¡Hola!** *('oh-lah)*
Good morning.	**Buenas días.** *('bweh-nohs 'dee-ahs)*
Good afternoon.	**Buenas tardes.** *('bweh-nahs 'tahr-dehs)*
Good evening.	**Buenas noches.** *('bweh-nahs 'noh-chehs)*
Good-bye!	**¡Adiós!** *(ah-dee-'ohs)*
See you later!	**¡Hasta luego!** *('ahs-tah 'lweh-goh)*
How are you?	**¿Cómo está?** *('koh-moh ehs-'tah)*
Very well.	**Muy bien.** *('moo-ee bee-'ehn)*
What's going on?	**¿Qué pasa?** *(keh 'pah-sah)*
Nothing much!	**¡Sin novedad!** *(seen noh-veh-'dahd)*
And you?	**¿Y usted?** *(ee oos-'tehd)*
How's it going?	**¡Qué tal!** *(keh tahl)*
So-so.	**Así-así.** *(ah-'see ah-'see)*
What's your name?	**¿Cómo se llama?** *('koh-moh seh 'yah-mah)*
My name is...	**Me llamo...** *(meh 'yah-moh)*
Nice to meet you!	**¡Mucho gusto!** *('moo-choh 'goos-toh)*
Same to you.	**Igualmente.** *(ee-gwahl-'mehn-teh)*
Excuse me.	**Con permiso.** *(kohn pehr-'mee-soh)*
Just a moment.	**Un momento.** *(oon moh-'mehn-toh)*
Go ahead!	**¡Pase!** *('pah-seh)*
I'm sorry.	**Lo siento.** *(loh see-'ehn-toh)*
May I come in?	**¿Se puede?** *(seh 'pweh-deh)*
Yes!	**¡Sí!** *(see)*
Come in!	**¡Adelante!** *(ah-deh-'lahn-teh)*
Pardon me.	**Perdón.** *(pehr-'dohn)*

Welcome!	**¡Bienvenidos!** *(bee-ehn-veh-'nee-dohs)*
Congratulations!	**¡Felicitaciones!** *(feh-lee-see-tah-see-'oh-nehs)*
Good luck!	**¡Buena suerte!** *('bweh-nah soo-'ehr-teh)*
Have a nice day!	**¡Que le vaya bien!** *(keh leh 'vah-yah bee-'ehn)*
Have a nice trip!	**¡Buen viaje!** *(bwehn vee-'ah-heh)*
Have a good time!	**¡Que disfrute!** *(keh dees-'froo-teh)*
Give my regards to...	**Me saluda a...** *(meh sah-'loo-dah ah)*

All the better!	**¡Tanto mejor!** *('tahn-toh meh-'hohr)*
Good idea!	**¡Buena idea!** *('bweh-nah ee-'deh-ah)*
It doesn't matter!	**¡No importa!** *(noh eem-'pohr-tah)*
Maybe!	**¡Quizas!** *(kee-'sahs)*
More or less!	**¡Más o menos!** *(mahs oh 'meh-nohs)*
No wonder!	**¡Con razón!** *(kohn rah-'sohn)*
Of course!	**¡Por supuesto!** *(pohr soo-poo-'ehs-toh)*
Really?	**¿Verdad?** *(vehr-'dahd)*
That depends!	**¡Depende!** *(deh-'pehn-deh)*
That's for sure!	**¡Es cierto!** *(ehs see-'ehr-toh)*
That's OK!	**¡Está bien!** *(ehs-'tah bee-'ehn)*
Sure!	**¡Claro!** *('klah-roh)*
I agree!	**¡De acuerdo!** *(deh ah-'kwehr-doh)*
I hope so!	**¡Ojalá!** *(oh-hah-'lah)*
I see!	**¡Ya veo!** *(yah 'veh-oh)*
I'm so glad!	**¡Me alegro!** *(meh ah-'leh-groh)*
I think so!	**¡Creo que sí!** *('kreh-oh keh see)*
I remember!	**¡Yo recuerdo!** *(yoh reh-'kwehr-doh)*
Me, neither!	**¡Yo tampoco!** *(yoh tahm-'poh-koh)*
Me, too!	**¡Yo también!** *(yoh tahm-bee-'ehn)*

Extra Info!

See how the word **Qué** (how) can be used in the expressions below:

How sad!	**¡Qué triste!** *(keh 'trees-teh)*
So what!	**¡Qué importa!** *(keh eem-'pohr-tah)*
What a shame!	**¡Qué lástima!** *(keh 'lahs-tee-mah)*
That's great!	**¡Qué bueno!** *(keh 'bweh-noh)*

Combine your Spanish words with *y* (and), *o* (or), and *pero* (but):

Juan y María comen tacos o enchiladas, pero no comen frijoles.
('hwahn ee mah-'ree-ah 'koh-mehn 'tah-kohs oh ehn-chee-'lah-dahs 'peh-roh noh 'koh-mehn free-'hoh-lehs)
Juan **and** María eat tacos **or** enchiladas, **but** they don't eat beans.

The Culture!
La cultura
(lah kool-'too-rah)

Latin America is predominantly Catholic, and several common expressions include the word God, or **Dios** *(dee-'ohs)*:

God willing!	**¡Que Dios quiera!** *(keh dee-'ohs kee-'eh-rah)*
Oh my gosh!	**¡Dios mío!** *(dee-'ohs 'mee-oh)*
Thank goodness!	**¡Gracias a Dios!** *('grah-see-ahs ah dee-'ohs)*
Go with God!	**¡Vaya con Dios!** *('vah-yah kohn dee-'ohs)*
God bless you!	**¡Dios le bendiga!** *(dee-'ohs leh behn-'dee-gah)*

Commands*
Las órdenes
(lahs 'ohr-deh-nehs)

Commands are considered expressions, too. This is a collection of one-word command phrases:

Walk!	**¡Camine!** *(kah-'mee-neh)*
Write!	**¡Escriba!** *(ehs-'kree-bah)*
Run!	**¡Corra!** *('kohr-rah)*
Read!	**¡Lea!** *('leh-ah)*
Go!	**¡Vaya!** *('vah-yah)*
Come!	**¡Venga!** *('vehn-gah)*
Leave!	**¡Salga!** *('sahl-gah)*
Answer!	**¡Conteste!** *(kohn-'tehs-teh)*
Sign!	**¡Firme!** *('feer-meh)*
Work!	**¡Trabaje!** *(trah-'bah-heh)*

*For a more extensive list of employer commands, see the back of the book.

Employers spend much of their time giving instructions or telling employees what to do. Notice the different ways you can create a simple command in Spanish:

Bring it to me!	**¡Tráigamelo!** *('trah-ee-gah-meh-loh)*
Take a seat.	**Tome un asiento.** *('toh-meh oon ah-see-'ehn-toh)*
No smoking, please.	**Favor de no fumar.** *(fah-'vohr deh noh foo-'mahr)*
Close the door.	**Cierre la puerta.** *(see-'eh-rreh lah 'pwehr-tah)*
Let's get to work!	**¡Vamos a trabajar!** *('vah-mohs ah trah-bah-'hahr)*

As we mentioned at the beginning of the book, all commands in this book are formal. Experience tells us that conflict may arise when some people feel that they are treated a bit too informally.

Do You Understand?
¿Entiende usted?
(ehn-tee-'ehn-deh oos-'tehd)

The following one-liners will help when there is a breakdown in communication:

Again, please.
Otra vez, por favor. *('oh-trah vehs pohr fah-'vohr)*

I don't know.
No sé. *(noh seh)*

I don't understand.
No entiendo. *(noh ehn-tee-'ehn-doh)*

I speak a little Spanish.
Hablo poquito español. *('ah-bloh poh-'kee-toh ehs-pahn-'yohl)*

I'm learning Spanish.
Estoy aprendiendo español. *(ehs-'toh-ee ah-prehn-dee-'ehn-doh ehs-pahn-'yohl)*

More slowly.
Más despacio. *(mahs dehs-'pah-see-oh)*

What does it mean?
¿Qué significa? *(keh seeg-nee-'fee-kah)*

Thanks for your patience.
Gracias por su paciencia. *('grah-see-ahs pohr soo pah-see-'ehn-see-ah)*

Do you need an interpreter?
¿Necesita un intérprete? *(neh-seh-'see-tah oon een-'tehr-preh-teh)*

How do you spell it?
¿Cómo se deletrea? *('koh-moh seh deh-leh-'treh-ah)*

Please write it down.
Por favor, escríbalo. *(pohr fah-'vohr ehs-'kree-bah-loh)*

How do you say it?
¿Cómo se dice? *('koh-moh seh 'dee-seh)*

Say it in English.
Dígalo en inglés. *('dee-gah-loh ehn een-'glehs)*

Letter by letter.
Letra por letra. *('leh-trah pohr 'leh-trah)*

Number by number.
Número por número. *('noo-meh-roh pohr 'noo-meh-roh)*

Word for word.
Palabra por palabra. *(pah-'lah-brah pohr pah-'lah-brah)*

 ## Let's Practice (2)

Connect each phrase with its appropriate response:

1. ¿Cómo está?	Adiós.
2. Gracias.	No, lo siento.
3. ¿Entiende?	De nada.
4. Hasta luego.	Bien. ¿Y usted?
5. ¿Qué pasa?	Sin novedad.

Basic Vocabulary
El vocabulario básico
(ehl voh-kah-boo-'lah-ree-oh 'bah-see-koh)

You'll get nowhere without the following vocabulary items, so work on this set before anything else:

bathroom	**el baño** *(ehl 'bahn-yoh)*
book	**el libro** *(ehl 'leeb-roh)*
car	**el carro** *(ehl 'kahr-roh)*
chair	**la silla** *(lah 'see-yah)*
clothing	**la ropa** *(lah 'roh-pah)*
door	**la puerta** *(lah 'pwehr-tah)*
floor	**el piso** *(ehl 'pee-soh)*
food	**la comida** *(lah koh-'mee-dah)*
house	**la casa** *(lah 'kah-sah)*
light	**la luz** *(lah loos)*
money	**el dinero** *(ehl dee-'neh-roh)*
paper	**el papel** *(ehl pah-'pehl)*
pen	**el lapicero** *(ehl lah-pee-'seh-roh)*
pencil	**el lápiz** *(ehl 'lah-pees)*
people	**la gente** *(lah 'hehn-teh)*
room	**el cuarto** *(ehl 'kwahr-toh)*
table	**la mesa** *(lah 'meh-sah)*
telephone	**el teléfono** *(ehl teh-'leh-foh-noh)*
water	**el agua** *(ehl 'ah-gwah)*
work	**el trabajo** *(ehl trah-'bah-hoh)*

The Articles
Los artículos
(lohs ahr-'tee-koo-lohs)

Notice that the names for people, places, and things need the definite articles **el** (*ehl*) or **la** (*lah*) in front to indicate gender (either masculine or feminine). Here are a few guidelines:

Generally, if the word ends in the letter **o**, it's considered masculine and the "the" in front is **el** (e.g., **el cuarto** [*ehl 'kwahr-toh*], **el niño** [*ehl 'nee-nyoh*]). Conversely, if the word ends in an **a**, it's considered feminine and there's a **la** in front (e.g., **la mesa** [*lah 'meh-sah*], **la persona** [*lah pehr-'soh-nah*]). Some Spanish words are exceptions: **el agua** (*ehl 'ah-gwah*), **la mano** (*lah 'mah-noh*), **el sofá** (*ehl soh-'fah*), etc.

Words not ending in either an **o** or **a** need to be memorized (e.g., **el amor** [*ehl ah-'mohr*], **la paz** [*lah pahs*]). In the case of single objects, use **el** and **la** much like the word "the" in English:

The house is big.   **La casa es grande.** (*lah 'kah-sah ehs 'grahn-deh*).

Remember too, that **el** and **la** are used in Spanish to indicate a person's sex: **El doctor** (*ehl dohk-'tohr*) is a male doctor, while **la doctora** (*lah dohk-'toh-rah*) is a female doctor. Here's how we refer to the female gender: **la muchacha** (*lah moo-'chah-chah*), **la niña** (*lah 'nee-nyah*), **la bebé** (*lah beh-'beh*), etc.

And, when referring to more than one item in Spanish, the words **el** and **la** become **los** and **las**, respectively:

el baño	**los baños** *(lohs 'bahn-yohs)*
el muchacho	**los muchachos** *(lohs moo-'chah-chohs)*
la mesa	**las mesas** *(lahs 'meh-sahs)*
la señorita	**las señoritas** *(lahs sehn-yoh-'ree-tahs)*

Extra Info!

There are two contractions in Spanish, so blend these words together when you speak:

of or *from the*	**de + el = del** *(dehl)*
It's from the boss.	**Es del jefe.** *(ehs dehl 'heh-feh)*
to the	**a + el = al** *(ahl)*
I'm going to the bathroom.	**Voy al baño.** *('voh-ee ahl 'bahn-yoh)*

Let's Practice ③

A. Fill in the blank with an English translation:

1. el libro _____
2. la mesa _____
3. el trabajo _____

B. Now change these words from the singular to the plural form:

1. la casa _____
2. el baño _____
3. el papel _____

The Culture

Friendly greetings in Spanish are used all day long. Being courteous is the key to establishing trust with your employee. Throughout the Spanish-speaking world, a smile and a pleasant word can lead to respect and complete cooperation.

The Numbers
Los números
(lohs 'noo-meh-rohs)

Regardless of the job, every employer needs these. Keep a list of the numbers with you at all times:

0	**cero** *('seh-roh)*	14	**catorce** *(kah-'tohr-seh)*
1	**uno** *('oo-noh)*	15	**quince** *('keen-seh)*
2	**dos** *(dohs)*	16	**dieciséis** *(dee-ehs-ee-'seh-ees)*
3	**tres** *(trehs)*	17	**diecisiete** *(dee-ehs-ee-see-'eh-teh)*
4	**cuatro** *('kwah-troh)*	18	**dieciocho** *(dee-ehs-ee-'oh-choh)*
5	**cinco** *('seen-koh)*	19	**diecinueve** *(dee-ehs-ee-noo-'eh-veh)*
6	**seis** *('seh-ees)*	20	**veinte** *('veh-een-teh)*
7	**siete** *(see-'eh-teh)*	30	**treinta** *('treh-een-tah)*
8	**ocho** *('oh-choh)*	40	**cuarenta** *(kwah-'rehn-tah)*
9	**nueve** *(noo-'eh-veh)*	50	**cincuenta** *(seen-'kwehn-tah)*
10	**diez** *(dee-'ehs)*	60	**sesenta** *(seh-'sehn-tah)*
11	**once** *('ohn-seh)*	70	**setenta** *(seh-'tehn-tah)*
12	**doce** *('doh-seh)*	80	**ochenta** *(oh-'chehn-tah)*
13	**trece** *('treh-seh)*	90	**noventa** *(noh-'vehn-tah)*

For all the numbers in-between, just add **y** *(ee)*, which means "and":

21   **veinte y uno** *('veh-een-teh ee 'oo-noh)*
22   **veinte y dos** *('veh-een-teh ee dohs)*
23   **veinte y tres** *('veh-een-teh ee trehs)*

You'll also need to know how to say the larger numbers in Spanish:

100   **cien** *(se-'ehn)*
200   **doscientos** *(dohs-see-'ehn-tohs)*
300   **trescientos** *(trehs-see-'ehn-tohs)*
400   **cuatrocientos** *(kwah-troh-see-'ehn-tohs)*
500   **quinientos** *(keen-ee-'ehn-tohs)*
600   **seiscientos** *(seh-ee-see-'ehn-tohs)*
700   **setecientos** *(seh-teh-see-'ehn-tohs)*
800   **ochocientos** *(oh-choh-see-'ehn-tohs)*
900   **novecientos** *(noh-veh-see-'ehn-tohs)*
1000   **mil** *(meel)*

Extra Info!

You'll need some of the ordinal numbers also:

first	**primero** *(pree-'meh-roh)*
second	**segundo** *(seh-'goon-doh)*
third	**tercero** *(tehr-'seh-roh)*
fourth	**cuarto** *('kwahr-toh)*
fifth	**quinto** *('keen-toh)*
sixth	**sexto** *('sehks-toh)*
seventh	**séptimo** *('sehp-tee-moh)*
eighth	**octavo** *(ohk-'tah-voh)*
ninth	**noveno** *(noh-'veh-noh)*
tenth	**décimo** *('deh-see-moh)*

Descriptions
Las descripciones
(lahs dehs-kreep-see-'oh-nehs)

To learn descriptions quickly, start with those that can be grouped into pairs of opposites:

good	**bueno** *('bweh-noh)*
bad	**malo** *('mah-loh)*
big	**grande** *('grahn-deh)*
small	**chico** *('chee-koh)*
long	**largo** *('lahr-goh)*
short (in length)	**corto** *('kohr-toh)*
tall	**alto** *('ahl-toh)*
short (in height)	**bajo** *('bah-hoh)*
fat	**gordo** *('gohr-doh)*
thin	**delgado** *(dehl-'gah-doh)*

strong	**fuerte** *('fwehr-teh)*
weak	**débil** *('deh-beel)*
dirty	**sucio** *('soo-see-oh)*
clean	**limpio** *('leem-pee-oh)*
slow	**lento** *('lehn-toh)*
fast	**rápido** *('rah-pee-doh)*
easy	**fácil** *('fah-seel)*
difficult	**difícil** *(dee-'fee-seel)*
cold	**frío** *('free-oh)*
hot	**caliente** *(kah-lee-'ehn-teh)*

Read the following examples, translate, and create brief sentences with the other vocabulary you have just seen:

rich	**rico** *('ree-koh)*

El Sr. López es rico. *(ehl sehn-'yohr 'loh-pehs ehs 'ree-koh)*

poor	**pobre** *('poh-breh)*

La señora es pobre. *(lah sehn-'yoh-rah ehs 'poh-breh)*

inexpensive	**barato** *(bah-'rah-toh)*

El libro es barato. *(ehl 'lee-broh ehs bah-'rah-toh)*

expensive	**caro** *('kah-roh)*

La casa es cara. *(lah 'kah-sah ehs 'kah-rah)*

The Colors
Los colores
(lohs koh-'loh-rehs)

Speaking of descriptions, beginners in Spanish must know their colors:

black	**negro** *('neh-groh)*
blue	**azul** *(ah-'sool)*
brown	**café** *(kah-'feh)*
green	**verde** *('vehr-deh)*

orange	**anaranjado** *(ah-nah-rahn-'hah-doh)*
purple	**morado** *(moh-'rah-doh)*
red	**rojo** *('roh-hoh)*
white	**blanco** *('blahn-koh)*
yellow	**amarillo** *(ah-mah-'ree-yoh)*
gray	**gris** *(grees)*

Develop more sets of descriptive words on your own:

handsome	**guapo** *('gwah-poh)*
pretty	**bonito** *(boh-'nee-toh)*
ugly	**feo** *('feh-oh)*

new	**nuevo** *('nweh-voh)*
young	**joven** *('hoh-vehn)*
old	**viejo** *(vee-'eh-hoh)*

Let's Practice ④

A. Follow the examples:

doscientos, trescientos, <u>cuatrocientos</u>, quinientos

1. treinta, cuarenta, _____, sesenta
2. primero, segundo, tercero, _____,
3. _____, cinco, seis, siete

     I'm first.   *Soy el primero.*

4. I'm eighth.   _____

     It's green.   *Es verde.*

5. It's red.   _____

B. Now connect the words with opposite meanings:

1. alto	feo
2. malo	chico
3. bonito	corto
4. rico	bueno
5. frío	bajo
6. largo	caliente
7. grande	pobre

People
La gente
(lah 'hehn-teh)

This selection provides the names for people in Spanish:

baby	**el bebé** *(ehl beh-'beh)*
boy	**el niño** *(ehl 'neen-yoh)*
girl	**la niña** *(lah 'neen-yah)*
man	**el hombre** *(ehl 'ohm-breh)*
woman	**la mujer** *(lah moo-'hehr)*
person	**la persona** *(lah pehr-'soh-nah)*
teenager (female)	**la muchacha** *(lah moo-'chah-chah)*
teenager (male)	**el muchacho** *(ehl moo-'chah-choh)*
children	**los niños** *(lohs 'neen-yohs)*
friends	**los amigos** *(lohs ah-'mee-gohs)*
relatives	**los parientes** *(lohs pah-ree-'ehn-tehs)*

And here are the immediate family members.

brother	**el hermano** *(ehl ehr-'mah-noh)*
daughter	**la hija** *(lah 'ee-hah)*
father	**el padre** *(ehl 'pah-dreh)*
husband	**el esposo, el marido** *(ehl ehs-'poh-soh, ehl mah-'ree-doh)*
mother	**la madre** *(lah 'mah-dreh)*
sister	**la hermana** *(lah ehr-'mah-nah)*
son	**el hijo** *(ehl 'ee-hoh)*
wife	**la esposa** *(lah ehs-'poh-sah)*

These should be memorized right away:

Mr. or a man	**Señor (Sr.)** *(sehn-'yohr)*
Mrs. or a lady	**Señora (Sra.)** *(sehn-'yoh-rah)*
Miss or a young lady	**Señorita (Srta.)** *(sehn-yoh-'ree-tah)*

The Reversal Rule
La regla del reverso
(lah 'reh-glah dehl reh-'vehr-soh)

In Spanish, words are often positioned in reverse order. Generally, this reversal rule is applied when you give a description. The descriptive word usually goes after the word being described:

The white paper.
El papel blanco. *(ehl pah-'pehl 'blahn-koh)*

The important man.
El hombre importante. *(ehl 'ohm-breh eem-pohr-'tahn-teh)*

One small table.
Una mesa chica. *('oo-nah 'meh-sah 'chee-kah)*

When referring to more than one item in Spanish, all the words must then agree, that is, all the words must be in the plural form, and the genders must match as well:

Two white papers.
Dos papeles blancos. *(dohs pah-'peh-lehs 'blahn-kohs)*

Many important men.
Muchos hombres importantes. *('moo-chohs 'ohm-brehs eem-pohr-'tahn-tehs)*

Three small tables.
Tres mesas chicas. *(trehs 'meh-sahs 'chee-kahs)*

 Extra Info!

To say "a" or "an" in Spanish, use **un** or **una**, and to say "some" or "a few," use **unos** or **unas**:

A book	**Un libro** *(oon 'lee-broh)*
A blue book	**Un libro azul** *(oon 'lee-broh ah-'sool)*
A few blue books	**Unos libros azules** *('oo-nohs 'lee-brohs ah-'soo-lehs)*
A girl	**Una niña** *('oo-nah 'neen-yah)*
A pretty girl	**Una niña bonita** *('oo-nah 'neen-yah boh-'nee-tah)*
Some pretty girls	**Unas niñas bonitas** *('oo-nahs 'neen-yahs boh-'nee-tahs)*

Let's Practice (5)

Change these from the singular to the plural. Follow the example:

El carro grande   <u>Los carros grandes</u>
1. La silla amarilla   _____
2. Una señora alta   _____
3. La oficina nueva   _____
4. Un piso sucio   _____
5. El trabajo excelente   _____

The Question Words
Las preguntas
(lahs preh-'goon-tahs)

Very frequently used words in Spanish are the "question" words. Read them, read them again, and they will soon become familiar:

How?	**¿Cómo?** *('koh-moh)*
How many?	**¿Cuántos?** *('kwahn-tohs)*
How much?	**¿Cuánto?** *('kwahn-toh)*
What?	**¿Qué?** *(keh)*
When?	**¿Cuándo?** *('kwahn-doh)*
Where?	**¿Dónde?** *('dohn-deh)*
Which?	**¿Cuál?** *(kwahl)*
Who?	**¿Quién?** *(kee-'ehn)*
Whose?	**¿De quién?** *(deh kee-'ehn)*
Why?	**¿Por qué?** *(pohr keh)*

A few question words are common expressions used regularly in simple conversations. Notice how they are not always literal translations:

How's it going?	**¡Qué tal!** *(keh tahl)*
What's your name?	**¿Cómo se llama?** *('koh-moh seh 'yah-mah)*
How old are you?	**¿Cuántos años tiene?** *('kwahn-tohs 'ahn-yohs tee-'eh-neh)*
How much does it cost?	**¿Cuánto cuesta?** *('kwahn-toh 'kwehs-tah)*
Where are you from?	**¿De dónde es?** *(deh 'dohn-deh ehs)*

The Pronouns
Los pronombres
(lohs proh-'nohm-brehs)

To answer effectively questions about "who" or "whose," certain pronouns will be needed. These are the subject pronouns:

I	**Yo** *(yoh)*
We	**Nosotros** *(noh-'soh-trohs)*
You	**Usted** *(oos-'tehd)*; often written as **Ud.**
You (plural)	**Ustedes** *(oos-'teh-dehs)*; often written as **Uds.**
She	**Ella** *('eh-yah)*
He	**Él** *(ehl)*
They (feminine)	**Ellas** *('eh-yahs)*
They (masculine)	**Ellos** *('eh-yohs)*

Study these simple dialogs, but remember that you can drop the subject pronouns in these sentences if you like:

How are you?
¿Cómo está (Ud.)? *('koh-moh ehs-'tah oos-'tehd)*

I am fine.
(Yo) estoy bien. *(yoh ehs-'toh-ee bee-'ehn)*

How are you guys?
¿Cómo están (ustedes)? *('koh-moh ehs-'tahn oos-'teh-dehs)*

We are fine.
(Nosotros) estamos bien. *(noh-'soh-trohs ehs-'tah-mohs bee-'ehn)*

Now read through the possessive pronouns. Notice the sample sentences:

my	**mi, mis** *(mee, mees)*
your	**tu, tus / su, sus** *(too, toos / soo, soos)*
his	**su, sus** *(soo, soos)*
her	**su, sus** *(soo, soos)*
their	**su, sus** *(soo, soos)*
our	**nuestro, nuestros/ nuestra, nuestras** *('nwehs-troh, 'nwehs-trohs / 'nwehs-trah, 'nwehs-trahs)*

mine	**mío / mía** *('mee-oh, 'mee-ah)*
yours	**tuyo, tuyos / tuya, tuyas / suyo, suyos / suya, suyas**
	('too-yoh, 'too-yohs /'too-yah, 'too-yahs / 'soo-yoh, 'soo-yohs / 'soo-yah,
	'soo-yahs)
his	**suyo, suyos / suya, suyas** *('soo-yoh, 'soo-yohs / 'soo-yah, 'soo-yahs)*
hers	**suyo, suyos / suya, suyas** *('soo-yoh, 'soo-yohs / 'soo-ya, 'soo-yahs)*
theirs	**suyo, suyos / suya, suyas** *('soo-yoh, 'soo-yohs / 'soo-yah, 'soo-yahs)*

It's my house.	**Es mi casa.** *(ehs mee 'kah-sah)*
It's your, his, her, or their house.	**Es su casa.** *(ehs soo 'kah-sah)*
It's our house.	**Es nuestra casa.** *(ehs 'nwehs-trah 'kah-sah)*
It's mine.	**Es mía.** *(ehs 'mee-ah)*
It's hers.	**Es suya.** *(ehs 'soo-yah)*

And here's what happens when you refer to more than one:

mi casa *(mee 'kah-sah)*	**mis casas** *(mees 'kah-sahs)*
su casa *(soo 'kah-sah)*	**sus casas** *(soos 'kah-sahs)*
nuestra casa *('nweh-strah 'kah-sah)*	**nuestras casas** *('nwehs-trahs 'kah-sahs)*

If something belongs to someone else, use **de** to indicate possession:

It's Mary's.	**Es de Mary.** *(ehs deh 'mah-ree)*
It's his.	**Es de él.** *(ehs deh ehl)*

Let's Practice ⑥

A. Join the subject pronouns with their possessive forms:

1. Ella   mi
2. Yo   nuestro
3. Nosotros   su

B. Translate, and then answer each question aloud:

1. ¿Cuántos años tiene usted?   _____
2. ¿Quién es el presidente?   _____
3. ¿Cuándo es Thanksgiving?   _____

Where and When
Dónde y cuándo
(*'dohn-deh ee 'kwahn-doh*)

To answer the common question, **¿Dónde está?** (*'dohn-deh ehs-'tah,* Where is it?), simply say one or more of the following:

above	**encima** (*ehn-'see-mah*)
at the bottom	**en el fondo** (*ehn ehl 'fohn-doh*)
behind	**detrás** (*deh-'trahs*)
down	**abajo** (*ah-'bah-hoh*)
far	**lejos** (*'leh-hohs*)
here	**aquí** (*ah-'kee*)
in front	**enfrente** (*ehn-'frehn-teh*)
inside	**adentro** (*ah-'dehn-troh*)
near	**cerca** (*'sehr-kah*)
next to	**al lado** (*ahl 'lah-doh*)
outside	**afuera** (*ah-'fweh-rah*)
straight ahead	**adelante** (*ah-deh-'lahn-teh*)
there	**allí** (*ah-'yee*)
over there	**allá** (*ah-'yah*)
to the left	**a la izquierda** (*ah lah ees-kee-'ehr-dah*)
to the right	**a la derecha** (*ah lah deh-'reh-chah*)
under	**debajo** (*deh-'bah-hoh*)
up	**arriba** (*ahr-'ree-bah*)

And these are the one-word responses to the question, **¿Cuándo?** (*'kwahn-doh,* When?)

at the same time	**a la vez** (*ah lah vehs*)
after	**después** (*dehs-'pwehs*)
always	**siempre** (*see-'ehm-preh*)
before	**antes** (*'ahn-tehs*)
during	**durante** (*doo-'rahn-teh*)
early	**temprano** (*tehm-'prah-noh*)
late	**tarde** (*'tahr-deh*)
later	**luego** (*'lweh-goh*)
never	**nunca** (*'noon-kah*)
now	**ahora** (*ah-'oh-rah*)
since	**desde** (*'dehs-deh*)
sometimes	**a veces** (*ah 'veh-sehs*)

soon	**pronto** *('prohn-toh)*
then	**entonces** *(ehn-'tohn-sehs)*
today	**hoy** *(oh-ee)*
tomorrow	**mañana** *(mahn-'yah-nah)*
until	**hasta** *('ahs-tah)*
while	**mientras** *(mee-'ehn-trahs)*
yesterday	**ayer** *(ah-'yehr)*

Prepositions
Las preposiciones
(lahs preh-poh-see-see-'oh-nehs)

You will express yourself a lot better in Spanish once you acquire all the basic language words. Fill in the blanks with your own sentences, and don't worry about the spelling:

with	**con**	*Estoy con mis amigos.*
without	**sin**	*Carlos siempre está sin trabajo.*
to	**a**	*Vamos a la oficina.*
from, of	**de**	_____
in, on, at	**en**	_____
for	**para**	_____
by, through	**por**	_____
with me	**conmigo**	_____

Telling Time
Decir la hora
(deh-'seer lah 'oh-rah)

Time-telling is easy in Spanish:

| What time is it? | **¿Qué hora es?** *(keh 'oh-rah ehs)* |
| It's 7:00. | **Son las <u>siete</u>.** *(sohn lahs see-'eh-teh)* |

| At what time? | **¿A qué hora?** *(ah keh 'oh-rah)* |
| At 2:40. | **A las <u>dos y cuarenta</u>** *(ah lahs dohs ee kwah-'rehn-tah)* |

Look over these other words and phrases that refer to time-telling:

| A.M. | **de la mañana** *(deh lah mahn-'yah-nah)* |
| P.M. | **de la tarde** *(deh lah 'tahr-deh)* |

half past	**y media** *(ee 'meh-dee-ah)*
midnight	**medianoche** *(meh-dee-ah-'noh-cheh)*
noon	**mediodía** *(meh-dee-oh-'dee-ah)*
last night	**anoche** *(ah-'noh-cheh)*
an hour ago	**hace una hora** *('ah-seh 'oo-nah 'oh-rah)*

The Calendar
El calendario
(ehl kah-lehn-'dah-ree-oh)

Mark these new words on your calendar and review them every day:

DAYS OF THE WEEK **LOS DÍAS DE LA SEMANA**
(lohs 'dee-ahs deh lah seh-'mah-nah)

Monday	**lunes** *('loo-nehs)*
Tuesday	**martes** *('mahr-tehs)*
Wednesday	**miércoles** *(mee-'ehr-koh-lehs)*
Thursday	**jueves** *('hweh-vehs)*
Friday	**viernes** *(vee-'ehr-nehs)*
Saturday	**sábado** *('sah-bah-doh)*
Sunday	**domingo** *(doh-'meen-goh)*

MONTHS OF THE YEAR **LOS MESES DEL AÑO**
(lohs 'meh-sehs dehl 'ahn-yoh)

January	**enero** *(eh-'neh-roh)*
February	**febrero** *(feh-'breh-roh)*
March	**marzo** *('mahr-soh)*
April	**abril** *('ah-breel)*
May	**mayo** *('mah-yoh)*
June	**junio** *('hoo-nee-oh)*
July	**julio** *('hoo-lee-oh)*
August	**agosto** *(ah-'gohs-toh)*
September	**septiembre** *(sehp-tee-'ehm-breh)*
October	**octubre** *(ohk-'too-breh)*
November	**noviembre** *(noh-vee-'ehm-breh)*
December	**diciembre** *(dee-see-'ehm-breh)*

Now interject another word or two that refers to the calendar:

the date	**la fecha** *(lah 'feh-chah)*
weekend	**el fin de la semana** *(ehl feen deh lah seh-'mah-nah)*
next month	**el próximo mes** *(ehl 'prohk-see-moh mehs)*
last week	**la semana pasada** *(lah seh-'mah-nah pah-'sah-dah)*
the day after tomorrow	**pasado mañana** *(pah-'sah-doh mahn-'yah-nah)*
the day before yesterday	**anteayer** *(ahn-teh-ah-'yehr)*

The business world is full of time-related expressions:

Ready?	**¿Listo?** *('lees-toh)*
Not yet.	**Todavía no.** *(toh-dah-'vee-ah noh)*
Right away!	**¡En seguida!** *(ehn seh-'ghee-dah)*

The Weather
El tiempo
(ehl tee-'ehm-poh)

Note that "time" and "weather" are the same in Spanish: **tiempo.**

How's the weather?	**¿Qué tiempo hace?** *(keh tee-'ehm-poh 'ah-seh)*

It's…	**Hace…** *('ah-seh)*
cold	**frío** *('free-oh)*
hot (heat)	**calor** *(kah-'lohr)*
nice weather	**buen tiempo** *(bwehn tee-'ehm-poh)*
sunny	**sol** *(sohl)*
windy	**viento** *(vee-'ehn-toh)*

It's…	**Está…** *(ehs-'tah)*
cloudy	**nublado** *(noo-'blah-doh)*
raining	**lloviendo** *(yoh-vee-'ehn-doh)*
snowing	**nevando** *(neh-'vahn-doh)*

The Seasons
Las estaciones
(lahs ehs-tah-see-'oh-nehs):

I like...	**Me gusta...** *(meh 'goos-tah)*
spring	**la primavera** *(lah pree-mah-'veh-rah)*
summer	**el verano** *(ehl veh-'rah-noh)*
fall	**el otoño** *(ehl oh-'tohn-yoh)*
winter	**el invierno** *(ehl een-vee-'ehr-noh)*

Let's Practice ⑦

A. Fill in the blanks with the missing words:

1. enero, _____, marzo, _____, mayo, _____, julio, _____
2. _____, martes, _____, jueves, _____, sábado, _____

B. Connect each question with the best response:

1. ¿Qué hora es?	El diez de junio.
2. ¿Listo?	Está afuera.
3. ¿Qué tiempo hace?	Son las tres y media.
4. ¿Cuál es la fecha?	Sí, en seguida.
5. ¿Dónde está Paulo?	Está lloviendo.

Throughout this book there are sections titled **Verbs**, where you will be introduced to a variety of conjugated verb forms. By practicing the patterns, you'll soon be able to discuss past, present, and future events.

Verbs: To Be
Verbos: Estar y ser
('vehr-bohs ehs-'tahr ee sehr)

In order to join your Spanish words together, you'll need to understand the difference between **estar** *(ehs-'tahr)* and **ser** *(sehr)*. Both words mean "to be," but are used differently. Here are their forms in the present tense:

TO BE	ESTAR	SER
I'm	**estoy** *(ehs-'toh-ee)*	**soy** *('soh-ee)*
You are, He is, She is, It is	**está** *(ehs-'tah)*	**es** *(ehs)*
You are (pl.), They are	**están** *(ehs-'tahn)*	**son** *(sohn)*
We are	**estamos** *(ehs-'tah-mohs)*	**somos** *('soh-mohs)*

The verb **estar** expresses a temporary state, condition, or location. Look at these examples:

I am fine.	**Estoy bien.** *(ehs-'toh-ee bee-'ehn)*
The room is dirty.	**El cuarto está sucio.** *(ehl 'kwahr-toh ehs-'tah 'soo-see-oh)*
The books are on the table.	**Los libros están en la mesa.** *(lohs 'lee-brohs ehs-'tahn ehn lah 'meh-sah)*
We are in the car.	**Estamos en el carro.** *(ehs-'tah-mohs ehn ehl 'kahr-roh)*

The verb **ser**, on the other hand, expresses an inherent characteristic or quality, including origin and ownership. Notice the difference:

I am Lupe.	**Soy Lupe.** *('soh-ee 'loo-peh)*
The girl is small.	**La niña es chica.** *(lah 'neen-yah ehs 'chee-kah)*
The chairs are black.	**Las sillas son negras.** *(lahs 'see-yahs sohn 'neh-grahs)*
We are Cuban.	**Somos cubanos.** *('soh-mohs koo-'bah-nohs)*

Obviously, the best way to learn how to use **estar** and **ser** correctly is to listen to Spanish speakers in real-life conversations.

Extra Info!

Read through these other tips on how to use **estar** and **ser**:

You don't have to use the subject pronouns in every sentence. It's usually understood who's involved. For example, **nosotros somos** *(noh-'soh-trohs 'soh-mohs)* and **somos** *('soh-mohs)* both mean "we are."

Two other words, **estás** and **eres**, are used to express "you are" among family, friends, and small children. However, since most of your beginning conversations will be between yourself and an employee, we will not dwell on these words.

The little word **hay** means "there is" and "there are," and is used differently than **estar** and **ser**:

There's one job.	**Hay un trabajo.** *('ah-ee oon trah-'bah-hoh)*
There are two jobs.	**Hay dos trabajos.** *('ah-ee dohs trah-'bah-hohs)*

Let's Practice

Fill in each blank with the appropriate verb form. Look at the example:

Juan <u>es</u> mi amigo.
1. Yo _____ bien.
2. El libro _____ en la mesa.
3. Los libros _____ importantes.
4. Nosotros _____ amigos.
5. La niña _____ americana.

Verbs: To Have
Verbos: Tener
(teh-'nehr)

Tener (to have) is another common verb in Spanish, and its forms will become more necessary as you begin to create Spanish sentences on your own. Here are its present tense forms:

I have	**tengo** *('tehn-goh)*
You have, He has, She has, It has	**tiene** *(tee-'eh-neh)*
You have (pl.), They have	**tienen** *(tee-'eh-nehn)*
We have	**tenemos** *(teh-'neh-mohs)*

Study these examples:

I have a problem.	**Tengo un problema.**
	('tehn-goh oon proh-'bleh-mah)
She has a white car.	**Tiene un carro blanco.**
	(tee-'eh-neh oon 'kah-rroh 'blahn-koh)
They have four children.	**Tienen cuatro niños.**
	(tee-'eh-nehn 'kwah-troh 'neen-yohs)
We have the paper.	**Tenemos el papel.**
	(teh-'neh-mohs ehl pah-'pehl)

Even though **tener** literally means "to have," sometimes it is used instead of the verb **estar** to express a temporary condition:

(I am) afraid.	**(Tengo) miedo.** *(mee-'eh-doh)*
(We are) at fault.	**(Tenemos) la culpa.** *(lah 'kool-pah)*
(They are) cold.	**(Tiene) frío.** *('free-oh)*
(She is) 15 years old.	**(Tiene) quince años.** *('keen-seh 'ah-nyohs)*
(I am) hot.	**(Tengo) calor.** *(kah-'lohr)*
(They are) hungry.	**(Tienen) hambre.** *('ahm-breh)*
(He is) sleepy.	**(Tiene) sueño.** *('sweh-nyoh)*
(We are) thirsty.	**(Tenemos) sed.** *(sehd)*

Just Say No!
¡Simplemente diga no!
(seem-pleh-'mehn-teh 'dee-gah noh)

To say "not" in Spanish, insert the word **no** *(noh)* in front of the verb:

José is not my friend.
José no es mi amigo. *(hoh-'seh noh ehs mee ah-'mee-goh)*

I do not have the job.
No tengo el trabajo. *(noh 'tehn-goh ehl trah-'bah-hoh)*

There are no more.
No hay más. *(noh 'ah-ee mahs)*

Action Words!
¡Las palabras de acción!

(lahs pah-'lah-brahs deh ahk-see-'ohn)

Although **estar**, **ser**, and **tener** are extremely useful, they do not express action. Learning how to use Spanish verbs will allow us to talk about what's going on in the world around us. Notice that Spanish verb infinitives end in the letters *ar*, *er*, or *ir*:

to come	**venir** *(veh-'neer)*
to drive	**manejar** *(mah-neh-'hahr)*
to eat	**comer** *(koh-'mehr)*
to drink	**beber** *(beh-'behr)*
to go	**ir** *(eer)*
to listen	**escuchar** *(ehs-koo-'chahr)*
to look	**mirar** *(mee-'rahr)*
to read	**leer** *(leh-'ehr)*
to run	**correr** *(kohr-'rehr)*
to sleep	**dormir** *(dohr-'meer)*
to speak	**hablar** *(ah-'blahr)*
to walk	**caminar** *(kah-mee-'nahr)*
to wait	**esperar** *(ehs-peh-'rahr)*
to work	**trabajar** *(trah-bah-'hahr)*
to write	**escribir** *(ehs-kree-'beer)*

One of the most effective ways to put verbs to work for you is to combine them with simple phrases that create complete commands. For example, look what happens when you add these verb infinitives to **Favor de...** *(fah-'vohr deh)*, which implies, "Would you please...":

Please ...	**Favor de . . .** *(fah-'vohr deh)*
write everything.	**escribir todo.** *(ehs-kree-'beer 'toh-doh)*
come tomorrow.	**venir mañana.** *(veh-'neer mah-'nyah-nah)*
speak in English.	**hablar en inglés.** *(ah-'blahr ehn een-'glehs)*

Again, by adding the word **no** in front of the verb, you communicate the command "don't":

Please don't come tomorrow.
Favor de no venir mañana. *(fah-'vohr deh noh veh-'neer mahn-'yah-nah)*

Extra Info!

Several more verb infinitives are listed in the **GLOSSARY** at the end of this book, so use it as a reference tool. When you come across a verb as you study and practice, look it up in Spanish or English to learn its base form and meaning. The good news is that many Spanish verb infinitives that relate to employment are similar to those in English:

to converse	**conversar** *(kohn-vehr-'sahr)*
to observe	**observar** *(ohb-sehr-'vahr)*
to consult	**consultar** *(kohn-sool-'tahr)*

Let's Practice ⑨

A. Use forms of **tener** to translate the following:

1. They are cold. _____
2. I don't have the job. _____
3. We are hungry. _____

B. Insert the verb infinitive that best fits each sentence:

comer, hablar, manejar, leer, escuchar

1. Favor de _____ el carro.
2. No _____ el libro aquí.
3. Favor de _____ español.
4. Favor de _____ en el restaurante.
5. No _____ la música.

Verbs: The Present Progressive
Los verbos: el presente progresivo
(lohs 'vehr-bohs ehl preh-'sehn-teh proh-greh-'see-voh)

Let's begin with the Present Progressive tense, which refers to actions that are taking place at this moment. It is similar to our "-ing" form in English. You will have to change the base verb ending slightly, and then combine the forms of the verb **estar** *(ehs-'tahr)*. Note how the **-ar** verbs add the ending **-ando** *('ahn-doh)*, whereas the **-er** and **-ir** verbs add **-iendo** *(ee-'ehn-doh)*. Study these examples:

to work	**trabajar** *(trah-bah-'hahr)*
working	**trabajando** *(trah-bah-'hahn-doh)*
We're working.	**Estamos trabajando.**
	(ehs-'tah-mohs trah-bah-'hahn-doh)
to eat	**comer** *(koh-'mehr)*
eating	**comiendo** *(koh-mee-'ehn-doh)*
The man is eating.	**El hombre está comiendo.**
	(ehl 'ohm-breh ehs-'tah koh-mee-'ehn-doh)

to write	**escribir** *(ehs-kree-'beer)*
writing	**escribiendo** *(ehs-kree-bee-'ehn-doh)*
I'm writing my name.	**Estoy escribiendo mi nombre.** *(ehs-'toh-ee ehs-kree-bee-'ehn-doh mee 'nohm-breh)*

Verbs

Be aware that some verbs change in spelling and pronunciation when you add the **-ndo** ending:

to follow	**seguir** *(seh-'geer)*
following	**siguiendo** *(see-gee-'ehn-doh)*
to sleep	**dormir** *(dohr-'meer)*
sleeping	**durmiendo** *(door-mee-'ehn-doh)*
read	**leer** *(leh-'ehr)*
reading	**leyendo** *(leh-'yehn-doh)*

Let's Practice (10)

Follow the pattern as you create sentences:

manejar	<u>manejando</u>	<u>Estoy manejando.</u>
1. trabajar	_____	_____
2. hablar	_____	_____
3. consultar	_____	_____

The Culture

If you get stuck in the middle of a phrase or sentence, don't be afraid to send messages using hand gestures or facial expressions. Body signals are used frequently in conversations throughout the Spanish-speaking world. And remember, there's nothing wrong with repeating your message several times until you're understood!

Chapter Two

The Employee
El empleado
(ehl ehm-pleh-'ah-doh)

The Employee Interview
La entrevista con el empleado
(lah ehn-treh-'vees-tah kohn ehl ehm-pleh-'ah-doh)

Before you take on the employee interview, read over and practice the basic language material found in Chapter One. Let's start with a few greetings and introductions:

Employer: **Buenos días. ¿Cómo está?**
Spanish speaker: **Bien, gracias, ¿y usted?**
Employer: **Bien, gracias. Soy el Sr. Wilson. Usted se llama Juan García, ¿no?**
Spanish speaker: **No, señora. Mi nombre es Juan Carlos García.**
Employer: **Perdón. Su nombre es Juan Carlos García. Mucho gusto.**
Spanish speaker: **El gusto es mío.**

Now add a few more phrases that you know:

Tome un asiento.
('toh-meh oon ah-see-'ehn-toh)

Y cierre la puerta, por favor.
(ee see-'ehr-reh lah 'pwehr-tah pohr fah-'vohr)

¿Necesita un/una intérprete?
(neh-seh-'see-tah oon/'oo-nah een-'tehr-preh-teh)

Lo siento, pero no hablo español muy bien.
(loh see-'ehn-toh 'peh-roh noh 'ah-bloh ehs-pahn-'yohl 'moo-ee bee-'ehn)

Gracias por su paciencia.
('grah-see-ahs pohr soo pah-see-'ehn-see-ah)

Here are two new one-liners that will help get the interview started:

I have a few questions for you.
Tengo algunas preguntas para usted.
('tehn-goh ahl-'goo-nahs preh-'goon-tahs 'pah-rah oos-'tehd)

Please answer the questions in one or two words.
Favor de contestar las preguntas con una o dos palabras. *(fah-'vohr deh kohn-tehs-'tahr lahs preh-'goon-tahs kohn 'oo-nah oh dohs pah-'lah-brahs)*

The Job Application
La solicitud para el trabajo
(lah soh-lee-see-'tood 'pah-rah ehl trah-'bah-hoh)

One of the first things you'll need to do is confirm that all the personal information you have is correct. Notice the pattern:

What is your...	**¿Cuál es su...?** *(kwahl ehs soo)*
address	**dirección** *(dee-rehk-see-'ohn)*
area code	**código telefónico** *('koh-dee-goh teh-leh-'foh-nee-koh)*
cell phone	**teléfono celular** *(teh-'leh-foh-noh seh-loo-'lahr)*
date of birth	**fecha de nacimiento** *('feh-chah deh nah-see-mee-'ehn-toh)*
e-mail address	**correo electrónico** *(kohr-'reh-oh eh-lehk-'troh-nee-koh)*
first name	**primer nombre** *(pree-'mehr 'nohm-breh)*
full name	**nombre completo** *('nohm-breh kohm-'pleh-toh)*
last name	**apellido** *(ah-peh-'yee-doh)*
last place of employment	**último lugar de empleo** *('ool-tee-moh loo-'gahr deh ehm-'pleh-oh)*
license number	**número de licencia** *('noo-meh-roh deh lee-'sehn-see-ah)*
maiden name	**nombre de soltera** *('nohm-breh deh sohl-'teh-rah)*
marital status	**estado civil** *(ehs-'tah-doh see-'veel)*
name	**nombre** *('nohm-breh)*
nationality	**nacionalidad** *(nah-see-oh-nah-lee-'dahd)*
place of birth	**lugar de nacimiento** *(loo-'gahr deh nah-see-mee-'ehn-toh)*
relationship	**relación** *(reh-lah-see-'ohn)*
social security number	**número de seguro social** *('noo-meh-roh deh seh-'goo-roh soh-see-'ahl)*
telephone number	**número de teléfono** *('noo-meh-roh deh teh-'leh-foh-noh)*
zip code	**zona postal** *('soh-nah pohs-'tahl)*

You may also have to translate the following words for the job applicant:

benefits	**los beneficios** *(lohs beh-neh-'fee-see-ohs)*
days off	**los días de descanso** *(lohs 'dee-ahs deh dehs-'kahn-soh)*
full-time	**el tiempo completo** *(ehl tee-'ehm-poh kohm-'pleh-toh)*
part-time	**el tiempo parcial** *(ehl tee-'ehm-poh pahr-see-'ahl)*
pay	**el pago** *(ehl 'pah-goh)*
raise	**el aumento de sueldo**
	(ehl ah-oo-'mehn-toh deh 'swehl-doh)
salary	**el salario** *(ehl sah-'lah-ree-oh)*
shift	**el turno de trabajo** *(ehl 'toor-noh deh trah-'bah-hoh)*
wage	**el sueldo** *(ehl 'swehl-doh)*

And don't forget to ask about citizenship:

Are you a U.S. citizen?
¿Es usted ciudadano de Estados Unidos?
(ehs oos-'tehd see-oo-dah-'dah-noh deh ehs-'tah-dohs oo-'nee-dohs)

Do you have a green card?
¿Tiene usted una tarjeta de residencia?
(tee-'eh-neh oos-'tehd 'oo-nah tahr-'heh-tah deh reh-see-'dehn-see-ah)

What's your resident number?
¿Cuál es su número de residente?
(kwahl ehs soo 'noo-meh-roh deh reh-see-'dehn-teh)

Are you a naturalized citizen?
¿Es usted un ciudadano naturalizado?
(ehs oos-'tehd oon see-oo-dah-'dah-noh nah-too-rah-lee-'sah-doh)

Do you have a work permit?
¿Tiene usted un permiso de trabajo?
(tee-'eh-neh oos-'tehd oon pehr-'mee-soh deh trah-'bah-hoh)

Extra Info!

Acquire any word that might be useful in an interview:

Tell me (the)...	**Dígame...** *('dee-gah-meh)*
city	**la ciudad** *(lah see-oo-'dahd)*
country	**el país** *(ehl pah-'ees)*
county	**el condado** *(ehl kohn-'dah-doh)*
district	**el distrito** *(ehl dees-'tree-toh)*
town	**el pueblo** *(ehl 'pweh-bloh)*
Write your...	**Escriba su...** *(ehs-'kree-bah soo)*
age	**edad** *(eh-'dahd)*
height	**altura** *(ahl-'too-rah)*
race	**raza** *('rah-sah)*
sex	**sexo** *('sehk-soh)*
signature	**firma** *('feer-mah)*
weight	**peso** *('peh-soh)*
Is it...?	**¿Es...?** *(ehs)*
approved	**aprobado** *(ah-proh-'bah-doh)*
correct	**correcto** *(kohr-'rehk-toh)*
current	**actual** *(ahk-'twahl)*
expired	**vencido** *(vehn-'see-doh)*
legal	**legal** *(leh-'gahl)*
signed	**firmado** *(feer-'mah-doh)*
valid	**válido** *('vah-lee-doh)*
verified	**verificado** *(veh-ree-fee-'kah-doh)*

The Physical Exam
El examen físico
(ehl ex-'ah-mehn 'fee-see-koh)

The hiring process may also include a physical exam. General questions are all you need for now:

Are you taking any medication?
¿Está tomando medicamentos?
(ehs-'tah toh-'mahn-doh meh-dee-kah-'mehn-tohs)

Are you pregnant?
¿Está embarazada?
(ehs-'tah ehm-bah-rah-'sah-dah)

Have you had any surgeries?
¿Lo han operado alguna vez?
(loh ahn oh-peh-'rah-doh ahl-'goo-nah vehs)

Do you suffer from...	**Sufre de...** *('soo-freh deh)*
allergies	**las alergias** *(lahs ah-'lehr-hee-ahs)*
fainting spells	**los desmayos** *(lohs dehs-'mah-yohs)*
illnesses	**las enfermedades** *(lahs ehn-fehr-meh-'dah-dehs)*
pains	**los dolores** *(lohs doh-'loh-rehs)*
physical disabilities	**las incapacidades físicas** *(lahs een-kah-pah-see-'dah-dehs 'fee-see-kahs)*

Have you had...?	**¿Ha tenido...?** *(ah teh-'nee-doh)*
chicken pox	**la varicela** *(lah vah-ree-'seh-lah)*
measles	**el sarampión** *(ehl sah-rahm-pee-'ohn)*
mumps	**las paperas** *(lahs pah-'peh-rahs)*

To check on body parts and organs, utilize this easy phrase:

Do you have trouble with your...?	**¿Tiene problemas con...?** *(tee-'eh-neh proh-'bleh-mahs kohn)*
ankle	**el tobillo** *(ehl toh-'bee-yoh)*
arm	**el brazo** *(ehl 'brah-soh)*

back	**la espalda** *(lah ehs-'pahl-dah)*
chest	**el pecho** *(ehl 'peh-choh)*
ear	**el oído** *(ehl oh-'ee-doh)*
elbow	**el codo** *(ehl 'koh-doh)*
eye	**el ojo** *(ehl 'oh-hoh)*
face	**la cara** *(lah 'kah-rah)*
finger	**el dedo** *(ehl 'deh-doh)*
foot	**el pie** *(ehl pee-'eh)*
hair	**el pelo** *(ehl 'peh-loh)*
hand	**la mano** *(lah 'mah-noh)*
head	**la cabeza** *(lah kah-'beh-sah)*
heart	**el corazón** *(ehl koh-rah-'sohn)*
hip	**la cadera** *(lah kah-'deh-rah)*
jaw	**la mandíbula** *(lah mahn-'dee-boo-lah)*
kidneys	**los riñones** *(lohs reen-'yoh-nehs)*
knee	**la rodilla** *(lah roh-'dee-yah)*
liver	**el hígado** *(ehl 'ee-gah-doh)*
lungs	**los pulmones** *(lohs pool-'moh-nehs)*
mouth	**la boca** *(lah 'boh-kah)*
neck	**el cuello** *(ehl 'kweh-yoh)*
nose	**la nariz** *(lah nah-'rees)*
shoulder	**el hombro** *(ehl 'ohm-broh)*
skin	**la piel** *(lah pee-'ehl)*
stomach	**el estómago** *(ehl ehs-'toh-mah-goh)*
teeth	**los dientes** *(lohs dee-'ehn-tehs)*
tongue	**la lengua** *(lah 'lehn-gwah)*
wrist	**la muñeca** *(lah moon-'yeh-kah)*

Employment Tests
Exámenes pre-empleo
(ex-'ah-meh-nehs preh-ehm-'pleh-oh)

You can take (the)...	**Puede tomar...** *('pweh-deh toh-'mahr)*
AIDS test	**la prueba de SIDA** *(lah proo-'eh-bah deh 'see-dah)*
breath test	**la prueba de aliento** *(lah proo-'eh-bah deh ah-lee-'ehn-toh)*
drug test	**la prueba de drogas** *(lah proo-'eh-bah deh 'droh-gahs)*
eye exam	**el examen de la vista** *(ehl ex-'ah-mehn deh lah 'vees-tah)*
polygraph	**el detector de mentiras** *(ehl deh-tehk-'tohr deh mehn-'tee-rahs)*

What's Your Occupation?
¿Cuál es su ocupación?
(kwahl ehs soo oh-koo-pah-see-'ohn)

For practical purposes and unless noted, we refer to masculine nouns and adjectives. But please be aware that most such words are either masculine or feminine in Spanish. As a rule, to address a female, use the article **la** and simply change the **o** ending of nouns and adjectives to **a**, or add an **a** when the words end in **r**. Look at the following list, and you will notice that most nouns are distinctly masculine or feminine, whereas a few remain identical:

Are you (the)...?	**¿Es usted...?** *(ehs oos-'tehd)*
I'm looking for (the)...	**Estoy buscando a...** *(ehs-'toh-ee boos-'kahn-doh ah)*
accountant	**el contador/la contadora**
	(ehl kohn-tah-'dohr/lah kohn-tah-'doh-rah)
actor	**el actor** *(ehl ahk-'tohr)*
actress	**la actriz** *(lah ahk-'trees)*
applicant	**el candidato/la candidata**
	(ehl kahn-dee-'dah-toh/lah kahn-dee-'dah-tah)
architect	**el arquitecto/la arquitecta**
	(ehl ahr-kee-'tehk-toh/lah ahr-kee-'tehk-tah)
artist	**el/la artista** *(ehl/la ahr-'tees-tah)*
assistant	**el/la asistente** *(ehl/lah ah-sees-'tehn-teh)*
baker	**el panadero/la panadera**
	(ehl pah-nah-'deh-roh/lah pah-nah-'deh-rah)
banker	**el banquero/la banquera**
	(ehl bahn-'keh-roh/lah bahn-'keh-rah)
bartender	**el cantinero/la cantinera**
	(ehl kahn-tee-'neh-roh/lah kahn-tee-'neh-rah)
busboy	**el ayudante de camarero/la ayudanta de camarero**
	(ehl ah-yoo-'dahn-teh deh kah-mah-'reh-roh/lah ah-yoo-'dahn-tah deh kah-mah-'reh-roh)
butcher	**el carnicero/la carnicera**
	(ehl kahr-nee-'seh-roh/lah kahr-nee-'seh-rah)
carpenter	**el carpintero/la carpintera**
	(ehl kahr-peen-'teh-roh/lah kahr-peen'teh-rah)
cashier	**el cajero/la cajera** *(ehl kah-'heh-roh/lah kah-'heh-rah)*

clerk	**el dependiente/la dependienta** *(ehl deh-pehn-dee-'ehn-teh/lah deh-pehn-dee-'ehn-tah)*
cook	**el cocinero/la cocinera** *(ehl koh-see-'neh-roh/lah koh-see-'neh-rah)*
dentist	**el/la dentista** *(ehl/lah dehn-'tees-tah)*
dishwasher	**el/la lavaplatos** *(ehl/lah lah-vah 'plah-tohs)*
doctor	**el médico/la médica** *(ehl 'meh-dee-koh/lah 'meh-dee-kah)*
dressmaker	**el modisto/la modista** *(ehl moh-'dees-toh/lah moh-'dees-tah)*
engineer	**el ingeniero/la ingeniera** *(ehl een-heh-nee-'eh-roh/lah een-heh-nee-'eh-rah)*
farmer	**el granjero/la granjera** *(ehl grahn-'heh-roh/lah grahn-'heh-rah)*
firefighter	**el bombero/la bombera** *(ehl bohm-'beh-roh/lah bohm-'beh-rah)*
florist	**el/la florista** *(ehl/lah floh-'rees-tah)*
gardener	**el jardinero/la jardinera** *(ehl hahr-dee-'neh-roh/lah hahr-dee-'neh-rah)*
guide	**el/la guía** *(ehl/lah 'ghee-ah)*
hairdresser	**el peluquero/la peluquera** *(ehl peh-loo-'keh-roh/lah peh-loo-'keh-rah)*
helper	**el ayudante/la ayudanta** *(ehl ah-yoo-'dahn-teh/lah ah-yoo-'dahn-tah)*
housekeeper	**el criado/la criada** *(ehl kree-'ah-doh/lah kree-'ah-dah)*
janitor	**el/la conserje** *(ehl/lah kohn-'sehr-heh)*
laborer	**el obrero/la obrera** *(ehl oh-'breh-roh/lah oh-'breh-rah)*
lawyer	**el abogado/la abogada** *(ehl ah-boh-'gah-doh/lah ah-boh-'gah-dah)*
librarian	**el bibliotecario/la bibliotecaria** *(ehl beeb-lee-oh-teh-'kah-ree-oh/lah beeb-lee-oh-teh-'kah-ree-ah)*
machinist	**el operario/la operaria** *(ehl oh-peh-'rah-ree-oh/lah oh-peh-'rah-ree-ah)*
mail carrier	**el cartero/la cartera** *(ehl kahr-'teh-roh/lah kahr-'teh-rah)*
mechanic	**el mecánico/la mecánica** *(ehl meh-'kah-nee-koh/lah meh-'kah-nee-kah)*
merchant	**el/la comerciante** *(ehl/lah koh-mehr-see-'ahn-teh)*

musician	**el músico/la música** *(ehl 'moo-see-koh/lah 'moo-see-kah)*
nurse	**el enfermero/la enfermera** *(ehl ehn-fehr-'meh-roh/lah ehn-fehr-'meh-rah)*
painter	**el pintor/la pintora** *(ehl peen-'tohr/lah peen-'toh-rah)*
pilot	**el/la piloto** *(ehl/lah pee-'loh-toh)*
police officer	**el/la policía** *(ehl/lah poh-lee-'see-ah)*
priest	**el cura** *(ehl 'koo-rah)*
plumber	**el plomero/la plomera** *(ehl ploh-'meh-roh/lah ploh-'meh-rah)*
receptionist	**el/la receptionista** *(ehl/lah reh-sehp-see-oh-'nees-tah)*
salesperson	**el vendedor/la vendedora** *(ehl vehn-deh-'dohr/lah vehn-deh-'doh-rah)*
secretary	**el secretario/la secretaria** *(ehl seh-kreh-'tah-ree-oh/lah seh-kreh-'tah-ree-ah)*
tailor	**el/la sastre** *(ehl/lah 'sahs-treh)*
taxi driver	**el/la taxista** *(ehl/lah tahk-'sees-tah)*
teacher	**el maestro/la maestra** *(ehl mah-'ehs-troh/lah mah-'ehs-trah)*
technician	**el técnico/la técnica** *(ehl 'tehk-nee-koh/lah 'tehk-nee-kah)*
translator	**el traductor/la traductora** *(ehl trah-dook-'tohr/lah trah-dook-'toh-rah)*
truck driver	**el camionero/la camionera** *(ehl kah-mee-oh-'neh-roh/lah kah-mee-oh-'neh-rah)*
waiter/waitress	**el mesero/la mesera** *(ehl meh-'seh-roh/lah meh-'seh-rah)*
worker	**el trabajador/la trabajadora** *(ehl trah-bah-hah-'dohr/lah trah-bah-hah-'doh-rah)*
writer	**el escritor/la escritora** *(ehl ehs-kree-'tohr/lah ehs-kree-'toh-rah)*

Be sure to mention your job title as well:

I'm (the)...	**Soy...** *('soh-ee)*
administrator	**el administrador/la administradora** *(ehl ahd-mee-nees-trah-'dohr/lah ahd-mee-nees-trah-'doh-rah)*
boss	**el jefe/la jefa** *(ehl 'heh-feh/lah 'heh-fah)*
contractor	**el/la contratista** *(ehl/lah kohn-trah-'tees-tah)*

coordinator	**el coordinador/la coordinadora** *(ehl koh-ohr-dee-nah-'dohr/lah koh-ohr-dee-nah-'doh-rah)*
director	**el director/la directora** *(ehl dee-rehk-'tohr/lah dee-rehk-'toh-rah)*
employee	**el empleado/la empleada** *(ehl ehm-pleh-'ah-doh/lah ehm-pleh-'ah-dah)*
employer	**el empresario/la empresaria** *(ehl ehm-preh-'sah-ree-oh/lah ehm-preh-'sah-ree-ah)*
manager	**el/la gerente** *(ehl/lah heh-'rehn-teh)*
owner	**el dueño/la dueña** *(ehl 'dwehn-yoh/lah 'dwehn-yah)*
president	**el presidente/la presidenta** *(ehl preh-see-'dehn-teh/lah preh-see-'dehn-tah)*
supervisor	**el supervisor/la supervisora** *(ehl soo-pehr-vee-'sohr/lah soo-pehr-vee-'soh-rah)*
vice-president	**el/la vicepresidente** *(ehl/lah vee-seh-preh-see-'dehn-teh)*

 ## The Culture

When referring to others by name, it really helps if you are able to pronounce people's names correctly, as it makes them feel much more at ease. Always remember that Spanish is pronounced the way it is written. Also, it is not uncommon for someone in Spain or Latin America to have two last names. Don't get confused. Here's the order:

FIRST NAME	FATHER'S LAST NAME	MOTHER'S LAST NAME
primer nombre	**apellido paterno**	**apellido materno**
(pree-'mehr 'nohm-breh)	*(ah-peh-'yee-doh pah-'tehr-noh)*	*(ah-peh-'yee-doh mah-'tehr-noh)*
Juan Carlos	**García**	**Espinoza**
(hoo-'ahn 'kahr-lohs)	*(gahr-'see-ah)*	*(ehs-pee-'noh-sah)*

Remember, too, that not all Hispanics have two first names, and there is no middle name as we know it. In addition, when a woman marries, she keeps her father's last name, followed by her husband's.

Extra Info!

If you like, make an encouraging remark during the conversation. We will use "a" (**un**, *oon*, for masculine nouns and **una**, *'oo-nah*, for feminine nouns):

It's an excellent _____   **Es** _____ **excelente** *(ehs ___ ex-seh-'lehn-teh)*

business	**un negocio** *(oon neh-'goh-see-oh)*
career	**una carrera** *('oo-nah kahr-'reh-rah)*
job	**un trabajo** *(oon trah-'bah-hoh)*
occupation	**una ocupación** *('oo-nah oh-koo-pah-see-'ohn)*
opportunity	**una oportunidad** *('oo-nah oh-pohr-too-nee-'dahd)*
position	**un puesto** *(oon 'pwehs-toh)*
profession	**una profesión** *('oo-nah proh-feh-see-'ohn)*
shift	**un turno** *(oon 'toor-noh)*

Let's Practice   ⑪

A. Complete this form with answers about yourself:

1. nombre completo   _____
2. lugar de nacimiento   _____
3. correo electrónico   _____
4. zona postal   _____
5. edad   _____

B. Finish this pattern in Spanish using what you've learned:

We need...   **Necesitamos...**

1. carpenters   _____
2. your signature   _____
3. the job   _____

C. Read these sentences aloud and translate them:

1. Pedro es el nuevo jefe.   _____
2. ¿Quién es la empresaria?   _____
3. Soy el dueño de la compañía.   _____

D. From memory, name five body parts in Spanish:

_____   _____   _____   _____   _____

More Key Questions
Más preguntas claves
(mahs preh-'goon-tahs 'klah-vehs)

As you interview, listen for the answers, **sí** or **no**:

Can you...?	¿**Puede usted...**? *('pweh-deh oos-'tehd)*
begin tomorrow	**comenzar mañana** *(koh-mehn-'sahr mahn-'yah-nah)*
do the job	**hacer el trabajo** *(ah-'sehr ehl trah-'bah-hoh)*
drive	**manejar** *(mah-neh-'hahr)*
read and write	**leer y escribir** *(leh-'ehr ee ehs-kree-'beer)*
speak a little English	**hablar inglés un poco** *(ah-'blahr een-'glehs oon 'poh-koh)*
travel	**viajar** *(vee-ah-'hahr)*
understand everything	**entender todo** *(ehn-tehn-'dehr 'toh-doh)*
use one of these	**usar uno de éstos** *('oo-sahr 'oo-noh deh 'ehs-tohs)*
work at night	**trabajar de noche** *(trah-bah-'hahr deh 'noh-cheh)*
work with computers	**trabajar con computadoras** *(trah-bah-'hahr kohn kohm-poo-tah-'doh-rahs)*

Do you have (the)...?	¿**Tiene usted...**? *(tee-'eh-neh oos-'tehd)*
appointment	**la cita** *(lah 'see-tah)*
card	**la tarjeta** *(lah tahr-'heh-tah)*
certificate	**el certificado** *(ehl sehr-tee-fee-'kah-doh)*
contract	**el contrato** *(ehl kohn-'trah-toh)*
diploma	**el diploma** *(ehl dee-'ploh-mah)*
driver's license	**la licencia de manejar** *(lah lee-'sehn-see-ah deh mah-neh-'hahr)*
education	**la educación** *(lah eh-doo-kah-see-'ohn)*
equipment	**el equipo** *(ehl eh-'kee-poh)*
experience	**la experiencia** *(lah ex-peh-ree-'ehn-see-ah)*
form	**el formulario** *(ehl fohr-moo-'lah-ree-oh)*
identification	**la identificación** *(lah ee-dehn-tee-fee-kah-see-'ohn)*
information	**la información** *(lah een-fohr-mah-see-'ohn)*
insurance	**el seguro** *(ehl seh-'goo-roh)*
interview	**la entrevista** *(lah ehn-treh-'vees-tah)*
meeting	**la reunión** *(lah reh-oo-nee-'ohn)*
passport	**el pasaporte** *(ehl pah-sah-'pohr-teh)*
photo	**la foto** *(lah 'foh-toh)*

references	**las referencias** *(lahs reh-feh-'rehn-see-ahs)*
résumé	**el currículum** *(ehl koor-'ree-koo-loom)*
schedule	**el horario** *(ehl oh-'rah-ree-oh)*
tools	**las herramientas** *(lahs ehr-rah-mee-'ehn-tahs)*
training	**el entrenamiento** *(ehl ehn-treh-nah-mee-'ehn-toh)*
transcripts	**las transcripciones** *(lahs trahns-kreep-see-'oh-nehs)*
transportation	**el transporte** *(ehl trahns-'pohr-teh)*
uniform	**el uniforme** *(ehl oo-nee-'fohr-meh)*

As usual, the following descriptive words are directed at a male. When addressing a female, simply change words ending in **o** to **a** (except for **capaz**, which remains unchanged):

Are you...?	**¿Está usted... ?** *(ehs-'tah oos-'tehd)*
available	**disponible** *(dees-poh-'nee-bleh)*
busy	**ocupado** *(oh-koo-'pah-doh)*
capable	**capaz** *(kah-'pahs)*
employed	**empleado** *(ehm-pleh-'ah-doh)*
interested	**interesado** *(een-teh-reh-'sah-doh)*
qualified	**calificado** *(kah-lee-fee-'kah-doh)*
skilled	**especializado** *(ehs-peh-see-ah-lee-'sah-doh)*
trained	**entrenado** *(ehn-treh-'nah-doh)*

Try out this new question pattern:

Have you...?	**¿Ha... ?** *(ah)*
completed high school	**terminado la escuela secundaria**
	(tehr-mee-'nah-doh lah ehs-'kweh-lah seh-koon-'dah-ree-ah)
ever been arrested	**sido arrestado alguna vez**
	('see-doh ahr-rehs-'tah-doh ahl-'goo-nah vehs)
had training	**sido entrenado** *('see-doh ehn-treh-'nah-doh)*
taken courses in college	**tomado cursos en la universidad**
	(toh-'mah-doh 'koor-sohs ehn lah oo-nee-vehr-see-'dahd)
used that machine	**usado esa máquina** *(oo-'sah-doh 'eh-sah 'mah-kee-nah)*
worked here before	**trabajado aquí antes**
	(trah-bah-'hah-doh ah-'kee 'ahn-tehs)

Now collect information using the question words. These may look easy, but you'll have to listen carefully if you want to understand their responses:

What's your...?	¿Cuál es su... ? *(kwahl ehs soo)*
background	**origen** *(oh-'ree-hehn)*
expertise	**competencia** *(kohm-peh-'tehn-see-ah)*
field	**campo de trabajo** *('kahm-poh deh trah-'bah-hoh)*
level	**nivel** *(nee-'vehl)*
skill	**aptitud** *(ahp-tee-'tood)*
specialty	**especialidad** *(ehs-peh-see-ah-lee-'dahd)*
title	**título** *('tee-too-loh)*

Who's your...?	¿Quién es su... ? *(kee-'ehn ehs soo)*
closest relative	**pariente más cercano** *(pah-ree-'ehn-teh mahs sehr-'kah-noh)*
family physician	**médico familiar** *('meh-dee-koh fah-mee-lee-'ahr)*
friend	**amigo** *(ah-'mee-goh)*
neighbor	**vecino** *(veh-'see-noh)*
partner	**socio** *(soh-see-oh)*
previous employer	**empresario previo** *(ehm-preh-'sah-ree-oh 'preh-vee-oh)*
roommate	**el compañero/la compañera de cuarto** *(ehl kohm-pahn-'yeh-roh/lah kohm-pahn-'yeh-rah deh 'kwahr-toh)*

When...?	¿Cuándo... ? *('kwhan-doh)*
can you work	**puede trabajar** *('pweh-deh trah-bah-'hahr)*
can you finish	**puede terminar** *('pweh-deh tehr-mee-'nahr)*
can you start	**puede empezar** *('pweh-deh ehm-peh-'sahr)*
did you arrive	**llegó** *(yeh-'goh)*
did you graduate	**se graduó** *(she grah-doo-'oh)*
did you work there	**trabajó ahí** *(trah-bah-'hoh ah-'ee)*

Where ...?	¿Dónde... ? *('dohn-deh)*
were you born	**nació** *(nah-see-'oh)*
did you study	**estudió** *(ehs-too-dee-'oh)*
did you work before that	**trabajaba antes de eso** *(trah-bah-'hah-bah 'ahn-tehs deh 'eh-soh)*

do you work now	**trabaja ahora** *(trah-'bah-hah ah-'oh-rah)*
do you live	**vive** *('vee-veh)*
did you learn	**aprendió** *(ah-prehn-dee-'oh)*
Why...?	**¿Por qué...?** *(pohr keh)*
were you fired	**lo despidieron** *(loh dehs-pee-dee-'eh-rohn)*
should I hire you	**debiera contratarlo**
	(deh-bee-'eh-rah kohn-trah-'tahr-loh)
don't you like your job	**no le gusta su trabajo**
	(noh leh 'goos-tah soo trah-'bah-hoh)
did you quit	**renunció** *(reh-noon-see-'oh)*
aren't you working	**no está trabajando** *(noh ehs-'tah trah-bah-'hahn-doh)*
do you want to work here	**quiere trabajar aquí** *(kee-'eh-reh trah-bah-'hahr ah-'kee)*

Verbs

"To know something" requires the verb **saber**, whereas "to know someone" requires the verb **conocer**. Here's how **saber** can be used in an interview setting. Notice how the little pronoun **lo** means "it":

Do you know (how) to...	**¿Sabe usted... ?** *('sah-beh oos-'tehd)*
cook it	**cocinarlo** *(koh-see-'nahr-loh)*
clean it	**limpiarlo** *(leem-pee-'ahr-loh)*
drive it	**manejarlo** *(mah-neh-'hahr-loh)*
use it	**usarlo** *(oo-'sahr-loh)*
build it	**construirlo** *(kohns-troo-'eer-loh)*
do it	**hacerlo** *(ah-'sehr-loh)*
draw it	**dibujarlo** *(de-boo-'hahr-loh)*
say it	**decirlo** *(deh-'seer-loh)*
fix it	**repararlo** *(reh-pah-'rahr-loh)*
write it	**escribirlo** *(ehs-kree-'beer-loh)*

These are the two most common responses using **saber**:

I know.	**Yo sé.** *(yoh seh)*
I don't know.	**Yo no sé.** *(yoh noh seh)*

Tell Me About Yourself!
¡Hábleme de usted!
('ah-bleh-meh deh oos-'tehd)

Although they may require more effort, this next set of questions can really open things up during a private conversation. This time, you'll need to change the endings from the feminine **a** to **o** when addressing a male:

Are you...?	¿Es usted... ? *(ehs oos-'tehd)*
divorced	**divorciada** *(dee-vohr-see-'ah-dah)*
married	**casada** *(kah-'sah-dah)*
separated	**separada** *(seh-pah-'rah-dah)*
single	**soltera** *(sohl-'teh-rah)*
widowed	**viuda** *(vee-'oo-dah)*
Cuban	**cubana** *(koo-'bah-nah)*
Mexican	**mejicana** *(meh-hee-'kah-nah)*
Puerto Rican	**puertorriqueña** *(pwehr-tohr-re-'kehn-yah)*
South American	**sudamericana** *(soo-dah-meh-ree-'kah-nah)*
Salvadoran	**salvadoreña** *(sal-vah-doh-'rehn-yah)*
Guatemalan	**guatemalteca** *(gwah-teh-mahl-'teh-kah)*

Now ask how the applicant sees himself, and utilize the words below. Here we have a few adjectives (those with asterisks) that do not change with the sex of the person:

Are you...?	¿Es usted... ? *(ehs oos-'tehd)*
ambitious	**ambicioso** *(ahm-bee-see-'oh-soh)*
brave	**valiente*** *(vah-lee-'ehn-teh)*
clever	**hábil*** *('ah-beel)*
friendly	**amistoso** *(ah-mees-'toh-soh)*
healthy	**saludable*** *(sah-loo-'dah-bleh)*
industrious	**trabajador** *(trah-bah-hah-'dohr)*
mature	**maduro** *(mah-'doo-roh)*
patient	**paciente*** *(pah-see-'ehn-teh)*
polite	**cortés*** *(kohr-'tehs)*
punctual	**puntual*** *(poon-too-'ahl)*
quiet	**tranquilo** *(trahn-'kee-loh)*
reliable	**confiable*** *(kohn-fee-'ah-bleh)*
strong	**fuerte*** *('fwehr-teh)*

You also may need to address an obvious concern:

Let's talk about your...	**Vamos a hablar de su...** *('vah-mohs ah ah-'blahr deh soo)*
appearance	**aspecto** *(ahs-'pehk-toh)*
lack of experience	**falta de experiencia** *('falh-tah deh ex-peh-ree-'ehn-see-ah)*
language proficiency	**competencia en el lenguaje**
	(kohm-peh-'tehn-see-ah ehn ehl lehn-'gwah-heh)
legal status	**estado legal** *(ehs-'tah-doh leh-'gahl)*
medical problem	**problema médico** *(proh-'bleh-mah 'meh-dee-koh)*
personal problem	**problema personal** *(proh-'bleh-mah pehr-soh-'nahl)*

Interview-Related Phrases
Frases relacionadas con la entrevista
('frah-sehs reh-lah-see-oh-'nah-dahs kohn lah ehn-treh-'vees-tah)

job description	**la descripción del trabajo**
	(lah dehs-kreep-see-'ohn dehl trah-'bah-hoh)
work schedule	**el horario de trabajo**
	(ehl oh-'rah-ree-oh deh trah-'bah-hoh)
hiring procedure	**el procedimiento de contratación**
	(ehl proh-seh-dee-mee-'ehn-toh deh kohn-trah-tah-see-'ohn)
work experience	**la experiencia de trabajo**
	(lah ex-peh-ree-'ehn-see-ah deh trah-'bah-hoh)
education background	**los antecedentes académicos**
	(lohs ahn-teh-seh-'dehn-tehs ah-kah-'deh-mee-kohs)
equal opportunities	**la igualdad de oportunidades**
	(lah ee-gwahl-'dahd deh oh-pohr-too-nee-'dah-dehs)
job placement	**la colocación del personal**
	(lah koh-loh-kah-see-'ohn dehl pehr-soh-'nahl)
entry level	**el nivel básico** *(ehl nee-'vehl 'bah-see-koh)*

The Culture

Get to know the people you're looking to hire. Take an interest in their responses, and be careful to control your tone of voice and nonverbal actions. The more comfortable they feel, the more information they will share. One way to loosen things up is to mention their homeland or point out pictures of your own family members. Here are more words about the family and extended family that you should know:

It's the…	Es … *(ehs)*
aunt	**la tía** *(lah 'tee-ah)*
cousin (male)	**el primo** *(ehl 'pree-moh)*
cousin (female)	**la prima** *(lah 'pree-mah)*
father-in-law	**el suegro** *(ehl 'sweh-groh)*
granddaughter	**la nieta** *(lah nee-'eh-tah)*
grandfather	**el abuelo** *(ehl ah-'bweh-loh)*
grandmother	**la abuela** *(lah ah-'bweh-lah)*
grandson	**el nieto** *(ehl nee-'eh-toh)*
mother-in-law	**la suegra** *(lah 'sweh-grah)*
nephew	**el sobrino** *(ehl soh-'bree-noh)*
niece	**la sobrina** *(lah soh-'bree-nah)*
uncle	**el tío** *(ehl 'tee-oh)*

They are…	Son…*(sohn)*
close friends	**los buenos amigos** *(lohs 'bweh-nohs ah-'mee-gohs)*
parents	**los padres** *(lohs 'pah-drehs)*
relatives	**los parientes** *(lohs pah-ree-'ehn-tehs)*
step-children	**los hijastros** *(lohs ee-'hahs-trohs)*

Let's Practice (12)

A. Translate and then make up a sentence using each word. Look at the example:

Single: **soltero**   ¿Es Ud. soltero?
1. schedule: _____
2. contract: _____
3. tools: _____

B. Name one person you personally know to fill in the lines below:

pariente   _____
sobrino   _____
amiga   _____

C. Name three nationalities in Spanish:

_____
_____
_____

D. Can you create sentences using the descriptions you have learned?

Es un trabajador _____.
Es un hombre _____.
Es una gerente _____.

E. Now create questions using these important words:

¿Ha tenido...?
¿Puede usted...?
¿Sabe...?

The Benefits
Los beneficios
(los beh-neh-'fee-see-ohs)

Chat with the potential employee about the job offer in more detail. In some cases, you'll need to discuss payment and benefits, or share any insurance information that you have:

On this date, you receive (the)...	**En esta fecha, recibe usted...** *(ehn 'ehs-tah 'feh-chah reh-'see-beh oos-'tehd)*
check	**el cheque** *(ehl 'che-keh)*
commissions	**las comisiones** *(lahs koh-mee-see-'oh-nehs)*
earnings	**las ganancias** *(lahs gah-'nahn-see-ahs)*
payment	**la paga** *(lah 'pah-gah)*
Benefits include (the)...	**Los beneficios incluyen...** *(lohs beh-neh-'fee-see-ohs een-'kloo-yehn)*
Benefits don't include (the)...	**Los beneficios no incluyen...** *(lohs beh-neh-'fee-see-ohs noh een-'kloo-yehn)*
back pay	**los pagos atrasados** *(lohs 'pah-gohs ah-trah-'sah-dohs)*
bonuses	**las bonificaciones** *(lahs boh-nee-fee-kah-see-'oh-nehs)*
breaks	**las pausas para descansar** *(lahs 'pah-oo-sahs 'pah-rah dehs-kahn-'sahr)*
child care	**el cuidado de niños** *(ehl kwee-'dah-doh deh 'neen-yohs)*
discounts	**los descuentos** *(lohs dehs-'kwehn-tohs)*
incentive scheme	**el plan de incentivos** *(ehl plahn deh een-sehn-'tee-vohs)*
maternity pay	**el subsidio de maternidad** *(ehl soob-'see-dee-oh deh mah-tehr-nee-'dahd)*
medical insurance	**el seguro médico** *(ehl seh-'goo-roh 'meh-dee-koh)*
memberships	**las afiliaciones** *(lahs ah-fee-lee-ah-see-'oh-nehs)*
parking space	**el estacionamiento personal** *(ehl ehs-tah-see-oh-nah-mee-'ehn-toh pehr-soh-'nahl)*
perks	**los beneficios adicionales** *(lohs beh-neh-'fee-see-ohs ah-dee-see-oh-'nah-lehs)*
profit sharing	**la participación en los beneficios** *(lah pahr-tee-see-pah-see-'ohn ehn lohs beh-neh-'fee-see-ohs)*
promotions	**los ascensos** *(lohs ah-'sehn-sohs)*
retirement package	**el paquete de jubilación** *(ehl pah-'keh-teh deh hoo-bee-lah-see-'ohn)*

severence pay	**la indemnización por despedida**
	(lah een-dem-nee-sah-see-'ohn pohr dehs-peh-'dee-dah)
sick leave	**el permiso por enfermedad**
	(ehl pehr-'mee-soh pohr ehn-fehr-meh-'dahd)
Social Security	**el seguro de seguridad social**
Insurance	*(ehl seh-'goo-roh deh seh-goo-ree-'dahd soh-see-'ahl)*
time off for	**los días libres por luto**
bereavement	*(lohs 'dee-ahs 'leeb-rehs pohr 'loo-toh)*
vacation days	**los días de vacaciones**
	(lohs 'dee-ahs deh vah-kah-see-'oh-nehs)
Workman's	**la compensación laboral**
Compensation	*(lah kohm-pehn-sah-see-'ohn lah-boh-'rahl)*

Notice the familiar sentence patterns:

You can...	**Usted puede...** *(oos-'tehd 'pweh-deh)*
You cannot...	**Usted no puede...** *(oos-'tehd noh 'pweh-deh)*
attend special events	**asistir a eventos especiales**
	(ah-sees-'teer ah eh-'vehn-tohs ehs-peh-see-'ah-lehs)
drive company vehicles	**manejar los vehículos de la compañía**
	(mah-neh-'hahr lohs veh-'ee-koo-lohs del lah kohm-pah-'nee-ah)
join the union	**inscribirse con el sindicato**
	(eens-kree-'beer-seh kohn ehl seen-dee-'kah-toh)
keep the keys	**quedarse con las llaves**
	(keh-'dahr-seh kohn lahs 'yah-vehs)
open an expense	**abrir una cuenta de gastos reembolsables**
account	*(ahb-'reer 'oo-nah 'kwehn-tah deh 'gahs-tohs reh-ehm-bohl-'sah-blehs)*
use the executive	**usar los baños ejecutivos**
restrooms	*(oo-'sahr lohs 'bahn-yohs eh-heh-koo-'tee-vohs)*
There is/are...	**Hay...** *('ah-ee)*
There isn't/aren't...	**No hay...** *(noh 'ah-ee)*
compressed work	**semanas de trabajo reducidas**
weeks	*(seh-'mah-nahs deh trah-'bah-hoh reh-doo-'see-dahs)*
flexible schedules	**horarios flexibles** *(oh-'rah-ree-ohs flehk-'see-blehs)*
four-day workweeks	**cuatro días de trabajo por semana**
	('kwah-troh 'dee-ahs deh trah-'bah-hoh pohr seh-'mah-nah)

job sharing	**trabajos compartidos**
	(trah-'bah-hohs kohm-pahr-'tee-dohs)
overtime pay	**pagos por horas extra**
	('pah-gohs pohr 'oh-rahs 'ex-trah)
paid holidays	**días de fiesta pagados**
	('dee-ahs deh fee-'ehs-tah pah-'gah-dohs)
tax deductions	**deducciones de impuestos**
	(deh-dook-see-'oh-nehs deh eem-'pwehs-tohs)

Extra Info!

Take a moment to focus on insurance concerns:

Do you have...?	**¿Tiene usted...?** *(tee-'eh-neh oos-'tehd)*
We offer...	**Ofrecemos...** *(oh-freh-'seh-mohs)*
auto insurance	**el seguro de vehículos**
	(ehl seh-'goo-roh deh veh-'ee-koo-lohs)
dental insurance	**el seguro dental** *(ehl seh-'goo-roh dehn-'tahl)*
disability insurance	**el seguro de incapacidad**
	(ehl seh-'goo-roh deh een-kah-pah-see-'dahd)
home insurance	**el seguro de casa** *(ehl seh-'goo-roh deh 'kah-sah)*
life insurance	**el seguro de vida** *(ehl seh-'goo-roh deh 'vee-dah)*
unemployment insurance	**el seguro de desempleo**
	(ehl seh-'goo-roh deh deh-sehm-'pleh-oh)

To End the Interview
Para terminar la entrevista
('pah-rah tehr-mee-'nahr lah ehn-treh-'vees-tah)

Close the conversation with a few traditional one-liners:

Thank you for your time.
Gracias por su tiempo. *('grah-see-ahs pohr soo tee-'ehm-poh)*

Do you have any questions?
¿Tiene usted alguna pregunta? *(tee-'eh-neh oos-'tehd ahl-'goo-nah preh-'goon-tah)*

It was a pleasure meeting you.
Fue un gusto conocerlo. *(fweh oon 'goos-toh koh-noh-'sehr-loh)*

I'll let you know as soon as we decide.
Le avisaré tan pronto como decidamos.
(leh ah-vee-sah-'reh tahn 'prohn-toh 'koh-moh deh-see-'dah-mohs)

How did you hear about the job?
¿Cómo escuchó del trabajo? *('koh-moh ehs-koo-'choh dehl trah-'bah-hoh)*

You also might want to share what you plan to do next:

I would like...	**Quisiera...** *(kee-see-'eh-rah)*
to call you later	**llamarlo más tarde** *(yah-'mahr-loh mahs 'tahr-deh)*
to confirm everything	**confirmar todo** *(kohn-feer-'mahr 'toh-doh)*
to describe the position	**describir el puesto** *(dehs-kree-'beer ehl 'pwehs-toh)*
to explain why	**explicarle porqué** *(ex-plee-'kahr-leh pohr-'keh)*
to give you something	**darle algo** *('dahr-leh 'ahl-goh)*
to have a second interview	**tener una segunda entrevista** *(teh-'nehr 'oo-nah seh-'goon-dah ehn-treh-'vees-tah)*
to hire you	**contratarlo** *(kohn-trah-'tahr-loh)*
to know if you're interested	**saber si tiene interés** *(sah-'behr see tee-'eh-neh een-teh-'rehs)*
to offer you the job	**ofrecerle el trabajo** *(oh-freh-'sehr-leh ehl trah-'bah-hoh)*
to read your résumé	**leer su currículum** *(leh-'ehr soo koor-'ree-koo-loom)*
to send you an e-mail	**mandarle un correo electrónico** *(mahn-'dahr-leh oon kohr-'reh-oh eh-lehk-'troh-nee-koh)*
to talk to your previous boss	**hablar con su jefe previo** *(ah-'blahr kohn soo 'heh-feh 'preh-vee-oh)*
to think about it	**pensarlo** *(pehn-'sahr-loh)*

Not everyone gets the job, so learn how to share the bad news, too:

I'm sorry, but...	**Lo siento, pero...** *(loh see-'ehn-toh 'peh-roh)*
maybe later	**quizás más tarde** *(kee-'sahs mahs 'tahr-deh)*
the position has been filled	**ya no hay vacante** *(yah noh 'ah-ee vah-'kahn-teh)*

try back next month	**trate el próximo mes**
	('trah-teh ehl 'prok-see-moh mehs)
we hired someone else	**contratamos a otra persona**
	(kohn-trah-'tah-mohs ah 'oh-trah pehr-'soh-nah)
we're looking for	**estamos buscando a un/una _____**
a ____	*(ehs-'tah-mohs boos-'kahn-doh ah oon/'oo-nah)*
we're not hiring	**no estamos contratando**
	(noh ehs-'tah-mohs kohn-trah-'tahn-doh)
you need more	**necesita más experiencia**
experience	*(neh-seh-'see-tah mahs ex-peh-ree-'ehn-see-ah)*

Extra Info!

Learn all the one-liners you can!

Call me at this number.
Llámeme a este número. *('yah-meh-meh ah 'ehs-teh 'noo-meh-roh)*

Check out our website.
Revise nuestra página de web.
(reh-'vee-seh 'nwehs-trah 'pah-hee-nah deh web)

It's a great job offer.
Es una oferta de trabajo muy buena.
(ehs 'oo-nah oh-'fehr-tah deh trah-'bah-hoh 'moo-ee 'bweh-nah)

Sign this agreement.
Firme este contrato. *('feer-meh 'ehs-teh kohn-'trah-toh)*

Talk to your family.
Hable con su familia. *('ah-bleh kohn soo fah-'mee-lee-ah)*

You're a great applicant.
Usted es un buen solicitante.
(oos-'tehd ehs oon bwehn soh-lee-see-'tahn-teh)

Action Words!

To handle any conversation with an employee, you need verbs. Pronounce and memorize these infinitives, and create your own sentences:

to take	**tomar** *(toh-'mahr)*	*Favor de tomar el formulario.*
to sign	**firmar** *(feer-'mahr)*	*Estoy firmando aquí.*
to call	**llamar** *(yah-'mahr)*	_____
to accept	**aceptar** *(ah-sehp-'tahr)*	_____
to answer	**contestar** *(kohn-tehs-'tahr)*	_____
to apply	**solicitar** *(soh-lee-see-'tahr)*	_____
to bring	**traer** *(trah-'ehr)*	_____
to check	**revisar** *(reh-vee-'sahr)*	_____
to describe	**describir** *(dehs-kree-'beer)*	_____
to explain	**explicar** *(ex-plee-'kahr)*	_____
to give	**dar** *(dahr)*	_____
to hire	**contratar** *(kohn-trah-'tahr)*	_____
to learn	**aprender** *(ah-prehn-'dehr)*	_____
to listen	**escuchar** *(ehs-koo-'chahr)*	_____
to live	**vivir** *(vee-'veer)*	_____
to quit	**renunciar** *(reh-noon-see-'ahr)*	_____
to read	**leer** *(leh-'ehr)*	_____
to receive	**recibir** *(reh-see-'beer)*	_____
to recommend	**recomendar** *(reh-koh-mehn-'dahr)*	_____
to return	**regresar** *(reh-greh-'sahr)*	_____
to send	**mandar** *(mahn-'dahr)*	_____
to speak	**hablar** *(ah-'blahr)*	_____
to study	**estudiar** *(ehs-too-dee-'ahr)*	_____
to tell	**decir** *(deh-'seer)*	_____
to write	**escribir** *(ehs-kree-'beer)*	_____

Here's a more extensive list of phrases that are used before infinitives, some of which you already know. Study the example, and then add a few infinitives of your own:

I can…	**Puedo …**	_____ salir _____
I'd like to…	**Quisiera …**	_____
I have to…	**Tengo que …**	_____

I like (to)…	**Me gusta …**	_____
I'm going to…	**Voy a …**	_____
I need (to)…	**Necesito …**	_____
I prefer (to)…	**Prefiero …**	_____
I really want (to)…	**Deseo …**	_____
I should…	**Debo …**	_____
I want (to)…	**Quiero …**	_____

Verbs

The most common verb form at the workplace is the command. **A complete list of commands can be found at the end of this book.** Some of these were introduced earlier:

Take	**Tome.** *('toh-meh)*
Take a seat.	**Tome un asiento.** *('toh-meh oon ah-see-'ehn-toh)*
Sign	**Firme.** *('feer-meh)*
Sign here.	**Firme aquí.** *('feer-meh ah-'kee)*
Call	**Llame.** *('yah-meh)*
Call your supervisor.	**Llame a su supervisor.** *('yah-meh ah soo soo-pehr-vee-'sohr)*
Listen	**Escuche.** *(ehs-'koo-cheh)*
Listen to the question.	**Escuche la pregunta.** *(ehs-'koo-cheh lah preh-'goon-tah)*
Speak	**Hable.** *('ah-bleh)*
Speak more slowly.	**Hable más despacio.** *('ah-bleh mahs dehs-'pah-see-oh)*
Write	**Escriba.** *(ehs-'kree-bah)*
Write the number.	**Escriba el número.** *(ehs-'kree-bah ehl 'noo-meh-roh)*
Bring	**Traiga.** *('trah-ee-gah)*
Bring the form.	**Traiga el formulario.** *('trah-ee-gah ehl fohr-moo-'lah-ree-oh)*
Read	**Lea.** *('leh-ah)*
Read the application.	**Lea la solicitud.** *('leh-ah lah soh-lee-see-'tood)*

Return	**Regrese.** *(reh-'greh-seh)*
Return tomorrow.	**Regrese mañana.** *(reh-'greh-seh mah-'nyah-nah)*

Answer	**Conteste.** *(kohn-'tehs-teh)*
Answer in English.	**Conteste en inglés.** *(kohn-'tehs-teh ehn een-'glehs)*

Try a few more with your new employees:

Explain to me.	**Explíqueme.** *(ex-'plee-keh-meh)*
Tell me.	**Dígame.** *('dee-gah-meh)*
Call me.	**Llámeme.** *('yah-meh-meh)*
Give me.	**Déme.** *('deh-meh)*
Send me.	**Mándeme.** *('mahn-deh-meh)*
Answer me.	**Contésteme.** *(kohn-'tehs-teh-meh)*
Bring me.	**Tráigame.** *('trah-ee-gah-meh)*

Verbs: The Present Indicative
Los verbos: el presente indicativo
(lohs 'vehr-bohs ehl preh-'sehn-teh een-dee-kah-'tee-voh)

Like the commands, verb infinitives also must be changed when we refer to everyday activities. In the examples below, notice how the forms are altered based upon *who* completes the action. These final endings are the same for most verbs:

TO SPEAK	**HABLAR** *(ah-'blahr)*
I speak	habl**o** *('ah-bloh)*
you speak; he, she speaks	habl**a** *('ah-blah)*
you (plural), they speak	habl**an** *('ah-blahn)*
we speak	habl**amos** *(ah-'blah-mohs)*

<u>Hablo</u> español y mi amiga <u>habla</u> inglés.
('ah-bloh ehs-pan-'yohl ee mee ah-'mee-gah 'ah-blah een-'glehs)

TO EAT	**COM<u>ER</u>** *(koh-'mehr)*
I eat	com**o** *('koh-moh)*
you eat; he, she eats	come *('koh-meh)*
you (plural), they eat	com**en** *('koh-mehn)*
we eat	com**emos** *(koh-'meh-mohs)*

Usted <u>come</u> enchiladas y ellos <u>comen</u> tacos.
(oos-'tehd 'koh-meh ehn-chee-'lah-dahs ee 'eh-yohs 'koh-mehn 'tah-kohs)

TO WRITE	**ESCRIB<u>IR</u>** *(ehs-kree-'beer)*
I write	escri**bo** *(ehs-'kree-boh)*
you write; he, she writes	escri**be** *(ehs-'kree-beh)*
you (plural), they write	escri**ben** *(ehs-'kree-behn)*
we write	escri**bimos** *(ehs-kree-'bee-mohs)*

Ustedes <u>escriben</u> en el papel y nosotros <u>escribimos</u> en el libro. *(oos-'teh-dehs ehs-'kree-behn ehn ehl pah-'pehl ee noh-'soh-trohs ehs-kree-'bee-mohs ehn ehl 'lee-broh)*

Spanish verbs have three types of conjugation, depending on the verb ending: **-ar**, **-er**, or **-ir**. Notice how the endings of the **-ar** verb, **hablar**, don't change the same as the endings of the **-er** and **-ir** verbs! Also remember that some verbs are irregular because they don't follow the pattern shown above, as shown here:

TO BEGIN	**empezar** *(ehm-peh-'sahr)*
I begin:	**Empiezo.** *(ehm-pee-'eh-soh)*
TO BRING	**traer** *(trah-'ehr)*
I bring:	**Traigo.** *('trah-ee-goh)*
TO DO	**hacer** *(ah-'sehr)*
I do:	**Hago.** *('ah-goh)*
TO FIND	**encontrar** *(ehn-kohn-'trahr)*
I find:	**Encuentro.** *(ehn-'kwehn-troh)*
TO GIVE	**dar** *(dahr)*
I give:	**Doy.** *('doh-ee)*
TO LEAVE	**salir** *(sah-'leer)*
I leave:	**Salgo.** *('sahl-goh)*
TO OFFER	**ofrecer** *(oh-freh-'sehr)*
I offer:	**Ofrezco.** *(oh-'frehs-koh)*
TO SEE	**ver** *(vehr)*
I see:	**Veo.** *('veh-oh)*
TO TELL	**decir** *(deh-'seer)*
I tell:	**Digo.** *('dee-goh)*
TO THINK	**pensar** *(pehn-'sahr)*
I think:	**Pienso.** *(pee-'ehn-soh)*
TO UNDERSTAND	**entender** *(ehn-tehn-'dehr)*
I understand:	**Entiendo.** *(ehn-tee-'ehn-doh)*

And this is how you ask a question and express the negative in the present indicative:

Do they work here?   **¿Trabajan aquí?**
         (trah-'bah-hahn ah-'kee)
No, they don't work here. **No, no trabajan aquí.**
         (noh noh trah-'bah-hahn ah-'kee)

And, here are two more irregular verbs that you'll be using every day:

TO BE ABLE TO   **PODER** *(poh-'dehr)*
I can   **puedo** *('pweh-doh)*
you, he, she, it can **puede** *('pweh-deh)*
you (plural), they can **pueden** *('pweh-dehh)*
we can   **podemos** *(poh-'deh-mohs)*

<u>Puedo</u> **leer y él <u>puede</u> escribir.**
('pweh-doh leh-'ehr ee ehl 'pweh-deh ehs-kree-'beer)

TO WANT   **QUERER** *(keh-'rehr)*
I want   **quiero** *(kee-'eh-roh)*
you want; he, she wants **quiere** *(kee-'eh-reh)*
you (plural), they want **quieren** *(kee-'eh-rehn)*
we want   **queremos** *(keh-'reh-mohs)*

<u>Quiero</u> **trabajar hoy y ella <u>quiere</u> trabajar mañana.**
(kee-'eh-roh trah-bah-'hahr 'oh-ee ee 'eh-yah kee-'eh-reh trah-bah-'hahr mahn-'yah-nah)

 ## The Culture

Did your employee just move to this country? Is he or she a bit confused about our language and culture? When you find the time, share a few insights on U.S. customs toward tipping, dress, dating, holidays, and social skills. Make immigrants feel welcome by respecting their perspectives, and watch your relationship grow!

Let's Practice (13)

A. These expressions are important, so look up the translations if you forgot them:

1. Workman's Compensation _____
2. medical insurance _____
3. overtime pay _____

B. Using what you learned about the present indicative tense, conjugate the verbs according to the sentence and then translate the sentences.

| to eat: comer | Yo como temprano. | (<u>I eat early.</u>) |

1. to work: trabajar   Ella _____ mucho.   (_____)
2. to send: mandar   Nosotros _____ el dinero.   (_____)
3. to return: regresar   Ellos _____ tarde.   (_____)
4. to write: escribir   Yo _____ la información.   (_____)
5. to use: usar   Él _____ el lápiz.   (_____)

C. Now choose the best command word and write it on the line provided:

Traiga, Conteste, Firme

1. _____ la pregunta.
2. _____ su nombre.
3. _____ la silla.

D. Connect the words with opposite meanings:

1. hablar   leer
2. contestar   escuchar
3. escribir   contratar
4. despedir   dar
5. recibir   preguntar

Chapter Three

The Workplace
El lugar de empleo
(ehl loo-'gahr deh ehm-'pleh-oh)

On the Job
En el trabajo
(ehn ehl trah-'bah-hoh)

You've learned how to conduct an interview **en español**, but you still need those words that describe the workplace itself. Begin by naming some of the buildings around the worksite:

That's (the)…	**Ese es…** *('eh-seh ehs)*
building	**el edificio** *(ehl eh-dee-'fee-see-oh)*
factory	**la fábrica** *(lah 'fah-bree-kah)*
office	**la oficina** *(lah oh-fee-'see-nah)*
shop	**el taller** *(ehl tah-'yehr)*
store	**la tienda** *(lah tee-'ehn-dah)*
warehouse	**el almacén** *(ehl ahl-mah-'sehn)*

It's part of (the)…	**Es parte de…** *(ehs 'pahr-teh deh)*
agency	**la agencia** *(lah ah-'hehn-see-ah)*
business	**el negocio** *(ehl neh-'goh-see-oh)*
chain	**la cadena** *(lah kah-'deh-nah)*
corporation	**la corporación** *(lah kohr-poh-rah-see'ohn)*
facility	**la instalación** *(lah eens-tah-lah-see-'ohn)*
firm	**la firma** *(lah 'feer-mah)*
franchise	**la concesión** *(lah kohn-seh-see-'ohn)*
industrial complex	**el complejo industrial** *(ehl kohm-'pleh-hoh een-doos-tree-'ahl)*

institution	**la institución** *(lah eens-tee-too-see-'ohn)*
organization	**la organización** *(lah ohr-gah-nee-sah-see-'ohn)*
plant	**la planta** *(lah 'plahn-tah)*
property	**la propiedad** *(lah proh-pee-eh-'dahd)*

Job sites differ, so select words from the list below:

The job is at (the) …	**El trabajo está en…**
	(ehl trah-'bah-hoh ehs-'tah ehn)

airport	**el aeropuerto** *(ehl ah-eh-roh-'pwehr-toh)*
bank	**el banco** *(ehl 'bahn-koh)*
car lot	**el lote de carros** *(ehl 'loh-teh deh 'kahr rohs)*
church	**la iglesia** *(lah eeg-'leh-see-ah)*
clinic	**la clínica** *(lah 'klee-nee-kah)*
gas station	**la gasolinera** *(lah gah-soh-lee-'neh-rah)*
hospital	**el hospital** *(ehl ohs-pee-'tahl)*
hotel	**el hotel** *(ehl oh-'tehl)*
movie theater	**el cine** *(ehl 'see-neh)*
museum	**el museo** *(ehl moo-'seh-oh)*
park	**el parque** *(ehl 'pahr-keh)*
restaurant	**el restaurante** *(ehl rehs-tah-oo-'rahn-teh)*
school district	**el distrito escolar** *(ehl dees-'tree-toh ehs-koh-'lahr)*
supermarket	**el supermercado** *(ehl soo-pehr-mehr-'kah-doh)*

You work for (the)…	**Trabaja usted para…**
	(trah-'bah-hah oos-'tehd 'pah-rah)

amusement park	**el parque de diversiones**
	(ehl 'pahr-keh deh dee-vehr-see-'oh-nehs)
resort	**el lugar de vacaciones**
	(ehl loo-'gahr deh vah-kah-see-'oh-nehs)
stadium	**el estadio** *(ehl ehs-'tah-dee-oh)*
theater	**el teatro** *(ehl teh-'ah-troh)*
university	**la universidad** *(lah oo-nee-vehr-see-'dahd)*
zoo	**el zoológico** *(ehl soh-oh-'loh-hee-koh)*

As always, the important word (noun) comes first in Spanish, and then is followed by the description (adjective):

The _____ center	El centro de _____
	(ehl 'sehn-troh deh)
community	**comunidad** *(koh-moo-nee-'dahd)*
convention	**convenciones** *(kohn-vehn-see-'oh-nehs)*
medical	**salud** *(sah-'lood)*
recreation	**recreo** *(reh-'kreh-oh)*
shopping	**comercio** *(koh-'mehr-see-oh)*
visitor	**visitantes** *(vee-see-'tahn-tehs)*

The _____ station	La estación de _____
	(lah ehs-tah-see-'ohn deh)
bus	**autobús** *(ah-oo-'boos)*
subway	**metro** *('meh-troh)*
train	**tren** *(trehn)*

Workers are needed everywhere:

Can you work at (the)... ?	¿Puede trabajar en... ?
	('pweh-deh trah-bah-'hahr ehn)
drilling rig	**la plataforma de perforación**
	(lah plah-tah-'fohr-mah deh pehr-foh-rah-see-'ohn)
foundry	**el taller de fundación**
	(ehl tah-'yehr deh foon-dah-see-'ohn)
mine	**la mina** *(lah 'mee-nah)*
quarry	**la cantera** *(lah kahn-'teh-rah)*
refinery	**la refinería** *(lah reh-fee-neh-'ree-ah)*
sawmill	**el asseradero** *(ehl ah-sehr-rah-'deh-roh)*

Extra Info!

Notice how the suffix **-sería** is sometimes added to a root word to indicate a specific shop or store:

Trabajo en la...   I work at (the)...
(trah-'bah-hoh ehn lah)

cafetería *(kah-feh-teh-'ree-ah)*   coffee shop (from **café**, coffee)
carnicería *(kahr-nee-seh-'ree-ah)*   butcher shop (from **carne**, meat)
floristería *(floh-rees-teh-'ree-ah)*   flower shop (from **flor**, flower)
frutería *(froo-teh-'ree-ah)*   fruit market (from **fruta**, fruit)
joyería *(ho-yeh-'ree-ah)*   jewelry shop (from **joya**, jewel)
juguetería *(hoo-geh-teh-'ree-ah)*   toy store (from **jugar**, to play)
librería *(lee-breh-'ree-ah)*   bookstore (from **libro**, book)
mueblería *(mweh-bleh-'ree-ah)*   furniture store (from **mueble**, furniture)
panadería *(pah-nah-deh-'ree-ah)*   bakery (from **pan**, bread)
peluquería *(peh-loo-keh-'ree-ah)*   beauty shop (from **peluca**, wig)
tapicería *(tah-pee-seh-'ree-ah)*   upholstery shop (from **tapiz**, tapestry)
tintorería *(teen-toh-reh-'ree-ah)*   dry cleaner's (from **tinte**, tint)
verdulería *(vehr-doo-leh-'ree-ah)*   vegetable market (from **verdura**, vegetable)
zapatería *(sah-pah-teh-'ree-ah)*   shoe store (from **zapato**, shoe)

Try to determine the root words here:

brewery	**la cervecería** *(lah sehr-veh-seh-'ree-ah)*	_____
cattle raising	**la ganadería** *(lah gah-nah-deh-'ree-ah)*	_____
dairy farming	**la lechería** *(lah leh-cheh-'ree-ah)*	_____
fishing industry	**la pesquería** *(lah pehs-keh-'ree-ah)*	_____
hotel business	**la hostelería** *(lah ohs-teh-leh-'ree-ah)*	_____

The Departments
Los departamentos
(lohs deh-pahr-tah-'mehn-tohs)

Use these phrases to place new employees where they belong:

Here is (the)...	**Aquí está...** *(ah-'kee ehs-'tah)*
area	**el área** *(ehl 'ah-reh-ah)*
branch	**la sucursal** *(lah soo-koor-'sahl)*
cubicle	**el cubículo** *(ehl koo-'bee-koo-loh)*
department	**el departamento** *(ehl deh-pahr-tah-'mehn-toh)*
district	**el distrito** *(ehl dees-'tree-toh)*
division	**la división** *(lah dee-vee-see-'ohn)*
floor	**el piso** *(ehl 'pee-soh)*
office	**la oficina** *(lah oh-fee-'see-nah)*
outlet	**la subdistribuidora** *(lah soob-dees-tree-boo-ee-'doh-rah)*
place	**el lugar** *(ehl loo-'gahr)*
region	**la región** *(lah reh-hee-'ohn)*
room	**el cuarto** *(ehl 'kwahr-toh)*
section	**la sección** *(lah sehk-see-'ohn)*
site	**el sitio** *(ehl 'see-tee-oh)*
station	**la estación** *(lah ehs-tah-see-'ohn)*
subdivision	**la subdivisión** *(lah soob-dee-vee-see-'ohn)*
territory	**el territorio** *(ehl tehr-ree-'toh-ree-oh)*
unit	**la unidad** *(lah oo-nee-'dahd)*
zone	**la zona** *(lah 'soh-nah)*
It's (the) _____ department.	**Es el departamento de _____.** *(ehs ehl deh-pahr-tah-'mehn-toh deh)*
accounting	**contabilidad** *(kohn-tah-bee-lee-'dahd)*
administration	**administración** *(ahd-mee-nees-trah-see-'ohn)*
advertising	**publicidad** *(poo-blee-see-'dahd)*
assembly	**montaje** *(mohn-'tah-heh)*
communications	**comunicaciones** *(koh-moo-nee-kah-see-'oh-nehs)*
credit	**crédito** *('kreh-dee-toh)*
customer service	**servicio para clientes** *(sehr-'vee-see-oh 'pah-rah klee-'ehn-tehs)*
finance	**finanzas** *(fee-'nahn-sahs)*

human resources	**recursos humanos** *(reh-'koor-sohs oo-'mah-nohs)*
maintenance	**mantenimiento** *(mahn-teh-nee-mee-'ehn-toh)*
manufacturing	**fabricación** *(fah-bree-kah-see-'ohn)*
marketing	**mercadeo** *(mehr-kah-'deh-oh)*
operations	**operaciones** *(oh-peh-rah-see'oh-nehs)*
packaging	**embalaje** *(ehm-bah-'lah-heh)*
production	**producción** *(proh-dook-see-'ohn)*
publicity	**publicidad** *(poo-blee-see-'dahd)*
quality control	**control de calidad** *(kohn-trohl deh kah-lee-'dahd)*
receiving	**recepción** *(reh-sehp-see-'ohn)*
research	**investigación** *(een-vehs-tee-gah-see-'ohn)*
sales	**ventas** *('vehn-tahs)*
security	**seguridad** *(seh-goo-ree-'dahd)*
shipping	**envíos** *(ehn-'vee-ohs)*

Let's Practice ⑭

A. Remember how to tell people which floor they're on. We learned these numbers earlier, so go ahead and fill in the blanks:

It's on the _____ floor.
Está en el _____ piso. *(ehs-'tah ehn ehl _____ 'pee-soh)*

1st	primer	6th	_____
2nd	segundo	7th	_____
3rd	_____	8th	_____
4th	_____	9th	_____
5th	_____	10th	_____

B. Translate these useful terms:

1. warehouse _____
2. factory _____
3. shopping center _____
4. business _____
5. sales department _____
6. office _____

Let's Practice

C. Now, connect the words that belong together:

1. estudiante	hospital
2. dinero	zoológico
3. medicina	gasolinera
4. hamburguesa	universidad
5. tigre	banco
6. carro	restaurante

The Home Office
La casa matriz
(lah 'kah-sah mah-'trees)

Once employees know their job's location, point out parts of the main office building. Open up with a welcome:

Welcome to (the)… **Bienvenido a…** *(bee-ehn-veh-'nee-doh ah)*

operations center **el centro de operaciones**
(ehl 'sehn-troh deh oh-peh-rah-see-'oh-nehs)

headquarters **la dirección general**
(lah dee-rehk-see-'ohn heh-neh-'rahl)

I'll show you (the)… **Le muestro…** *(leh 'mwehs-troh)*

cafeteria **la cafetería** *(lah kah-feh-teh-'ree-ah)*
lobby **el vestíbulo** *(ehl vehs-'tee-boo-loh)*
mailbox **el buzón** *(ehl boo-'sohn)*
parking area **el estacionamiento** *(ehl ehs-tah-see-oh-nah-mee-'ehn-toh)*
public telephone **el teléfono público** *(ehl teh-'leh-foh-noh 'poob-lee-koh)*
punch clock **el reloj registrador** *(ehl reh-'loh reh-hees-trah-'dohr)*
reception desk **la recepción** *(lah reh-sehp-see-'ohn)*
restroom **los servicios** *(lohs sehr-'vee-see-ohs)*
vending machine **la máquina vendedora**
(lah 'mah-kee-nah vehn-deh-'doh-rah)
water fountain **la fuente de agua** *(lah 'fwehn-teh deh 'ah-gwah)*

This is called (the) _____ .	**Esto se llama** _____ . *('ehs-toh seh 'yah-mah)*
conference room	**la sala de conferencias** *(lah 'sah-lah deh kohn-feh-'rehn-see-ahs)*
laboratory	**el laboratorio** *(ehl lah-boh-rah-'toh-ree-oh)*
library	**la biblioteca** *(lah bee-blee-oh-'teh-kah)*
loading bay	**la zona de carga y descarga** *(lah 'soh-nah deh 'kahr-gah ee dehs-'kahr-gah)*
mailroom	**la oficina de correos** *(lah oh-fee-'see-nah deh kohr-'reh-ohs)*
show room	**la sala de exhibición** *(lah 'sah-lah deh ex-ee-bee-see-'ohn)*
storeroom	**el depósito** *(ehl deh-'poh-see-toh)*
training room	**la sala de entrenamiento** *(lah 'sah-lah deh ehn-treh-nah-mee-'ehn-toh)*
waiting room	**la sala de espera** *(lah 'sah-lah deh ehs-'peh-rah)*
work center	**el centro de trabajo** *(ehl 'sehn-troh deh trah-'bah-hoh)*
Please use (the)…	**Favor de usar…** *(fah-'vohr deh oo-'sahr)*
double doors	**las puertas dobles** *(lahs 'pwehr-tahs 'doh-blehs)*
elevator	**el ascensor** *(ehl ah-sehn-'sohr)*
entrance	**la entrada** *(lah ehn-'trah-dah)*
escalator	**la escalera mecánica** *(lah ehs-kah-'leh-rah meh-'kah-nee-kah)*
exit	**la salida** *(lah sah-'lee-dah)*
gate	**el portón** *(ehl pohr-'tohn)*
hallway	**el corredor** *(ehl kohr-reh-'dohr)*
stairs	**las escaleras** *(lahs ehs-kah-'leh-rahs)*
steps	**los escalones** *(lohs ehs-kah-'loh-nehs)*

 # The Culture

Bear in mind that traditional American foods don't always appeal to a multi-ethnic workforce. Many Hispanics prefer to bring their home-made foods to work with them for lunch. To raise morale, consider asking employees about the foods they enjoy most, and then add those items to the current cafeteria menu.

Extra Info!

Identify the outstanding structures of your property:

Look at (the)...	**Mire...** *('mee-reh)*
balcony	**el balcón** *(ehl bahl-'kohn)*
bridge	**el puente** *(ehl 'pwehn-teh)*
ceiling	**el techo** *(ehl 'teh-choh)*
dock	**el muelle** *(ehl 'mweh-yeh)*
fence	**la cerca** *(lah 'sehr-kah)*
garden	**el jardín** *(ehl hahr-'deen)*
light post	**el farol** *(ehl fah-'rohl)*
ramp	**la rampa** *(lah 'rahm-pah)*
roof	**el tejado** *(ehl teh-'hah-doh)*
tower	**la torre** *(lah 'tohr-reh)*
walkway	**el sendero** *(ehl sehn-'deh-roh)*
wall	**la pared** *(lah pah-'rehd)*
window	**la ventana** *(lah vehn-'tah-nah)*

You may also need to use Spanish around the cafeteria, vending machine, lunch truck, or dining area:

This is the dining and break area.
Esta es la zona para comer y descansar.
('ehs-tah ehs lah 'soh-nah 'pah-rah koh-'mehr ee dehs-kahn-'sahr)

You may sit where you want.
Puede sentarse dónde quiera.
('pweh-deh sehn-'tahr-seh 'dohn-deh kee-'eh-rah)

These are the hours of service.
Estas son las horas de servicio.
('ehs-tahs sohn lahs 'oh-rahs deh sehr-'vee-see-oh)

The food is very good.
La comida es muy buena.
(lah koh-'mee-dah ehs 'moo-ee 'bweh-nah)

Extra Info!

You have to pay over there.
Tiene que pagar ahí. *(tee-'eh-neh keh pah-'gahr ah-'ee)*

They sell ...	**Venden ...** *('vehn-dehn)*
breakfast	**el desayuno** *(ehl deh-sah-'yoo-noh)*
dinner	**la cena** *(lah 'seh-nah)*
drinks	**las bebidas** *(lahs beh-'bee-dahs)*
lunch	**el almuerzo** *(ehl ahl-'mwehr-soh)*
snacks	**la comida ligera** *(lah koh-'mee-dah lee-'heh-rah)*

Office Furniture
Los muebles de oficina
(lohs 'mweh-blehs deh oh-fee-'see-nah)

Workplace Spanish vocabulary also includes the names for office equipment, furniture, and décor. One practice technique that really works is to apply removable stickers on everything, so that you can read the Spanish as you walk by. Start by naming the furnishings:

It has (the) _____.	**Tiene _____.** *(tee-'eh-neh)*
armchair	**el sillón** *(ehl see-'yohn)*
bench	**el banco** *(ehl 'bahn-koh)*
bookshelf	**el librero** *(ehl lee-'breh-roh)*
carpet	**la alfombra** *(lah ahl-'fohm-brah)*
chair	**la silla** *(lah 'see-yah)*
clock	**el reloj** *(ehl reh-'loh)*
counter	**el mostrador** *(ehl mohs-trah-'dohr)*
desk	**el escritorio** *(ehl ehs-kree-'toh-ree-oh)*
furniture (single piece)	**el mueble** *(ehl 'mweh-bleh)*
lamp	**la lámpara** *(lah 'lahm-pah-rah)*
seat	**el asiento** *(ehl ah-see-'ehn-toh)*

shelf	**la repisa** *(lah reh-'pee-sah)*
sofa	**el sofá** *(ehl soh-'fah)*
stool	**el banquillo** *(ehl bahn-'kee-yoh)*
table	**la mesa** *(lah 'meh-sah)*
trash basket	**el cesto de basura** *(ehl 'sehs-toh deh bah-'soo-rah)*
It's inside (the)...	**Está dentro de...** *(ehs-'tah 'dehn-troh deh)*
cabinet	**el gabinete** *(ehl gah-bee-'neh-teh)*
chest	**el baúl** *(ehl bah-'ool)*
closet	**el closet** *(ehl 'kloh-seht)*
cupboard	**el armario** *(ehl ahr-'mah-ree-oh)*
drawer	**el cajón** *(ehl kah-'hohn)*
file cabinet	**el archivo** *(ehl ahr-'chee-voh)*
safe	**la caja fuerte** *(lah 'kah-hah 'fwehr-teh)*
showcase	**la vitrina** *(lah vee-'tree-nah)*

Extra Info!

Here are more important words for the employer:

Carry (the)...	**Lleve...** *('yeh-veh)*
bottle	**la botella** *(lah boh-'teh-yah)*
box	**la caja** *(lah 'kah-hah)*
bundle	**el bulto** *(ehl 'bool-toh)*
can	**la lata** *(lah 'lah-tah)*
container	**el contenedor** *(ehl kohn-teh-neh-'dohr)*
roll	**el rollo** *(ehl 'roh-yoh)*

Office Equipment
El equipo de oficina
(ehl eh-'kee-poh deh oh-fee-'see-nah)

You should ask your office employees yes-no questions so that you'll be able to understand their responses more easily:

Do you need (the)…?	**¿Necesita usted…?** *(neh-seh-'see-tah oos-'tehd)*
calendar	**el calendario** *(ehl kah-lehn-'dah-ree-oh)*
cart	**el carrito** *(ehl kahr-'ree-toh)*
chart	**el gráfico** *(ehl 'grah-fee-koh)*
cushion	**la almohadilla** *(lah ahl-moh-ah-'dee-yah)*
map	**el mapa** *(ehl 'mah-pah)*
partition	**el divisor** *(ehl dee-vee-'sohr)*
pegboard	**el tablero perforado** *(ehl tah-'bleh-roh pehr-foh-'rah-doh)*
planner	**el planificador** *(ehl plah-nee-fee-kah-'dohr)*
podium	**el atril** *(ehl ah-'treel)*
schedule	**el horario** *(ehl oh-'rah-ree-oh)*
tray	**la bandeja** *(lah bahn-'deh-hah)*
whiteboard	**el pizarrón** *(ehl pee-sahr-'rohn)*
Do you know how to use…?	**¿Sabe usted usar…?** *('sah-beh oos-'tehd oo-'sahr)*
adding machine	**la sumadora** *(lah soo-mah-'doh-rah)*
air conditioner	**el acondicionador de aire** *(ehl ah-kohn-dee-see-oh-nah-'dohr deh 'ah-ee-reh)*
answering machine	**el contestador telefónico** *(ehl kohn-tehs-tah-'dohr teh-leh-'foh-nee-koh)*
calculator	**la calculadora** *(lah kahl-koo-lah-'doh-rah)*
camcorder	**la filmadora** *(lah feel-mah-'doh-rah)*
cash register	**la registradora** *(lah reh-gees-trah-'doh-rah)*
computer	**la computadora** *(lah kohm-poo-tah-'doh-rah)*
copier	**la copiadora** *(lah koh-pee-ah-'doh-rah)*
dictaphone	**el dictáfono** *(ehl deek-'tah-foh-noh)*
digital camera	**la cámara digital** *(lah 'kah-mah-rah dee-hee-'tahl)*
fan	**el ventilador** *(ehl vehn-tee-lah-'dohr)*

fax machine	**la máquina de fax** *(lah 'mah-kee-nah deh fahx)*
GPS	**el sistema de navegación portátil**
	(ehl sees-'teh-mah deh nah-veh-gah-see-'ohn pohr-'tah-teel)
headphones	**los auriculares** *(lohs aw-ree-koo-'lah-rehs)*
heater	**el calefactor** *(ehl kah-leh-fahk-'tohr)*
intercom	**el intercomunicador**
	(ehl een-tehr-koh-moo-nee-kah-'dohr)
laminator	**la laminadora** *(lah lah-mee-nah-'doh-rah)*
laptop	**la computadora portátil**
	(lah kohm-poo-tah-'doh-rah pohr-'tah-teel)
microphone	**el micrófono** *(ehl mee-'kroh-foh-noh)*
monitor	**el monitor** *(ehl moh-nee-'tohr)*
organizer	**el organizador** *(ehl ohr-gah-nee-sah-'dohr)*
paper shredder	**la desmenuzadora** *(lah dehs-meh-noo-sah-'doh-rah)*
PDA	**la computadora de bolsillo**
	(lah kohm-poo-tah-'doh-rah deh bohl-'see-yoh)
pencil sharpener	**el sacapuntas** *(ehl sah-kah-'poon-tahs)*
player	**el tocador** *(ehl toh-kah-'dohr)*
pointer	**el señalador** *(ehl sehn-yah-lah-'dohr)*
printer	**la impresora** *(lah eem-preh-'soh-rah)*
projector	**el proyector** *(ehl proh-yehk-'tohr)*
recorder	**la grabadora** *(lah grah-bah-'doh-rah)*
remote control	**el control remoto** *(ehl kohn-'trohl reh-'moh-toh)*
scale	**la báscula** *(lah 'bahs-koo-lah)*
scanner	**el escáner** *(ehl ehs-'kah-nehr)*
screen	**la pantalla** *(lah pahn-'tah-yah)*
speaker	**el altavoz** *(ehl ahl-tah-'vohs)*
translator	**la traductora** *(lah trah-dook-'toh-rah)*
TV	**el televisor** *(ehl teh-leh-vee-'sohr)*
Do you want (the)…?	**¿Quiere usted…?** *(kee-'eh-reh oos-'tehd)*
accessories	**los accesorios** *(lohs ahk-seh-'soh-ree-ohs)*
appliances	**los electrodomésticos**
	(lohs eh-lehk-troh-doh-'mehs-tee-kohs)
devices	**los aparatos** *(lohs ah-pah-'rah-tohs)*
equipment	**el equipo** *(ehl eh-'kee-poh)*
furniture	**los muebles** *(lohs 'mweh-blehs)*

instruments	**los instrumentos** *(lohs eens-troo-'mehn-tohs)*
machines	**las máquinas** *(lahs 'mah-kee-nahs)*
materials	**los materiales** *(lohs mah-teh-ree-'ah-lehs)*
merchandise	**las mercancías** *(lahs mehr-kahn-'see-ahs)*
stationery	**los objetos de escritorio**
	(lohs ohb-'heh-tohs deh ehs-kree-'toh-ree-oh)
supplies	**los suministros** *(lohs soo-mee-'nees-trohs)*
tools	**las herramientas** *(lahs ehr-rah-mee-'ehn-tahs)*

Extra Info!

This vocabulary combines well with words of location:

It's...	**Está...** *(ehs-'tah)*
in back	**detrás** *(deh-'trahs)*
in front	**en frente** *(ehn 'frehn-teh)*
in the middle	**en medio** *(ehn 'meh-dee-oh)*

Some offices are a bit more elaborate than others:

Be careful with (the)...	**Tenga cuidado con...** *('tehn-gah kwee-'dah-doh kohn)*
ashtray	**el cenicero** *(ehl seh-nee-'seh-roh)*
flowerpot	**la maceta** *(lah mah-'seh-tah)*
mat	**el tapete** *(ehl tah-'peh-teh)*
mirror	**el espejo** *(ehl ehs-'peh-hoh)*
painting	**el cuadro** *(ehl 'kwah-droh)*
photograph	**la fotografía** *(lah foh-toh-grah-'fee-ah)*
pottery	**la cerámica** *(lah seh-'rah-mee-kah)*
statue	**la estatua** *(lah ehs-'tah-too-ah)*
vase	**el florero** *(ehl flo-'reh-roh)*

Office Supplies
Los suministros de oficina
(lohs soo-mee-'nees-trohs deh oh-fee-'see-nah)

When office employees have limited English skills, you may have to use a lot of commands:

Bring (the)…	**Traiga…** *('trah-ee-gah)*
hole punch	**la perforadora** *(lah pehr-foh-rah-'doh-rah)*
paper cutter	**la cortapapeles** *(lah kohr-tah-pah-'peh-lehs)*
ruler	**la regla** *(lah 'reh-glah)*
scissors	**las tijeras** *(lahs tee-'heh-rahs)*
stapler	**la engrapadora** *(lah ehn-grah-pah-'doh-rah)*
Use (the)…	**Use…** *('oo-seh)*
binder	**la carpeta** *(lah kahr-'peh-tah)*
card	**la tarjeta** *(lah tahr-'heh-tah)*
cardboard	**el cartón** *(ehl kahr-'tohn)*
envelope	**el sobre** *(ehl 'soh-breh)*
eraser	**el borrador** *(ehl bohr-rah-'dohr)*
highlighter	**el resaltador** *(ehl reh-sahl-tah-'dohr)*
label	**la etiqueta** *(lah eh-tee-'keh-tah)*
marker	**el marcador** *(ehl mahr-kah-'dohr)*
notebook	**el cuaderno** *(ehl kwah-'dehr-noh)*
paper clips	**los sujetapapeles** *(lohs soo-heh-tah-pah-'peh-lehs)*
paper	**el papel** *(ehl pah-'pehl)*
pen	**el lapicero** *(ehl lah-pee-'seh-roh)*
pencil	**el lápiz** *(ehl 'lah-pees)*
poster board	**el cartel** *(ehl kahr-'tehl)*
rubber bands	**los elásticos** *(lohs eh-'lahs-tee-kohs)*
scotch tape	**la cinta adhesiva** *(lah 'seen-tah ah-deh-'see-vah)*
stamps	**las estampillas** *(lahs ehs-tahm-'pee-yahs)*
staples	**las grapas** *(lahs 'grah-pahs)*
tacks	**las tachuelas** *(lahs tah-choo-'eh-lahs)*

Take (the)…	**Tome…** *('toh-meh)*
batteries	**las pilas** *(lahs 'pee-lahs)*
bulbs	**las bombillas** *(lahs bohm-'bee-yahs)*
film	**la película** *(lah peh-'lee-koo-lah)*
ink	**la tinta** *(lah 'teen-tah)*
ribbon	**la cinta** *(lah 'seen-tah)*
toner	**el tóner** *(ehl 'toh-nehr)*

Extra Info!

Keep speaking Spanglish!

el Whiteout®
el glue-stick
el Post-it®

Search online or in a dictionary for the names of specific items around the workplace:

ballpoint pen	**el bolígrafo** *(ehl boh-'lee-grah-foh)*
fountain pen	**la pluma** *(lah 'ploo-mah)*
pen refill	**el recambio de lapicero**
	(ehl reh-'kahm-bee-oh deh lah-pee-'seh-roh)
photo paper	**el papel fotográfico**
	(ehl pah'pehl foh-toh-'grah-fee-koh)
ink jet paper	**el papel de chorro de tinta**
	(ehl pah-'pehl deh 'chohr-roh deh 'teen-tah)
graph paper	**el papel cuadriculado**
	(ehl pah-'pehl kwah-dree-koo-'lah-doh)

Let's Practice (15)

A. Fill in the word that completes each series:

caja, asiento, ascensor, gabinete, lápiz, planificador, impresora

1. escalones, escaleras, _____
2. horario, calendario, _____
3. archivo, armario, _____
4. copiadora, computadora, _____
5. lata, botella, _____
6. sofá, silla, _____
7. borrador, lapicero, _____

B. Fill in these lines with words you have just learned:

¿Dónde está _____?
¡_____ es muy grande!
No trabajo con _____.

The Workshop
El taller
(ehl tah-'yehr)

Use simple questions to practice with the items present in the workshop, warehouse, or factory:

Where's (the)...?	¿Dónde está...? *('dohn-deh ehs-'tah)*
belt	**la correa** *(lah kohr-'reh-ah)*
blade	**la navaja** *(lah nah-'vah-hah)*
block	**el bloque** *(ehl 'bloh-keh)*
board	**la tabla** *(lah 'tah-blah)*
fastener	**el cierre** *(ehl see-'ehr-reh)*
brace	**el soporte** *(ehl soh-'pohr-teh)*
cart	**la carretilla** *(lah kahr-reh-'tee-yah)*
clamp	**la abrazadera** *(lah ah-brah-sah-'deh-rah)*
clasp	**el broche** *(ehl 'broh-cheh)*
dolly	**el travelín** *(ehl trah-veh-'leen)*
filter	**el filtro** *(ehl 'feel-troh)*

hook	**el gancho** *(ehl 'gahn-choh)*
hose	**la manguera** *(lah mahn-'geh-rah)*
ladder	**la escalera** *(lah ehs-kah-'leh-rah)*
ladle	**el cucharón** *(ehl koo-chah-'rohn)*
magnet	**el imán** *(ehl ee-'mahn)*
moulding	**el molde** *(ehl 'mohl-deh)*
net	**la red** *(lah rehd)*
pallet	**el soporte de madera** *(ehl soh-'pohr-teh deh mah-'deh-rah)*
plate	**la plancha** *(lah 'plahn-chah)*
pulley	**la polea** *(lah poh-'leh-ah)*
stake	**la estaca** *(lah ehs-'tah-kah)*
stick	**el palo** *(ehl 'pah-loh)*
tray	**la bandeja** *(lah bahn-'deh-hah)*
tripod	**el trípode** *(ehl 'tree-poh-deh)*
wheel	**la rueda** *(lah 'rweh-dah)*

Do you see (the)…?	**¿Ve usted…?** *(veh oos-'tehd)*

barrier	**la barrera** *(lah bahr-'reh-rah)*
duct	**el conducto** *(ehl kohn-'dook-toh)*
hatch	**la compuerta** *(lah kohm-'pwehr-tah)*
joist	**la vigueta** *(lah vee-'gheh-tah)*
landing	**el descanso** *(ehl dehs-'kahn-soh)*
partition	**el divisor** *(ehl dee-vee-'sohr)*
platform	**la plataforma** *(lah plah-tah-'fohr-mah)*
post	**el poste** *(ehl 'pohs-teh)*
rafter	**la viga** *(lah 'vee-gah)*
railing	**la baranda** *(lah bah-'rahn-dah)*
ramp	**la rampa** *(lah 'rahm-pah)*
scaffold	**el andamio** *(ehl ahn-'dah-mee-oh)*
shaft	**el pozo** *(ehl 'poh-soh)*
track	**el carril** *(ehl kahr-'reel)*

Do you like (the)…?	**¿Le gusta…?** *(leh 'goos-tah)*

booth	**el puesto** *(ehl 'pwehs-toh)*
cage	**la jaula** *(lah 'ha-oo-lah)*
shed	**el cobertizo** *(ehl koh-behr-'tee-soh)*
station	**la estación** *(lah ehs-tah-see-'ohn)*
work table	**la mesa de trabajo** *(lah 'meh-sah deh trah-'bah-hoh)*
workbench	**el banco de trabajo** *(ehl 'bahn-koh deh trah-'bah-hoh)*

Now shift to Spanish commands as the work begins:

Turn on (the) ...	**Prenda** ... *('prehn-dah)*
control panel	**el tablero de control** *(ehl tah-'bleh-roh deh kohn-'trohl)*
device	**el aparato** *(ehl ah-pah-'rah-toh)*
engine	**el motor** *(ehl moh-'tohr)*
equipment	**el equipo** *(ehl eh-'kee-poh)*
machine	**la máquina** *(lah 'mah-kee-nah)*
power	**la electricidad** *(lah eh-lehk-tree-see-'dahd)*

Check (the)…	**Revise**… *(reh-'vee-seh)*
battery	**la batería** *(lah bah-teh-'ree-ah)*
breaker	**el cortacircuitos** *(ehl kohr-tah-seer-koo-'ee-tohs)*
bulb	**el foco** *(ehl 'foh-koh)*
cable	**el cable** *(ehl 'kah-bleh)*
charger	**el cargador** *(ehl kahr-gah-'dohr)*
circuit	**el circuito** *(ehl seer-koo-'ee-toh)*
connection	**la conexión** *(lah koh-nehk-see-'ohn)*
drain	**el drenaje** *(ehl dreh-'nah-heh)*
electrical cable	**el cable eléctrico** *(ehl 'kah-bleh eh-'lehk-tree-koh)*
electrical outlet	**la toma de corriente** *(lah 'toh-mah deh kohr-ree-'ehn-teh)*
extension cord	**el cable de extensión** *(ehl 'kah-bleh deh ex-tehn-see-'ohn)*
fan	**el ventilador** *(ehl vehn-tee-lah-'dohr)*
faucet	**el grifo** *(ehl 'gree-foh)*
fuse	**el fusible** *(ehl foo-'see-bleh)*
gauge	**el indicador** *(ehl een-dee-kah-'dohr)*
gear	**el engranaje** *(ehl ehn-grah-'nah-heh)*
generator	**el generador** *(ehl heh-neh-rah-'dohr)*
meter	**el medidor** *(ehl meh-dee-'dohr)*
pipe	**la tubería** *(lah too-beh-'ree-ah)*
plug	**el enchufe** *(ehl ehn-'choo-feh)*
power line	**el cable eléctrico** *(ehl 'kah-bleh eh-'lehk-tree-koh)*
thermometer	**el termómetro** *(ehl tehr-'moh-meh-troh)*
thermostat	**el termostato** *(ehl tehr-mohs-'tah-toh)*
transformer	**el transformador** *(ehl trahns-fohr-mah-'dohr)*
valve	**la válvula** *(lah 'vahl-voo-lah)*
wire	**el alambre** *(ehl ah-'lahm-breh)*

Fill (the)…	**Llene…** *('yeh-neh)*
bag	**la bolsa** *(lah 'bohl-sah)*
barrel	**el barril** *(ehl bahr-'reel)*
basket	**la canasta** *(lah kah-'nahs-tah)*
box	**la caja** *(lah 'kah-hah)*
bucket	**el balde** *(ehl 'bahl-deh)*
crate	**la caja de transporte** *(lah 'kah-hah deh trahns-'pohr-teh)*
tank	**el tanque** *(ehl 'tahn-keh)*
tub	**la tina** *(lah 'tee-nah)*

Press (the)…	**Oprima…** *(oh-'pree-mah)*
button	**el botón** *(ehl boh-'tohn)*
buzzer	**el timbre** *(ehl 'teem-breh)*
dial	**el dial** *(ehl dee-'ahl)*
key	**la tecla** *(lah 'teh-klah)*
knob	**el tirador** *(ehl tee-rah-'dohr)*
switch	**el interruptor** *(ehl een-tehr-roop-'tohr)*
timer	**el cronógrafo** *(ehl kroh-'noh-grah-foh)*

Extra Info!

Regardless of the workplace, you can't do much without this next group:

Does it have…?	**¿Tiene…?** *(tee-'eh-neh)*
air conditioning	**el aire acondicionado** *(ehl 'ah-ee-reh ah-kohn-dee-see-oh-'nah-doh)*
gas meter	**el medidor de gas** *(ehl meh-dee-'dohr deh gahs)*
heating	**la calefacción** *(lah kah-leh-fahk-see-'ohn)*
lighting	**la iluminación** *(lah ee-loo-mee-nah-see-'ohn)*
plumbing	**la plomería** *(lah ploh-meh-'ree-ah)*
security system	**el sistema de seguridad** *(ehl sees-'tee-mah deh seh-goo-ree-'dahd)*
sprinkler system	**el sistema de regadío** *(ehl sees-'teh-mah deh reh-gah-'dee-oh)*
water valve	**la válvula de agua** *(lah 'vahl-voo-lah deh 'ah-gwah)*

The Culture

Although Spanglish (the blending of Spanish and English) is a fact of life in our country, it's always a good idea to use the correct Spanish words to communicate with your employees. Here are a few examples:

ENGLISH	SPANGLISH	SPANISH
lunch	**el lonche**	**el almuerzo**
	(ehl 'lohn-cheh)	*(ehl ahl-moo-'ehr-soh)*
elevator	**el elevador**	**el ascensor**
	(ehl eh-leh-vah-'dohr)	*(ehl ah-sehn-'sohr)*
truck	**la troca**	**el camión**
	(lah 'troh-kah)	*(ehl kah-mee-'ohn)*

Look at these others. Then create your own list of Spanglish words:

el typing

la party

el parking

el freeway

_____ _____

_____ _____

_____ _____

Let's Practice

(16)

A. Review by translating these command phrases aloud:

1. Press the button!
2. Fill the box!
3. Check the meter!

B. Connect the words that go well together:

1. máquina   estaca
2. barrera   broche
3. balde   alambre
4. cable   tina
5. cierre   divisor
6. palo   motor

Heavy Machinery
La maquinaria pesada
(lah mah-kee-'nah-ree-ah peh-'sah-dah)

This next group of vocabulary refers to heavy equipment and machinery:

Here is (the)…	**Aquí está…** *(ah-'kee ehs-'tah)*
blower	**el soplador** *(ehl soh-plah-'dohr)*
boiler	**la caldera** *(lah kahl-'deh-rah)*
compressor	**el compresor** *(ehl kohm-preh-'sohr)*
conveyor belt	**la correa transportadora** *(lah kohr-'reh-ah trahns-pohr-tah-'doh-rah)*
crane	**la grúa** *(lah 'groo-ah)*
drill	**la taladradora** *(lah tah-lah-drah-'doh-rah)*
forge	**la fragua** *(lah 'frah-gwah)*
forklift	**la carretilla elevadora** *(lah kahr-reh-'tee-yah eh-leh-vah-'doh-rah)*
furnace	**el horno** *(ehl 'ohr-noh)*
grinder	**el molinero** *(ehl moh-lee-'neh-roh)*
lathe	**el torno** *(ehl 'tohr-noh)*
mill	**el molino** *(ehl moh-'lee-noh)*
pump	**la bomba** *(lah 'bohm-bah)*
robot	**el robot** *(ehl roh-'boht)*
simulator	**la simuladora** *(lah see-moo-lah-'doh-rah)*
torch	**la antorcha** *(lah ahn-'tohr-chah)*
turbine	**la turbina** *(lah toor-'bee-nah)*

Do you know how to use (the)…	**¿Sabe manejar…** *('sa-beh mah-neh-'hahr)*
backhoe	**la retroexcavadora** *(lah reh-troh-ex-kah-vah-'doh-rah)*
bulldozer	**el tractor oruga** *(ehl trahk-'tohr oh-'roo-gah)*
cement truck	**el camión hormigonero** *(ehl kah-mee-'ohn ohr-mee-goh-'neh-roh)*
crane truck	**el camión grúa** *(ehl kah-mee-'ohn 'groo-ah)*
dump truck	**el camión volquete** *(ehl kah-mee-'ohn vohl-'keh-teh)*
flatbed truck	**el camión de plataforma** *(ehl kah-mee-'ohn deh plah-tah-'fohr-mah)*
loader	**la cargadora** *(lah kahr-gah-'doh-rah)*
semitrailer	**el semirremolque** *(ehl seh-mee-rreh-'mohl-keh)*

tanker truck	**el camión cisterna** *(ehl kah-mee-'ohn sees-'tehr-nah)*
tractor trailer	**el camión tractor** *(ehl kah-mee-'ohn trahk-'tohr)*

Many machines in Spanish are identified by their specific operation or function:

Check (the)...	**Revise...** *(reh-'vee-seh)*
burner	**la quemadora** *(lah keh-mah-'doh-rah)* (from **quemar**, to burn)
compactor	**la compactadora** *(lah kohm-pahk-tah-'doh-rah)* (from **compactar**, to compact)
cutter	**la cortadora** *(lah kohr-tah-'doh-rah)* (from **cortar**, to cut)
feeder	**la alimentadora** *(lah ah-lee-mehn-tah-'doh-rah)* (from **alimentar**, to feed)
stacker	**la apiladora** *(lah ah-pee-lah-'doh-rah)* (from **apilar**, to stack)

Extra Info!

Most businesses utilize the following vehicles every day:

car	**el carro** *(ehl 'kahr-roh)*
pickup	**la camioneta** *(lah kah-mee-oh-'neh-tah)*
truck	**el camión** *(ehl kah-mee-'ohn)*
van	**la vagoneta** *(lah vah-goh-'neh-tah)*

Electronic Devices
Los aparatos electrónicos
(lohs ah-pah-'rah-tohs eh-lehk-'troh-nee-kohs)

Many Spanish words related to electronics are used in descriptive phrases. Why not practice a few:

WE WORK ON...	**TRABAJAMOS CON...**
the _____ system	**el sistema de _____** *(ehl sees-'teh-mah deh)*
alarm	**alarmas** *(ah-'lahr-mahs)*
computer	**computadoras** *(kohm-poo-tah-'doh-rahs)*
telecommunications	**telecomunicaciones** *(teh-leh-koh-moo-nee-kah-see-'oh-nehs)*

the electronic _____   _____ **electrónica** *(eh-lehk-'troh-nee-kah)*

cash register   **la registradora** *(lah reh-hees-trah-'doh-rah)*
scale   **la báscula** *(lah 'bahs-koo-lah)*
copier   **la copiadora** *(lah koh-pee-ah-'doh-rah)*

the _____ equipment **el equipo de** _____ *(ehl eh-'kee-poh deh)*

measuring   **medición** *(meh-dee-see-'ohn)*
pressurizing   **presión** *(preh-see-'ohn)*
pumping   **bombeo** *(bohm-'beh-oh)*

It's (the)…   **Es…** *(ehs)*

amperage   **el amperaje** *(ehl ahm-peh-'rah-heh)*
cell   **la célula** *(lah 'seh-loo-lah)*
channel   **el canal** *(ehl kah-'nahl)*
current   **la corriente** *(lah kohr-ree-'ehn-teh)*
filament   **el filamento** *(ehl fee-lah-'mehn-toh)*
laser   **el láser** *(ehl 'lah-sehr)*
memory   **la memoria** *(lah meh-'moh-ree-ah)*
remote   **el control remoto** *(ehl kohn-'trohl reh-'moh-toh)*
voltage   **el voltaje** *(ehl vohl-'tah-heh)*

They are (the)…   **Son…** *(sohn)*

adapters   **los adaptadores** *(lohs ah-dahp-tah-'doh-rehs)*
capacitors   **los capacitores** *(lohs kah-pah-see-'toh-rehs)*
condensers   **los condensadores** *(lohs kohn-dehn-sah-'doh-rehs)*
detectors   **los detectores** *(lohs deh-tehk-'toh-rehs)*
diodes   **los diodos** *(lohs dee-'oh-dohs)*
electrodes   **los electrodos** *(lohs eh-lehk-'troh-dohs)*
integrated circuits **los circuitos integrados**
                     (los seer-koo-'ee-tohs een-teh-'grah-dohs)
microprocessors   **los microprocesadores**
                     (lohs mee-kroh-proh-seh-sah-'doh-rehs)
oscillators   **los osciladores** *(lohs oh-see-lah-'doh-rehs)*
resistors   **los resistores** *(lohs reh-sees-'toh-rehhs)*
semiconductors   **los semiconductores** *(lohs seh-mee-kohn-dook-'toh-rehs)*
sensors   **los sensores** *(lohs sehn-'soh-rehs)*
transducers   **los transductores** *(lohs trahns-dook-'toh-rehs)*
transformers   **los transformadores** *(lohs trahns-fohr-mah-'doh-rehs)*
transistors   **los transistores** *(lohs trahn-sees-'toh-rehs)*

Notice the word order in these examples:

AC	**corriente alterna** *(kohr-ree-'ehn-teh ahl-'tehr-nah)*
DC	**corriente directa** *(kohr-ree-'ehn-teh dee-'rehk-tah)*
high voltage	**alto voltaje** *('ahl-toh vohl-'tah-heh)*
low voltage	**bajo voltaje** *('bah-hoh vohl-'tah-heh)*
positive charge	**carga positiva** *('kahr-gah poh-see-'tee-vah)*
negative charge	**carga negativa** *('kahr-gah neh-gah-'tee-vah)*

Not all words in electronics are easy to recognize. Say these examples aloud:

coil	**la bobina** *(lah boh-'bee-nah)*
dry cell battery	**la pila** *(lah 'pee-lah)*
insulator	**el aislador** *(ehl ah-ees-lah-'dohr)*
switch	**el interruptor** *(ehl een-tehr-roop-'tohr)*
watt	**el vatio** *(ehl 'vah-tee-oh)*

Extra Info!

One way to remember job-specific vocabulary is to focus on the endings of the words. Note the simple patterns in both languages:

activation	**la activación** *(lah ahk-tee-vah-see-'ohn)*
concentration	**la concentración** *(lah kohn-sehn-trah-see-'ohn)*
installation	**la instalación** *(lah eens-tah-lah-see-'ohn)*
reduction	**la reducción** *(lah reh-dook-see-'ohn)*
hydraulic	**hidráulico** *(eed-'rah-oo-lee-koh)*
static	**estático** *(ehs-'tah-tee-koh)*
automatic	**automático** *(aw-toh-'mah-tee-koh)*
electronic	**electrónico** *(eh-lehk-'troh-nee-koh)*
capacity	**la capacidad** *(lah kah-pah-see-'dahd)*
intensity	**la intensidad** *(lah een-tehn-see-'dahd)*
polarity	**la polaridad** *(lah poh-lah-ree-'dahd)*
electricity	**la electricidad** *(lah eh-lehk-tree-see-'dahd)*

Let's Practice

(17)

A. Study the following pattern in Spanish and fill in the lines on your own:

It's...   Es... *(ehs)*

chemical   **químico** *('kee-mee-koh)*
1. _____   **técnico** *('tehk-nee-koh)*
2. _____   **mecánico** *(meh-'kah-nee-koh)*
3. _____   **eléctrico** *(eh-'lehk-tree-koh)*

B. These electronic devices are easy to identify:

1. el estéreo   _____
2. la fotocopiadora   _____
3. el escáner   _____
4. el micrófono   _____
5. la cámara   _____

C. How many work-related vocabulary words that are spelled exactly the same in both languages can you remember? Look at this list, and add your own:

digital	gradual	el radio	el sensor
virtual	el detector	artificial	el monitor
	normal	el conductor	
_____	_____	_____	
_____	_____	_____	
_____	_____	_____	

Common Tools
Las herramientas comunes
(lahs ehr-rah-mee-'ehn-tahs koh-'moo-nehs)

No matter what the field of employment, most of us know what to do with these:

Do you need (the)...?	¿Necesita...? *(neh-seh-'see-tah)*
ax	**el hacha** *(ehl 'ah-chah)*
chisel	**el cincel** *(ehs seen-'sehl)*
crowbar	**la palanca** *(lah pah-'lahn-kah)*
file	**la lima** *(lah 'lee-mah)*
hack saw	**la sierra de metales** *(lah see-'ehr-rah deh meh-'tah-lehs)*
hammer	**el martillo** *(ehl mahr-'tee-yoh)*
hand saw	**el serrucho** *(ehl sehr-'roo-choh)*
measuring tape	**la cinta de medir** *(lah 'seen-tah deh meh-'deer)*
level	**el nivel** *(ehl nee-'vehl)*
paint brush	**la brocha de pintar** *(lah 'broh-chah deh peen-'tahr)*
pliers	**las pinzas** *(lahs 'peen-sahs)*
sandpaper	**el papel de lija** *(ehl pah-'pehl deh 'lee-hah)*
scraper	**el raspador** *(ehl rahs-pah-'dohr)*
screwdriver	**el destornillador** *(ehl dehs-tohr-nee-yah-'dohr)*
Philips head	**el destornillador de cruz** *(ehl dehs-tohr-nee-yah-'dohr deh kroos)*
tape measure	**la cinta de medir** *(lah 'seen-tah deh meh-'deer)*
tongs	**las tenazas** *(lahs teh-'nah-sahs)*
trowel	**la paleta** *(lah pah-'leh-tah)*
utility knife	**la cuchilla** *(lah koo-'chee-yah)*
vise	**la prensa** *(lah 'prehn-sah)*
wrench	**la llave inglesa** *(lah 'yah-veh een-'gleh-sah)*

Do you have (the)...?	¿Tiene...? *(tee-'eh-neh)*
chain saw	**la motosierra** *(lah moh-toh-see-'ehr-rah)*
compressor	**el compresor de aire** *(ehl kohm-preh-'sohr deh 'ah-ee-reh)*
cordless drill	**el taladro a pilas** *(ehl tah-'lah-droh ah 'pee-lahs)*
jack hammer	**el martillo neumático** *(ehl mahr-'tee-yoh neh-oo-'mah-tee-koh)*
nail gun	**la pistola clavadora** *(lah pees-'toh-lah klah-vah-'doh-rah)*

Do you want (the)...?	¿Quiere...? *(kee-'eh-reh)*
mallet	**el mazo** *(ehl 'mah-soh)*
pick	**el pico** *(ehl 'pee-koh)*
rake	**el rastrillo** *(ehl rahs-'tree-yoh)*
shovel	**la pala** *(lah 'pah-lah)*
sledgehammer	**la almádena** *(lah ahl-'mah-deh-nah)*
wheelbarrow	**la carretilla** *(lah kahr-reh-'tee-yah)*

Keep putting your tools, equipment, and supplies into separate lists:

Bring...	**Traiga...** *('trah-ee-gah)*
glue	**el pegamento** *(ehl peh-gah-'mehn-toh)*
paint	**la pintura** *(lah peen-'too-rah)*
paste	**la pasta** *(lah 'pahs-tah)*
putty	**la masilla** *(lah mah-'see-yah)*
sealant	**el aislante** *(ehl ah-ees-'lahn-teh)*
tape	**la cinta** *(lah 'seen-tah)*

Grab (the)...	**Agarre...** *(ah-'gahr-reh)*
cable	**el cable** *(ehl 'kah-bleh)*
chain	**la cadena** *(lah kah-'deh-nah)*
cord	**el cordón** *(ehl kohr-'dohn)*
rope	**la soga** *(lah 'soh-gah)*
string	**la cuerda** *(lah 'kwehr-dah)*
thread	**el hilo** *(ehl 'ee-loh)*

Look for (the)...	**Busque...** *('boos-keh)*.
bit	**la broca** *(lah 'broh-kah)*
bolt	**el perno** *(ehl 'pehr-noh)*
nail	**el clavo** *(ehl 'klah-voh)*
nut	**la tuerca** *(lah 'twehr-kah)*
screw	**el tornillo** *(ehl tohr-'nee-yoh)*
washer	**la arandela** *(lah ah-rahn-'deh-lah)*

Use (the)...	**Use...** *('oo-seh)*
broom	**la escoba** *(lah ehs-'koh-bah)*
brush	**el cepillo** *(ehl seh-'pee-yoh)*
dust pan	**la recogebasura** *(lah reh-koh-heh-bah-'soo-rah)*
mop	**el trapeador** *(ehl trah-peh-ah-'dohr)*
sponge	**la esponja** *(lah ehs-'pohn-hah)*
towel	**la toalla** *(lah toh-'ah-yah)*

These items can be seen at job sites everywhere:

Move (the)...	**Mueva...** *(moo-'eh-vah)*
dumpster	**el basurero de hierro** *(ehl bah-soo-'reh-roh deh ee-'ehr-roh)*
trashbag	**la bolsa de basura** *(lah 'bohl-sah deh bah-'soo-rah)*
trashcan	**el bote de basura** *(ehl 'boh-teh deh bah-'soo-rah)*

The Materials
Los materiales
(lohs mah-teh-ree-'ah-lehs)

The materials and the tools used to work on them go hand in hand. Look at these sample sentences, and continue the pattern on your own:

We use (the)...	**Usamos...** *(oo-'sah-mohs)*
We don't use (the)...	**No usamos...** *(noh oo-'sah-mohs)*

alloy	**la aleación** *(lah ah-leh-ah-see-'ohn)*
aluminum	**el aluminio** *(ehl ah-loo-'mee-nee-oh)*
asbestos	**el amianto** *(ehl ah-mee-'ahn-toh)*
asphalt	**el asfalto** *(ehl ahs-'fahl-toh)*
brass	**el latón** *(ehl lah-'tohn)*
brick	**el ladrillo** *(ehl lah-'dree-yoh)*
bronze	**el bronce** *(ehl 'brohn-seh)*
canvas	**la lona** *(lah 'loh-nah)*
cardboard	**el cartón** *(ehl kahr-'tohn)*
cement	**el cemento** *(ehl seh-'mehn-toh)*
copper	**el cobre** *(ehl 'koh-breh)*
cotton	**el algodón** *(ehl ahl-goh-'dohn)*
fabric	**la tela** *(lah 'teh-lah)*

fiberglass	**la fibra de vidrio** *(lah 'fee-brah deh 'vee-dree-oh)*
floor tire	**la baldosa** *(lah bahl-'doh-sah)*
foam	**la espuma** *(lah ehs-'poo-mah)*
glass	**el vidrio** *(ehl 'vee-dree-oh)*
gravel	**la gravilla** *(lah grah-'vee-yah)*
iron	**el hierro** *(ehl ee-'ehr-roh)*
leather	**el cuero** *(ehl 'kweh-roh)*
lumber	**el madero** *(ehl mah-'deh-roh)*
mesh	**la malla** *(lah 'mah-yah)*
pipe	**la tubería** *(lah too-beh-'ree-ah)*
plaster	**el yeso** *(ehl 'yeh-soh)*
plastic	**el plástico** *(ehl 'plahs-tee-koh)*
plywood	**la madera terciada** *(lah mah-'deh-rah tehr-see-'ah-dah)*
rubber	**la goma** *(lah 'goh-mah)*
sand	**la arena** *(lah ah-'reh-nah)*
steel	**el acero** *(ehl ah-'seh-roh)*
stone	**la piedra** *(lah pee-'eh-drah)*
tin	**el estaño** *(ehl ehs-'tahn-yoh)*
wood	**la madera** *(lah mah-'deh-rah)*
wool	**la lana** *(lah 'lah-nah)*
They use (the)…	**Usan…** *('oo-sahn)*
They don't use (the)…	**No usan…** *(noh 'oo-sahn)*
gas	**el gas** *(ehl gahs)*
liquid	**el líquido** *(ehl 'lee-kee-doh)*
metal	**el metal** *(ehl meh-'tahl)*
powder	**el polvo** *(ehl 'pohl-voh)*
It uses (the)…	**Usa…** *('oo-sah)*
It doesn't use (the)…	**No usa…** *(noh 'oo-sah)*
coal	**el carbón** *(ehl kahr-'bohn)*
electricity	**la electricidad** *(lah eh-lehk-tree-see-'dahd)*
fuel	**el combustible** *(ehl kohm-boos-'tee-bleh)*
gasoline	**la gasolina** *(lah gah-soh-'lee-nah)*
kerosene	**la parafina** *(lah pah-rah-'fee-nah)*
oil	**el petróleo** *(ehl peh-'troh-leh-oh)*
propane	**el propano** *(ehl proh-'pah-noh)*
steam	**el vapor** *(ehl vah-'pohr)*

Let's Practice (18)

A. Link the words that seem to belong together:

1. gasolina	acero
2. soga	algodón
3. hierro	pintura
4. lana	arena
5. brocha	cordón
6. grava	broca
7. taladro	combustible

B. Which is bigger? **¿Cuál es más grande?**
(kwahl ehs mahs 'grahn-deh)

1. el destornillador o el tornillo _____
2. la paleta o la motosierra _____
3. el cepillo o el trapeador _____

Action Words!

Out in the warehouse or factory, there are dozens of useful Spanish verbs— or "action words"—that you'll need to know. Try out this list with more catch phrases that are used before infinitives:

You have to ...	**Tiene que ...** *(tee-'eh-neh keh)*
You should ...	**Debe ...** *('deh-beh).*
You need to …	**Necesita ...** *(neh-seh-'see-tah)*

Do you like to …?	**¿Le gusta …?** *(leh 'goos-tah)*
Can you …?	**¿Puede …?** *('pweh-deh)*
Do you want to …?	**¿Quiere …?** *(kee-'eh-reh)*

to bring	**traer** *(trah-'ehr)*
to carry	**llevar** *(yeh-'vahr)*
to clean	**limpiar** *(leem-pee-'ahr)*

to cut	**cortar** *(kohr-'tahr)*
to empty	**vaciar** *(vah-see-'ahr)*
to fill	**llenar** *(yeh-'nahr)*
to grab	**agarrar** *(ah-gahr-'rahr)*
to load	**cargar** *(kahr-'gahr)*
to look for	**buscar** *(boos-'kahr)*
to lower	**bajar** *(bah-'hahr)*
to move	**mover** *(moh-'vehr)*
to pick up	**recoger** *(reh-koh-'hehr)*
to plug in	**enchufar** *(ehn-choo-'fahr)*
to pull	**jalar** *(hah-'lahr)*
to push	**empujar** *(ehm-poo-hahr)*
to put away	**guardar** *(gwahr-'dahr)*
to put inside	**meter** *(meh-'tehr)*
to raise	**subir** *(soo-'beer)*
to remove	**sacar** *(sah-'kahr)*
to throw away	**tirar** *(tee-'rahr)*
to turn off	**apagar** *(ah-pah-'gahr)*
to turn on	**prender** *(prehn-'dehr)*
to turn	**voltear** *(vohl-teh-'ahr)*
to unload	**descargar** *(dehs-kahr-'gahr)*
to unplug	**desenchufar** *(dehs-ehn-choo-'fahr)*
to use	**usar** *(oo-'sahr)*
to wash	**lavar** *(lah-'vahr)*

Verbs: The Future
Los verbos: el futuro *(lohs 'vehr-bohs ehl foo-'too-roh)*

There are two ways to discuss *what's going to happen* in Spanish. The easiest is to use the basic forms of the verb "to go" (**ir**):

I'm going to...	**Voy a...** *('voh-ee ah)*
You're, He's, She's, It's going to...	**Va a...** *('vah ah)*
You're (pl.), They're going to...	**Van a...** *('vahn ah)*
We're going to...	**Vamos a...** *('vah-mohs ah)*

Notice how these statements refer to future actions when you add a verb infinitive:

I'm going to the office.
Voy a la oficina.
('voh-ee ah lah oh-fee-'see-nah)

I'm going <u>to call</u>.
Voy a <u>llamar</u>.
('voh-ee ah yah-'mahr)

We're going to the bathroom.
Vamos al baño.
('vah-mohs ahl 'bahn-yoh)

We're going <u>to clean</u>.
Vamos a <u>limpiar</u>.
('vah-mohs ah leem-pee-'ahr)

She's going to the factory.
Ella va a la fábrica.
('eh-yah vah ah lah 'fah-bree-kah)

She's going to <u>turn off</u> the machine.
Ella va a <u>apagar</u> la máquina.
('eh-yah vah ah ah-pah-'gahr lah 'mah-kee-nah)

The second way to talk about the future is the old-fashioned way: learn the future tense of every verb. But do not despair: it is fairly easy. Although some infinitives have irregular changes, notice the pattern for most **-ar, -er,** and **-ir** verbs:

TO GIVE
DAR *(dahr)*
I will give
daré *(dah-'reh)*
you, he, she, it will give
dará *(dah-'rah)*
you (plural), they will give
darán *(dah-'rahn)*
we will give
daremos *(dah-'reh-mohs)*

I'll work on Monday.
<u>Trabajaré</u> el lunes. *(trah-bah-hah-'reh ehl 'loo-nehs)*

He'll eat at six.
<u>Comerá</u> a las seis. *(koh-meh-'rah ah lahs 'seh-ees)*

They'll go in August.
<u>Irán</u> en agosto. *(ee-'rahn ehn ah-'gohs-toh)*

We'll finish tomorrow.
<u>Terminaremos</u> mañana. *(tehr-mee-nah-'reh-mohs mahn-'yah-nah)*

Let's Practice (19)

A. Look up the opposites of the following words and then complete the sentences. The first one is done for you:

bajar	subir	Necesita <u>subir la escalera</u>.
1. desenchufar	_____	Tiene que _____.
2. vaciar	_____	¿Quiere _____?
3. jalar	_____	Debe _____.
4. apagar	_____	¿Puede _____?
5. cargar	_____	¿Le gusta _____?

B. Answer these questions about future events:

¿Dónde va a comer su almuerzo?
¿Ud. va a trabajar mañana?
¿Cuándo va a estudiar español?
¿Quién va a leer este libro?
¿Cuántas personas en su familia van a mirar televisión hoy?

The Culture

Many employers work with new immigrants who are unfamiliar with local, state, or federal laws and regulations. If you plan to establish a long-term relationship, you can prevent potential problems by giving them as much legal information as possible. By contacting a variety of service agencies, you can pick up literature in Spanish concerning citizenship, taxes, health care, education, transportation, and residence, as well as personal rights and privileges.

Chapter Four

(kah-'pee-too-loh 'kwah-troh)

The Training
El entrenamiento
(ehl ehn-treh-nah-mee-'ehn-toh)

General Instructions
Instrucciones generales
(eens-trook-see-'oh-nehs heh-neh-'rah-lehs)

Once your employees are familiar with the workplace, give a few basic instructions related to their job assignments. This first selection can work wonders in a training session:

These are (the) _____	**Estos/Estas son** _____ *('ehs-tohs/'ehs-tahs sohn)*
assignments	**las tareas** *(lahs tah-'reh-ahs)*
chores	**las labores domésticas** *(lahs lah-'boh-rehs doh-'mehs-tee-kahs)*
duties	**los deberes** *(lohs deh-'beh-rehs)*
jobs	**los trabajos** *(lohs trah-'bah-hohs)*
responsibilities	**las responsabilidades** *(lahs rehs-pohn-sah-bee-lee-'dah-dehs)*

Watch and listen.
Mire y escuche. *('mee-reh ee ehs-'koo-cheh)*

Pay attention.
Preste atención. *('prehs-teh ah-tehn-see-'ohn)*

This is the procedure.
Este es el procedimiento. *('ehs-teh ehs ehl proh-seh-dee-mee-'ehn-toh)*

This is what I want.
Esto es lo que quiero. *('ehs-toh ehs loh keh kee-'eh-roh)*

This is how we do it.
Esto es cómo lo hacemos. *('ehs-toh ehs 'koh-moh loh ah-'seh-mohs)*

This way.
De esta manera. *(deh 'ehs-tah mah-'neh-rah)*

Like this.
Así. *(ah-'see)*

Remember this.
Recuerde esto. *(reh-'kwehr-deh 'ehs-toh)*

It's very important.
Es muy importante. *(ehs 'moo-ee eem-pohr-'tahn-teh)*

Try some more, but this time picture how, when, or where each one-liner can be used. Note that the components of the sentence must agree in gender and number.

Again.	**Otra vez.** *('oh-trah vehs)*
The same thing.	**La misma cosa.** *(lah 'mees-mah 'koh-sah)*
And this, too.	**Y este, también.** *(ee 'ehs-teh tahm-bee-'ehn)*
	Y esta, también. *(ee 'ehs-tah tahm-bee-'ehn)*
Like this one.	**Uno como este.** *('oo-noh 'koh-moh 'ehs-teh)*
	Una como esta. *('oo-nah 'koh-moh 'ehs-tah)*
Now, the other one.	**Ahora, el otro.** *(ah-'oh-rah ehl 'oh-troh)*
	Ahora, la otra. *(ah-'oh-rah lah 'oh-trah)*

This group can almost be used all by itself:

Not like that.	**Así no.** *(ah-'see noh)*
That's better.	**Está mejor.** *(ehs-'tah meh-'hohr)*
Keep going.	**Siga.** *('see-gah)*
You got it?	**¿Lo entiende?** *(loh ehn-tee-'ehn-deh)*
Great!	**¡Muy bien!** *('moo-ee bee-'ehn)*

Sometimes, pairs of opposite phrases are easier to remember:

That's it.	**Eso es.** *('eh-soh ehs)*
That's not it.	**Eso no es.** *('eh-soh noh ehs)*

A little more.	**Un poco más.** *(oon 'poh-koh mahs)*
A little less.	**Un poco menos.** *(oon 'poh-koh 'meh-nohs)*

Faster.	**Más rápido.** *(mahs 'rah-pee-doh)*
Slower.	**Más despacio.** *(mahs dehs-'pah-see-oh)*

Sometimes a phrase can be used as a command:

Backwards!	**¡Al revés!** *(ahl reh-'vehs)*
The other side!	**¡El otro lado!** *(ehl 'oh-troh 'lah-doh)*
Upside down!	**¡Boca abajo!** *('boh-kah ah-'bah-hoh)*

More Key Words
Más palabras claves
(mahs pah-'lah-brahs klah-'vehs)

When it comes to training, sometimes all that is required is a key word or two to communicate your message:

almost	**casi** *('kah-see)*
alone	**solo** *('soh-loh)*
enough	**bastante** *(bahs-'tahn-teh)*
most of it	**la mayor parte** *(lah mah-'yohr 'pahr-teh)*
none	**ninguno** *(neen-'goo-noh)*
not yet	**todavía no** *(toh-dah-'vee-ah noh)*
only one	**solamente uno** *(soh-lah-'mehn-teh 'oo-noh)*
the rest of it	**lo que queda** *(loh keh 'keh-dah)*
too much	**demasiado** *(deh-mah-see-'ah-doh)*
with me	**conmigo** *(kohn-'mee-goh)*

This list provides trainers with vocabulary to create sentences, along with quick, generic one-word responses:

anyone	**cualquier persona** *(kwahl-kee-'ehr pehr-'soh-nah)*
anything	**cualquier cosa** *(kwahl-kee-'ehr 'koh-sah)*
anywhere	**en cualquier sitio** *(ehn kwahl-kee-'ehr 'see-tee-oh)*
everyone	**todos** *('toh-dohs)*
everything	**todo** *('toh-doh)*
everywhere	**por todas partes** *(pohr 'toh-dahs 'pahr-tehs)*
no one	**nadie** *('nah-dee-eh)*
nothing	**nada** *('nah-dah)*
nowhere	**en ningún sitio** *(ehn neen-'goon 'see-tee-oh)*
someone	**alguien** *('ahl-gee-ehn)*
something	**algo** *('ahl-goh)*
somewhere	**en algún sitio** *(ehn ahl-'goon 'see-tee-oh)*

Read these practice dialogs aloud:

¿Quién trabaja el domingo?	Nadie.
¿Cuánto agua quiere usted?	Lo que queda.
¿Dónde están las computadoras?	Por todas partes.

Extra Info!

These instructional phrases communicate caution or warning:

Do not touch it.	**No lo toque.** *(noh loh 'toh-keh)*
It doesn't work.	**No funciona.** *(noh foon-see-'oh-nah)*
Be very careful.	**Tenga mucho cuidado.**
	('tehn-gah 'moo-choh koo-ee-'dah-doh)

The Schedule
El horario
(ehl oh-'rah-ree-oh)

After you set up a work schedule, use the following lines to tell your new employee how the system works.

This is the calendar.
Este es el calendario. *('ehs-teh ehs ehl kah-lehn-'dah-ree-oh)*

Check the schedule.
Revise el horario. *(reh-'vee-seh ehl oh-'rah-ree-oh)*

These are your hours.
Estas son sus horas de trabajo. *('ehs-tahs sohn soos 'oh-rahs deh trah-'bah-hoh)*

I'll send you (the) …	**Le voy a mandar…** *(leh 'voh-ee ah mahn-'dahr)*
agenda	**el programa** *(ehl proh-'grah-mah)*
change	**el cambio** *(ehl 'kahm-bee-oh)*
plan	**el plan** *(ehl plahn)*

You start ____	**Empieza ___** *(ehm-pee-'eh-sah)*
You finish ____	**Termina___** *(tehr-'mee-nah)*
Day in ___	**Día de entrada ___** *('dee-a deh ehn-'trah-dah)*
Day out ____	**Día de descanso ___** *('dee-ah deh dehs-'kahn-soh)*
From ___	**De ___** *(deh)*
Until ___	**Hasta ___** *('ahs-tah)*

Listen for (the) …	**Escuche …** *(ehs-'koo-cheh)*
bell	**la campana** *(lah-kahm-'pah-nah)*
horn	**la bocina** *(lah boh-'see-nah)*
whistle	**el silbato** *(ehl seel-'bah-toh)*

Your lunch is at _____.
Almuerza usted a _____. *(ahl-'mwehr-sah oos-'tehd ah)*

We are closed on _____.
Estamos cerrados los _____. *(ehs-'tah-mohs sehr-'rah-dohs lohs)*

We'll see you on _____.
Nos veremos el _____. *(nohs veh-'reh-mohs ehl)*

Of course, there are a variety of ways to explain a work schedule:

Be here at _____.
Esté aquí a _____. *(ehs-'teh ah-'kee ah)*

You may leave at _____.
Se puede ir a _____. *(seh 'pweh-deh eer ah)*

Take a break at _____.
Tome un descanso a _____. *('toh-meh oon dehs-'kahn-soh ah)*

You will work on _____.
Va a trabajar el _____. *(vah ah trah-bah-'hahr ehl)*

You don't work on _____.
No trabaja el _____. *(noh trah-'bah-hah ehl)*

 # The Culture

Some cultures put less emphasis on beating the clock than others, but our rules are demanding:

Don't be late!
¡No llegue tarde! *(noh 'yeh-geh 'tahr-deh)*

If you're late again, I'll have to let you go.
Si llega tarde otra vez, tendré que despedirlo.
(see 'yeh-gah 'tahr-deh 'oh-trah vehs, tehn-'dreh keh dehs-peh-'deer-loh)

We need to start on time.
Necesitamos comenzar a tiempo.
(neh-seh-see-'tah-mohs koh-mehn-'sahr ah tee-'ehm-poh)

Extra Info!

Be firm about tardiness and attendance right from the start:

Be here for sure!
¡Esté aquí sin falta! *(ehs-'teh ah-'kee seen 'fahl-tah)*

Please arrive early!
¡Favor de llegar temprano! *(fah-'vohr deh yeh-'gahr tehm-'prah-noh)*

Do not miss work!
¡No falte al trabajo! *(noh 'falh-teh ahl trah-'bah-hoh)*

Call if you have a problem!
¡Llame si tiene un problema! *('yah-meh see tee-'eh-neh oon proh-'bleh-mah)*

You will need a medical certificate!
¡Necesitará un certificado médico!
(neh-seh-see-tah-'rah oon sehr-tee-fee-'kah-doh 'meh-dee-koh)

Let's Practice   (20)

A. Translate:

1. Pay attention!   _____
2. This is what I want.   _____
3. That's it!   _____

B. Join these opposites:

1. algo   nadie
2. alguién   diferente
3. mismo   nada

C. Refer to a clock as you complete your work schedule for today:

1. Empiezo a las _____.
2. Termino a las _____.
3. Como mi almuerzo a las _____.

Everyday Procedures
Los procedimientos diarios
(lohs proh-seh-dee-mee-'ehn-tohs dee-'ah-ree-ohs)

Here's the employee ____.	**Aquí está _____ para los empleados.** *(ah-kee ehs-'tah ___ 'pah-rah lohs ehm-pleh-'ah-dohs)*
cafeteria	**la cafetería** *(lah kah-feh-teh-'ree-ah)*
entrance	**la entrada** *(lah ehn-'trah-dah)*
exit	**la salida** *(lah sah-'lee-dah)*
parking area	**el estacionamiento** *(ehl ehs-tah-see-oh-nah-mee-'ehn-toh)*
restroom	**el servicio** *(ehl sehr-'vee-see-oh)*
Use (the) ...	**Use ...** *('oo-seh)*
authorized password	**la contraseña autorizada** *(lah kohn-trah-'sehn-yah aw-toh-ree-'sah-dah)*
badge number	**el número de la placa** *(ehl 'noo-meh-roh deh lah 'plah-kah)*
company keys	**las llaves de la compañía** *(lahs 'yah-vehs deh lah kohm-pah-'nee-ah)*
metal detector	**el detector de metales** *(ehl deh-tehk-'tohr deh meh-'tah-lehs)*
personal identification	**la identificación personal** *(lah ee-den-tee-fee-kah-see-'ohn pehr-soh-'nahl)*
security code	**el código de seguridad** *(ehl 'koh-dee-goh deh seh-goo-ree-'dahd)*
sign-in sheet	**la lista de registración** *(lah 'lees-tah deh reh-hees-trah-see-'ohn)*
timecard	**el horario** *(ehl oh-'rah-ree-oh)*
time clock	**el reloj de trabajo** *(ehl reh-'loh deh trah-'bah-hoh)*

If possible, have most of your written instructions translated into Spanish. Then, utilize words that can help employees follow along:

Look at (the) ...	**Mire ...** *('mee-reh)*
announcement	**el anuncio** *(ehl ah-'noon-see-oh)*
bulletin board	**el tablero de anuncios** *(ehl tah-'bleh-roh deh ah-'noon-see-ohs)*
calendar	**el calendario** *(ehl kah-lehn-'dah-ree-oh)*

disk	**el disco** *(ehl 'dees-koh)*
document	**el documento** *(ehl doh-koo-'mehn-toh)*
e-mail	**el correo electrónico**
	(ehl kohr-'reh-oh eh-lehk-'troh-nee-koh)
letter	**la carta** *(lah 'kahr-tah)*
list	**la lista** *(lah 'lees-tah)*
mail	**el correo** *(ehl kohr-'reh-oh)*
memo	**el memorándum** *(ehl meh-moh-'rahn-doom)*
message	**el mensaje** *(ehl mehn-'sah-heh)*
notice	**la noticia** *(lah noh-'tee-see-ah)*
page	**la página** *(lah 'pah-hee-nah)*
poster	**el cartel** *(ehl kahr-'tehl)*
report	**el reporte** *(ehl reh-'pohr-teh)*
schedule	**el horario** *(ehl oh-'rah-ree-oh)*
sheet	**la hoja** *(lah 'oh-hah)*
sign	**el letrero** *(ehl leh-'treh-roh)*
text	**el texto** *(ehl 'tehks-toh)*
whiteboard	**la pizarra** *(lah pee-'sahr-rah)*

Extra Info!

Vocabulary when things at the workplace are tough to find:

It's in (the)...	**Está en...** *(ehs-'tah ehn)*.
drawer	**el cajón** *(ehl kah-'hohn)*
envelope	**el sobre** *(ehl 'soh-breh)*
file	**el archivo** *(ehl ahr-'chee-voh)*
kit	**el estuche** *(ehl ehs-'too-cheh)*
package	**el paquete** *(ehl pah-'keh-teh)*
briefcase	**el maletín** *(ehl mah-leh-'teen)*
They're in (the)...	**Están en...** *(ehs-'tahn ehn)*
aisle	**el pasillo** *(ehl pah-'see-yoh)*
group	**el grupo** *(ehl 'groo-poh)*
row	**la fila** *(lah 'fee-lah)*
series	**la serie** *(lah 'seh-ree-eh)*
set	**el juego** *(ehl 'hweh-goh)*

Staff Meeting
La reunión del personal
(lah reh-oo-nee-'ohn del pehr-soh-'nahl)

Gather your Spanish-speaking employees together for training, and tell what the training is all about:

Welcome to (the) ...	**Bienvenidos** ... *(bee-ehn-veh-'nee-dohs)*
class	**a la clase** *(ah lah 'klah-seh)*
committee	**al comité** *(ahl koh-mee-'teh)*
conference	**a la conferencia** *(ah lah kohn-feh-'rehn-see-ah)*
lesson	**a la lección** *(ah lah lehk-see-'ohn)*
meeting	**a la reunión** *(ah lah reh-oo-nee-'ohn)*
seminar	**al seminario** *(ahl seh-mee-'nah-ree-oh)*
session	**a la sesión** *(ah lah seh-see-'ohn)*
We're going to...	**Vamos a** ... *('vah-mohs ah)*
clarify	**aclarar** *(ah-klah-'rahr)*
discuss	**tratar** *(trah-'tahr)*
learn	**aprender** *(ah-prehn-'dehr)*
listen	**escuchar** *(ehs-koo-'chahr)*
participate	**participar** *(pahr-tee-see-'pahr)*
practice	**practicar** *(prahk-tee-'kahr)*
receive	**recibir** *(reh-see-'beer)*
review	**repasar** *(reh-pah-'sahr)*
watch	**mirar** *(mee-'rahr)*
It includes...	**Incluye a...** *(een-'kloo-yeh ah)*
conference speakers	**los conferenciantes** *(lohs kohn-feh-rehn-see-'ahn-tehs)*
multimedia	**medios de difusión múltiples** *('meh-dee-ohs deh dee-foo-see-'ohn 'mool-tee-plehs)*
video conferencing	**la conferencia por video** *(lah kohn-feh-'rehn-see-ah pohr vee-'deh-oh)*

Don't forget to go over the basic goals of the business:

We try to ...	**Tratamos de ...** *(trah-'tah-mohs deh)*
check our inventory	**inspeccionar nuestro inventario** *(eens-pehk-see-oh-'nahr 'nwehs-troh een-vehn-'tah-ree-oh)*
improve our skills	**mejorar nuestras habilidades** *(meh-hoh-'rahr 'nwehs-trahs ah-bee-lee-'dah-dehs)*
make a team effort	**hacer un esfuerzo unido** *(ah-'sehr oon ehs-'fwehr-soh oo-'nee-doh)*
provide excellent service	**proveer servicio excelente** *(proh-veh-'ehr sehr-'vee-see-oh ex-seh-'lehn-teh)*
reward our employees	**recompensar a nuestros empleados** *(reh-kohm-pehn-'sahr ah 'nwehs-trohs ehm-pleh-'ah-dohs)*
satisfy our customers	**satisfacer a los clientes** *(sah-tees-fah-'sehr ah lohs klee-'ehn-tehs)*
Let's see (the)...	**Veamos...** *(veh-'ah-mohs)*
concept	**el concepto** *(ehl kohn-'sehp-toh)*
goal	**la meta** *(lah 'meh-tah)*
idea	**la idea** *(lah ee-'deh-ah)*
motto	**el lema** *(ehl 'leh-mah)*
objective	**el objetivo** *(ehl ohb-heh-'tee-voh)*
principle	**el principio** *(ehl preen-'see-pee-oh)*
purpose	**el propósito** *(ehl proh-'poh-see-toh)*
slogan	**el eslogan** *(ehl ehs-'loh-gahn)*
theme	**el tema** *(ehl 'teh-mah)*

Now, distribute the training materials and review what the employees are supposed to do:

Open (the)...	**Abra ...** *('ah-brah)*
binder	**la carpeta** *(lah kahr-'peh-tah)*
book	**el libro** *(ehl 'lee-broh)*
booklet	**el librito** *(ehl lee-'bree-toh)*
pamphlet	**el folleto** *(ehl foh-'yeh-toh)*
portfolio	**el portafolio** *(ehl pohr-tah-'foh-lee-oh)*
training manual	**el manual de entrenamiento** *(ehl mah-'nwahl deh ehn-treh-nah-mee-'ehn-toh)*

Follow (the) ...   **Siga ...** *('see-gah)*

codes	**los códigos** *(lohs 'koh-dee-gohs)*
directions	**los pasos a seguir** *(lohs 'pah-sohs ah seh-'geer)*
guidelines	**las pautas** *(lahs 'pah-oo-tahs)*
instructions	**las instrucciones** *(lahs eens-trook-see-'oh-nehs)*
laws	**las leyes** *(lahs 'leh-yehs)*
measures	**las medidas** *(lahs meh-'dee-dahs)*
policies	**las políticas** *(lahs poh-'lee-tee-kahs)*
procedures	**los procedimientos** *(lohs proh-seh-dee-mee-'ehn-tohs)*
regulations	**los reglamentos** *(lohs reh-glah-'mehn-tohs)*
rules	**las reglas** *(lahs 'reh-glahs)*
steps	**los pasos** *(lohs 'pah-sohs)*

Study (the)...   **Estudie...** *(ehs-'too-dee-eh)*

chapter	**el capítulo** *(ehl kah-'pee-too-loh)*
chart	**el diagrama** *(ehl dee-ah-'grah-mah)*
drawing	**el dibujo** *(ehl dee-'boo-hoh)*
graph	**el gráfico** *(ehl 'grah-fee-koh)*
illustration	**el cuadro** *(ehl 'kwah-droh)*
map	**el mapa** *(ehl 'mah-pah)*
photo	**la foto** *(lah 'foh-toh)*

When it's time to close the meeting, keep things brief:

Are there any questions?
¿Hay alguna pregunta?
('ah-ee ahl-'goo-nah pre-'goon-tah)

I hope this meeting has been helpful.
Espero que la reunión haya sido útil.
(ehs-'peh-roh keh lah reh-oo-nee-'ohn 'ah-yah 'see-doh 'oo-teel)

Thank you all for coming.
Gracias a todos por venir. *('grah-see-ahs ah 'toh-dohs pohr veh-'neer)*

Extra Info!

Providing skills training may require some of the following vocabulary.
Notice how they work with different commands:

Look for (the) ...	**Busque** ... *('boos-keh)*
Remember (the) ...	**Recuerde** ... *(reh-'kwehr-deh)*
Use (the) ...	**Use** ... *('oo-seh)*

angle	**el ángulo** *(ehl 'ahn-goo-loh)*
corner	**la esquina** *(lah ehs-'kee-nah)*
curve	**la curva** *(lah 'koor-vah)*
design	**el diseño** *(ehl dee-'sehn-yoh)*
edge	**el borde** *(ehl 'bohr-deh)*
groove	**la muesca** *(lah 'mwehs-kah)*
letter	**la letra** *(lah 'leh-trah)*
line	**la línea** *(lah 'lee-neh-ah)*
mark	**la marca** *(lah 'mahr-kah)*
model	**el modelo** *(ehl moh-'deh-loh)*
pattern	**el patrón** *(ehl pah-'trohn)*
point	**la punta** *(lah 'poon-tah)*
shape	**la forma** *(lah 'fohr-mah)*
space	**el espacio** *(ehl ehs-'pah-see-oh)*
symbol	**el símbolo** *(ehl 'seem-boh-loh)*

Let's Practice

(21)

A. Select the word that belongs with the others:

1. el modelo, el patrón, _____	la ley
2. el documento, la página, _____	el diseño
3. el reglamento, la regla, _____	la hoja

B. Translate into Spanish:

1. We try to provide excellent service. _____
2. Use the authorized password. _____
3. We're going to practice and review. _____

Special Skills
Las habilidades especiales
(lahs ah-bee-lee-'dah-dehs ehs-peh-see-'ah-lehs)

Most employees today are required to have some specialized skills training. For example, a knowledge of basic measurements is a must:

Take (the)…	**Tome…** *('toh-meh)*
dozen	**la docena** *(lah doh-'seh-nah)*
gross	**la gruesa** *(lah groo-'eh-sah)*
pair	**el par** *(ehl pahr)*
Use (the)…	**Use…** *('oo-seh)*
third	**el tercio** *(ehl 'tehr-see-oh)*
half	**la mitad** *(lah mee-'tahd)*
quarter	**el cuarto** *(ehl 'kwahr-toh)*
It's measured by…	**Se mide por…** *(seh 'mee-deh pohr)*
centimeter	**el centímetro** *(ehl sehn-'tee-meh-troh)*
cup	**la taza** *(lah 'tah-sah)*
fluid ounce	**la onza fluida** *(lah 'ohn-sah floo-'ee-dah)*
foot	**el pie** *(ehl pee-'eh)*
gallon	**el galón** *(ehl gah-'lohn)*
gram	**el gramo** *(ehl 'grah-moh)*
inch	**la pulgada** *(lah pool-'gah-dah)*
kilogram	**el kilogramo** *(ehl kee-loh-'grah-moh)*
kilometer	**el kilómetro** *(ehl kee-'loh-meh-troh)*
liter	**el litro** *(ehl 'lee-troh)*
meter	**el metro** *(ehl 'meh-troh)*
metric ton	**la tonelada métrica** *(lah toh-neh-'lah-dah 'meh-tree-kah)*
mile	**la milla** *(lah 'mee-yah)*
milliliter	**el mililitro** *(ehl mee-lee-'lee-troh)*
millimeter	**el milímetro** *(ehl mee-'lee-meh-troh)*
ounce	**la onza** *(lah 'ohn-sah)*
pint	**la pinta** *(lah 'peen-tah)*
pound	**la libra** *(lah 'lee-brah)*
quart	**el cuarto** *(ehl 'kwahr-toh)*
tablespoon	**la cucharada** *(lah koo-chah-'rah-dah)*

teaspoon	**la cucharadita** *(lah koo-chah-rah-'dee-tah)*
ton	**la tonelada** *(lah toh-neh-'lah-dah)*
yard	**la yarda** *(lah 'yahr-dah)*

Sometimes, measurements are more general than exact:

Give me (the)…	**Deme …** *('deh-meh)*
bunch	**el montón** *(ehl mohn-'tohn)*
handful	**el puñado** *(ehl poon-'yah-doh)*
pallet	**la tarima** *(lah tah-'ree-mah)*
piece	**el pedazo** *(ehl peh-'dah-soh)*
portion	**la porción** *(lah pohr-see-'ohn)*
segment	**el segmento** *(ehl sehg-'mehn-toh)*
truckload	**la camionada** *(lah kah-mee-oh-'nah-dah)*
unit	**la unidad** *(lah oo-nee-'dahd)*

Sentences with Measurements
Frases con medidas
('frah-sehs kohn meh-'dee-dahs)

Why not practice saying these questions involving measurements aloud:

How long?	**¿Cuán largo?** *(kwahn 'lahr-goh)*
How high?	**¿Cuán alto?** *(kwahn 'ahl-toh)*
How cold?	**¿Cuán frío?** *(kwahn 'free-oh)*

How much does it weigh?	**¿Cuánto pesa?** *('kwahn-toh 'peh-sah)*
What's it measure?	**¿Cuánto mide?** *('kwahn-toh 'mee-deh)*
How much do you need?	**¿Cuánto necesita?** *('kwahn-toh neh-seh-'see-tah)*

Speaking of measurements, can you guess what these words mean?

decímetro cúbico	_____
miligramos	_____
hectárea	_____
por ciento	_____
millas naúticas	_____
año luz	_____
acres	_____

The Culture

Latin America uses temperatures in Celsius rather than Fahrenheit. To convert temperatures from Fahrenheit to Celsius, subtract 32 and multiply the result by 0.555. To convert temperatures from Celsius to Fahrenheit, multiply the temperature by 1.8 and add 32.

Notice the difference:

98.6°F	=	37°C
32°F	=	0°C
212°F	=	100°C

Common Containers
Los recipientes comunes
(los reh-see-pee-'ehn-tehs koh-'moo-nehs)

Train your employees how to handle materials and merchandise:

Fill the ...	**Llene** ... *('yeh-neh)*
Empty the ...	**Vacíe** ... *(vah-'see-eh)*
Carry the ...	**Lleve** ... *('yeh-veh)*
bag	**la bolsa** *(lah 'bohl-sah)*
basket	**la canasta** *(lah kah-'nahs-tah)*
bottle	**la botella** *(lah boh-'teh-yah)*
box	**la caja** *(lah 'kah-hah)*
bucket	**el balde** *(ehl 'bahl-deh)*
canister	**el bote** *(ehl 'boh-teh)*
crate	**la caja para transporte** *(lah 'kah-hah 'pah-rah trahns-'pohr-teh)*
cup	**la taza** *(lah 'tah-sah)*
drum	**el barril** *(ehl bahr-'reel)*
glass	**el vaso** *(ehl 'vah-soh)*
jar	**la jarra** *(lah 'har-rah)*
package	**el paquete** *(ehl pah-'keh-teh)*
pallet	**la plataforma** *(lah plah-tah-'fohr-mah)*

sack	**el saco** *(ehl 'sah-koh)*
small bottle	**el frasco** *(ehl 'frahs-koh)*
tank	**el tanque** *(ehl 'tahn-keh)*
thermos	**el termo** *(ehl 'tehr-moh)*
tub	**la cuba** *(lah 'koo-bah)*
tube	**el tubo** *(ehl 'too-boh)*

Extra Info!

When your instructions need to be more precise, beware of those words that are close in meaning:

It has to be...	**Tiene que ser...** *(tee-'eh-neh keh sehr)*
double	**el doble** *(ehl 'doh-bleh)*
twice that	**dos veces eso** *(dohs 'veh-sehs 'eh-soh)*
in two	**en dos partes** *(ehn dohs 'pahr-tehs)*

Do the Math
Saque la cuenta
('sah-keh lah 'kwehn-tah)

To explain simple computations in Spanish, you'll need these vocabulary groups:

You're going to...	**Usted va a...** *(oos-'tehd vah ah)*
to add	**sumar** *(soo-mahr)*
to divide	**dividir** *(dee-vee-'deer)*
to multiply	**multiplicar** *(mool-tee-plee-'kahr)*
to subtract	**restar** *(rehs-'tahr)*

It's 5 _____ 5.	**Son cinco _____ cinco** *(sohn 'seen-koh ___ 'seen-koh)*
divided by	**dividido entre** *(dee-vee-'dee-doh 'ehn-treh)*
equals	**es igual a** *(ehs ee-'gwahl ah)*
minus	**menos** *('meh-nohs)*
plus	**más** *(mahs)*
times	**por** *(pohr)*

Draw (the)…	**Dibuje**… *(dee-'boo-heh)*
circle	el **círculo** *(ehl 'seer-koo-loh)*
cone	el **cono** *(ehl 'koh-noh)*
cube	el **cubo** *(ehl 'koo-boh)*
cylinder	el **cilindro** *(ehl see-'leen-droh)*
line	la **línea** *(lah 'lee-neh-ah)*
point	el **punto** *(ehl 'poon-toh)*
rectangle	el **rectángulo** *(ehl rehk-'tahn-goo-loh)*
square	el **cuadrado** *(ehl kwah-'drah-doh)*
triangle	el **triángulo** *(ehl tree-'ahn-goo-loh)*

Write down…	**Anote** … *(ah-'noh-teh)*
depth	la **profundidad** *(lah proh-foon-dee-'dahd)*
height	la **altura** *(lah ahl-'too-rah)*
length	el **largo** *(ehl 'lahr-goh)*
percentage	el **porcentaje** *(ehl pohr-sehn-'tah-heh)*
ratio	la **proporción** *(lah proh-pohr-see-'ohn)*
size	el **tamaño** *(ehl tah-'mahn-yoh)*
width	el **ancho** *(ehl 'ahn-choh)*

Fractions (**las fracciones**, *lahs frahk-see-'oh-nehs*) are given in Spanish as in English, using a cardinal number for the numerator and an ordinal number for the denominator. The only exceptions are ½ (**un medio**, *oon 'meh-dee-oh*) and ⅓ (**un tercio**, *oon 'tehr-see-oh*):

¼	**un cuarto** *(oon 'kwahr-toh)*
⅜	**tres octavos** *(trehs ohk-'tah-vohs)*
⅔	**dos tercios** *(dohs 'tehr-see-ohs)*

Beyond one-tenth, the cardinal number adds the suffix **–avo(s)** *('ah-vohs)* to form the smaller fractions. Exceptions include one-hundredth (**un centésimo**, *oon sehn-'teh-see-moh*) and one-thousandth (**un milésimo**, *oon mee-'leh-see-moh*):

one-thirteenth	**un treceavo** *(oon treh-seh-'ah-voh)*
seven-twentieths	**siete veinteavos** *(see-'eh-teh veh-een-teh-'ah-vohs)*
two-hundredths	**dos centésimos** *(dohs sehn-'teh-see-mohs)*

Let's Practice (22)

Add one of these words to describe the job in greater detail. Follow the sentence pattern:

straight	*recto*	La línea es recta.
uneven	*desigual*	la caja es desigual.
level	*nivel*	_____
diagonal	*diagonal*	_____
horizontal	*horizontal*	_____
vertical	*vertical*	_____
parallel	*paralelo*	_____

When referring to percentages (**por ciento**, *pohr see-'ehn-toh*), **el** is generally placed before the number:

We received <u>ten</u> per cent discount.
Recibimos <u>el diez</u> por ciento de descuento.
(reh-see-'bee-mohs ehl dee-'ehs pohr see-'ehn-toh deh dehs-'kwehn-toh)

Information Technology
La tecnología informática
(lah tehk-noh-loh-'hee-ah een-fohr-'mah-tee-kah)

Learn the words that will help you communicate in simple terms with those who work with computers:

Bring (the)...	**Traiga...** *('trah-ee-'gah)*
adapter	**el adaptador** *(ehl ah-dahp-tah-'dohr)*
burner	**el reproductor** *(ehl reh-proh-dook-tohr)*
camcorder	**la filmadora** *(lah feel-mah-'doh-rah)*
charger	**la cargadora** *(lah kahr-gah-'doh-rah)*
cell phone	**el teléfono celular** *(ehl teh-'leh-foh-noh seh-loo-'lahr)*
digital camera	**la cámara digital** *(lah 'kah-mah-rah dee-hee-'tahl)*
GPS	**el sistema de navegación portátil**
	(ehl sees-'teh-mah deh nah-veh-gah-see-'ohn pohr-'tah-teel)
headphones	**los auriculares** *(lohs aw-ree-koo-'lah-rehs)*

laptop	**la computadora portátil**
	(lah kohm-poo-tah-'doh-rah pohr-'tah-teel)
microphone	**el micrófono** *(ehl mee-'kroh-foh-noh)*
PDA	**la computadora de bolsillo**
	(lah kohm-poo-tah-'doh-rah deh bohl-'see-yoh)
player	**el tocador** *(ehl toh-kah-'dohr)*
recorder	**la grabadora** *(lah grah-bah-'doh-rah)*
remote control	**el control remoto** *(ehl kohn-'trohl reh-'moh-toh)*
router	**el encaminador** *(ehl ehn-kah-mee-nah-'dohr)*
scanner	**el escáner** *(ehl ehs-'kah-nehr)*
speakers	**los altavoces** *(lohs ahl-tah-'voh-sehs)*

Check (the)…	**Revise…** *(reh-'vee-seh)*
cable	**el cable** *(ehl 'kah-bleh)*
connection	**la conexión** *(lah koh-nehk-see-'ohn)*
disk drive	**la disquetera** *(lah dees-keh-'teh-rah)*
hard drive	**el disco duro** *(ehl 'dees-koh 'doo-roh)*
keyboard	**el teclado** *(ehl teh-'klah-doh)*
memory	**la memoria** *(lah meh-'moh-ree-ah)*
monitor	**el monitor** *(ehl moh-nee-'tohr)*
mother board	**la placa madre** *(lah 'plah-kah 'mah-dreh)*
mouse	**el ratón** *(ehl rah-'tohn)*
power	**la corriente** *(lah kohr-ree-'ehn-teh)*
screen	**la pantalla** *(lah pahn-'tah-yah)*

You'll need …	**Necesitará…** *(neh-seh-see-tah-'rah)*
to click	**hacer "clic"** *(ah-'sehr kleek)*
to connect	**conectar** *(koh-nehk-'tahr)*
to delete	**eliminar** *(eh-lee-mee-'nahr)*
to download	**bajar** *(bah-'hahr)*
to drag	**arrastrar** *(ahr-rahs-'trahr)*
to file	**archivar** *(ahr-chee-'vahr)*
to find	**encontrar** *(ehn-kohn-'trahr)*
to forward	**reenviar** *(reh-ehn-vee-'ahr)*
to press	**oprimir** *(oh-pree-'meer)*
to print	**imprimir** *(eem-pree-'meer)*
to receive	**recibir** *(reh-see-'beer)*
to reply	**responder** *(rehs-pohn-'dehr)*
to save	**ahorrar** *(ah-ohr-'rahr)*

to scroll down	**desplazar hacia abajo**
	(dehs-plah-'sahr 'ah-see-ah ah-'bah-hoh)
to search	**buscar** *(boos-'kahr)*
to select	**escoger** *(ehs-koh-'hehr)*
to send	**enviar** *(ehn-vee-'ahr)*
to upgrade	**actualizar** *(ahk-too-ah-lee-'sahr)*

Where's (the)…	**¿Dónde está…?** *('dohn-deh ehs-'tah)*
application	**el formulario** *(ehl fohr-moo-'lah-ree-oh)*
attachment	**el adjunto** *(ehl ahd-'hoon-toh)*
browser	**el navegador** *(ehl nah-veh-gah-'dohr)*
computer file	**el fichero** *(ehl fee-'cheh-roh)*
curser	**la flechita** *(lah fleh-'chee-tah)*
database	**la base de datos** *(lah 'bah-seh deh 'dah-tohs)*
disc	**el disco** *(ehl 'dees-koh)*
e-mail	**el correo electrónico**
	(ehl kohr-'reh-oh eh-lehk-'troh-nee-koh)
folder	**el directorio** *(ehl dee-rekh-'toh-ree-oh)*
font	**la tipografía** *(lah tee-poh-grah-'fee-ah)*
home page	**la página inicial** *(lah 'pah-hee-nah ee-nee-see-'ahl)*
icon	**el ícono** *(ehl 'ee-koh-noh)*
mailbox	**el buzón** *(ehl boo-'sohn)*
menu	**el menú** *(ehl meh-'noo)*
message	**el mensaje** *(ehl mehn-'sah-heh)*
network	**la red** *(lah rehd)*
password	**la contraseña** *(lah kohn-trah-'sehn-yah)*
program	**el programa** *(ehl proh-'grah-mah)*
search engine	**el buscador** *(ehl boos-kah-'dohr)*
server	**el servidor** *(ehl sehr-vee-'dohr)*
trash	**la basura** *(lah bah-'soo-rah)*
web site	**el sitio web** *(ehl 'see-tee-oh ueb)*

And these are the basic parts of an e-mail in Spanish:

Silvia	@	*alegre*	.	*provider*	.	*es*
nombre del usario	**arroba**	**nombre del dominio**	**punto**	**proveedor**	**punto**	**país**
user name	at	domain name	dot	provider	dot	country

Extra Info!

Notice that *.com*, *.edu*, *.org*, etc. are not normal closings to an e-mail in other countries. In many cases, the country such as **fr** (France), **es** (Spain), and **pe** (Peru) each have their own abbreviation.

And, as you can guess, a lot of technical terminology is the same in both Spanish and English:

CD	DVD	PC	gPhone	Blu-ray
DSL	Wifi	podcast	Google	Bluetooth
iPod	MP3	webcam	HDTV	flash drive
url	LED	plasma	iPhone	Apple
USB	Blackberry	LCD	software	

Let's Practice (23)

A. Write these in Spanish:

1. ¼ _____
2. 7 mi. _____
3. 100° _____
4. 5 oz. _____
5. ½ _____
6. 25% _____
7. 3 lbs. _____
8. 12 in. _____

B. Answer these questions in Spanish:

1. ¿Cuál es más grande—la taza o el balde?
2. ¿Cuál es más chica—el vaso o la jarra?
3. ¿Cuál es más alto—la botella o el frasco?
4. ¿Cuánto es tres por cinco?
5. ¿Cuántas líneas tiene un cuadrado?
6. ¿Cuánto son dos más cinco?

C. Name five major parts of a desktop computer in Spanish:

_____ _____ _____ _____

Appropriate Attire
La ropa apropiada
(lah 'roh-pah ah-proh-pee-'ah-dah)

At many companies there is a dress code. These items can be practiced daily at home as you get dressed and undressed:

You need (the)...	**Necesita...** *(neh-seh-'see-tah)*
cap	**la gorra** *(lah 'gohr-rah)*
outfit	**el conjunto** *(ehl kohn-'hoon-toh)*
uniform	**el uniforme** *(ehl oo-nee-'fohr-meh)*
You should wear (the)...	**Debe ponerse...** *('deh-beh poh-'nehr-seh)*
blouse	**la blusa** *(lah 'bloo-sah)*
dress	**el vestido** *(ehl vehs-'tee-doh)*
pants	**los pantalones** *(lohs pahn-tah-'loh-nehs)*
shirt	**la camisa** *(lah kah-'mee-sah)*
skirt	**la falda** *(lah 'fahl-dah)*
socks	**los calcetines** *(lohs kahl-seh-'tee-nehs)*
sportcoat	**el saco** *(el 'sah-koh)*
suit	**el traje** *(ehl 'trah-heh)*
tie	**la corbata** *(lah kohr-'bah-tah)*
Do not wear (the)...	**No use...** *(noh 'oo-seh)*
sandals	**las sandalias** *(lahs sahn-'dah-lee-ahs)*
shorts	**los pantalones cortos** *(lohs pahn-tah-'loh-nehs 'kohr-tohs)*
sneakers	**las zapatillas** *(lahs sah-pah-'tee-yahs)*
sweatsuit	**la sudadera** *(la soo-dah-'deh-rah)*
T-shirt	**la camiseta** *(lah kah-mee-'seh-tah)*

Extra Info!

People should be told what to do with their personal items:

Please put aside the ...	**Por favor, guarde ...** *(pohr fah'vohr 'gwahr-deh)*
briefcase	**el maletín** *(ehl mah-lee-'teen)*
cell phone	**el teléfono celular** *(ehl teh-'leh-foh-noh seh-loo-'lahr)*
comb	**el peine** *(ehl 'peh-ee-neh)*
electronic games	**los juegos electrónicos** *(lohs 'hweh-gohs eh-lehk-'troh-nee-kohs)*
hairbrush	**el cepillo** *(ehl seh-'pee-yoh)*
hairpin	**la horquilla** *(lah ohr-'kee-yah)*
hairspray	**la laca** *(lah 'lah-kah)*
headset	**los audífonos** *(lohs aw-'dee-foh-nohs)*
magazine	**la revista** *(lah reh-'vees-tah)*
make-up	**el maquillaje** *(ehl mah-kee-'yah-heh)*
nail file	**la lima de uñas** *(lah 'lee-mah deh 'oon-yahs)*
newspaper	**el periódico** *(ehl peh-ree-'oh-dee-koh)*
PDA	**la computadora de bolsillo** *(lah kohm-poo-tah-'doh-rah deh bohl-'see-yoh)*
perfume	**el perfume** *(ehl pehr-'foo-meh)*
sunglasses	**los lentes de sol** *(lohs 'lehn-tehs deh sohl)*
umbrella	**el paraguas** *(ehl pah-'rah-gwahs)*

Safety First
La seguridad primero
(lah seh-goo-ree-'dahd pree-'meh-roh)

Safety meetings are a must. Demand that your Spanish-speaking trainees are properly equipped to do the job:

Put on (the)…	**Póngase…** *('pohn-gah-seh)*
apron	**el mandil** *(ehl mahn-'deel)*
back support	**la faja** *(lah 'fah-hah)*
belt	**el cinturón** *(ehl seen-too-'rohn)*
boots	**las botas** *(lahs 'boh-tahs)*
ear plugs	**los tapones de oídos** *(lohs tah-'poh-nehs deh oh-'ee-dohs)*
fall equipment	**la protección contra caídas** *(lah proh-tehk-see-'ohn 'kohn-trah kah-'ee-dahs)*
gloves	**los guantes** *(lohs 'gwahn-tehs)*
goggles	**las gafas** *(lahs 'gah-fahs)*
hair net	**la redecilla** *(lah reh-deh-'see-yah)*
hard hat	**el casco duro** *(ehl 'kahs-koh 'doo-roh)*
harness	**el correaje** *(ehl kohr-reh-'ah-heh)*
hat	**el sombrero** *(ehl sohm-'breh-roh)*
helmet	**el casco** *(ehl 'kahs-koh)*
jacket	**la chaqueta** *(lah chah-'keh-tah)*
knee pads	**las rodilleras** *(lahs roh-dee-'yeh-rahs)*
long sleeves	**la camisa de manga larga** *(lah kah-'mee-sah deh 'mahn-gah 'lahr-gah)*
mask	**la máscara** *(lah 'mahs-kah-rah)*
overalls	**los pantalones de peto** *(lohs pahn-tah-'loh-nehs deh 'peh-toh)*
overcoat	**el abrigo** *(ehl ah-'bree-goh)*
raincoat	**el impermeable** *(ehl eem-pehr-meh-'ah-bleh)*
reflectors	**los reflectores** *(los reh-flehk-'toh-rehs)*
respirator	**el respirador** *(ehl rehs-pee-rah-'dohr)*
safety glasses	**los lentes de seguridad** *(lohs 'lehn-tehs deh seh-goo-ree-'dahd)*
safety line	**la cuerda de seguridad** *(lah 'kwehr-dah deh seh-goo-ree-'dahd)*
safety outfit	**el conjunto de seguridad** *(ehl kohn-'hoon-toh deh seh-goo-ree-'dahd)*

scarf	**la bufanda** *(lah boo-'fahn-dah)*
shin guards	**las espinilladeras** *(lahs ehs-pee-nee-yah-'deh-rahs)*
strap	**la correa** *(lah kohr-'reh-ah)*
sunscreen	**la protección contra el sol**
	(lah proh-tehk-see-'ohn 'kohn-trah ehl sohl)
uniform	**el uniforme** *(ehl oo-nee-'fohr-meh)*
vest	**el chaleco** *(ehl chah-'leh-koh)*

More Instructions
Más instrucciones
(mahs eens-trook-see-'oh-nehs)

Here are sentence patterns that can be used effectively time and again:

Make sure that (you) ...	**Asegúrese de ...** *(ah-seh-'goo-reh-seh deh)*
arrive early	**llegar temprano** *(yeh-'gahr tehm-'prah-noh)*
ask me if you don't understand	**preguntarme si no entiende** *(preh-goon-'tahr-meh see noh ehn-tee-'ehn-deh)*
call me at this number	**llamarme a este número** *(yah-'mahr-meh ah 'ehs-teh 'noo-meh-roh)*
check on the materials	**vigilar los materiales** *(vee-hee-'lahr lohs mah-teh-ree-'ah-lehs)*
clean up the mess	**limpiar la basura** *(leem-pee-'ahr lah bah-'soo-rah)*
lock all the doors	**cerrar todas las puertas** *(sehr-'rahr 'toh-dahs lahs 'pwehr-tahs)*
look at the schedule	**mirar el horario** *(mee-'rahr ehl oh-'rah-ree-oh)*
put everything away	**guardar todo** *(gwahr-'dahr 'toh-doh)*
read the directions	**leer las instrucciones** *(leh-'ehr lahs eens-trook-see-'oh-nehs)*
turn off the machine	**apagar la máquina** *(ah-pah-'gahr lah 'mah-kee-nah)*

These also work well with training notes or messages:

Remember that ...
Recuerde que ... *(reh-'kwehr-deh keh)*

It's important that...
Es importante que ... *(ehs eem-pohr-'tahn-teh keh)*

When you finish ...
Cuando termine ... *('kwahn-doh tehr-'mee-neh)*

If it's possible...
Si es posible ... *(see ehs poh-'see-bleh)*

Before you go ...
Antes de irse ... *('ahn-tehs deh 'eer-seh)*

You can make a variety of suggestions or comments with this next group of phrases. They introduce, break up, transition from, or close out any topic you're discussing at the time. After pronouncing the new word, complete the sentence.

Above all...	**Sobre todo...** *('soh-breh 'toh-doh)*
	...no llegar tarde.
According to...	**Según...** *(seh-'goon)*
	...Juan, todo está bien.
Although...	**Aunque...** *(ah-'oon-keh)*
At first...	**Al principio...** *(ahl preen-'see-pee-oh)*
At last...	**Por fin...** *(pohr feen)*
At least...	**Por lo menos...** *(pohr loh 'meh-nohs)*
Besides...	**Además...** *(ah-deh-'mahs)*
By the way...	**A propósito...** *(ah proh-'poh-see-toh)*
For example...	**Por ejemplo...** *(pohr eh-'hehm-ploh)*
However...	**Sin embargo...** *(seen ehm-'bahr-goh)*
In general...	**En general...** *(ehn heh-neh-'rahl)*

In other words...	**Es decir...** *(ehs deh-'seer)*
In spite of...	**A pesar de...** *(ah peh-'sahr deh)*
Little by little...	**Poco a poco...** *('poh-koh ah 'poh-koh)*
On the contrary...	**Por lo contrario...** *(pohr loh kohn-'trah-ree-oh)*
On the other hand...	**En cambio...** *(ehn 'kahm-bee-oh)*
So...	**Así que...** *(ah-'see keh)*
Still...	**Aún...** *(ah-'oon)*
Then...	**Entonces...** *(ehn-'tohn-sehs)*
Therefore...	**Por eso...** *(pohr 'eh-soh)*
Without a doubt...	**Sin duda...** *(seen 'doo-dah)*

How Not to Do Something
Cómo no hacer algo
('koh-moh noh ah-'sehr 'ahl-goh)

For simple instructions in the negative, stick with the phrase you learned earlier:

Please, don't ...	**Favor de no ...** *(fah-'vohr deh noh)*
do that	**hacer eso** *(ah-'sehr 'eh-soh)*
leave them here	**dejarlos aquí** *(deh-'hahr-lohs ah-'kee)*
move the equipment	**mover el equipo** *(moh-'vehr ehl eh-'kee-poh)*
park there	**estacionar allí** *(ehs-tah-see-oh-'nahr ah-'ee)*
touch it	**tocarlo** *(toh-'kahr-loh)*
turn it off	**apagarla** *(ah-pah-'gahr-lah)*
use this machine	**usar esta máquina** *(oo-'sahr 'ehs-tah 'mah-kee-nah)*

In some cases, employers will have to tell Spanish-speaking supervisors or managers what needs to be communicated to the rest of the crew:

Tell them that ...	**Dígales que ...** *('dee-gah-lehs keh)*
everything looks good	**todo se ve bien** *('toh-doh seh veh bee-'ehn)*
I want to talk to them	**quiero hablarles** *(kee-'eh-roh ah-'blahr-lehs)*
it is required	**es obligatorio** *(ehs oh-blee-gah-'toh-ree-oh)*
there is a problem	**hay un problema** *('ah-ee oon proh-'bleh-mah)*
they have to finish it all	**tienen que terminar todo** *(tee-'eh-nehn keh tehr-mee-'nahr 'toh-doh)*
they must go to the meeting	**tienen que ir a la reunión** *(tee-'eh-nehn keh eer ah lah reh-oo-nee-'ohn)*
they need to get started	**necesitan empezar** *(neh-seh-'see-tahn ehm-peh-'sahr)*
they should hurry	**deben apurarse** *('deh-behn ah-poo-'rahr-seh)*
we have more work to do	**tenemos más trabajo que hacer** *(teh-'neh-mohs mahs trah-'bah-hoh keh ah-'sehr)*

 ## Let's Practice

A. Correctly put the words in order in each sentence below:

1. apagar   asegúrese   la   de   máquina
2. problema   que   hay   dígales   un
3. allí   no   estacionar   de   favor
4. lentes   traer   sol   puede   de   los
5. manga   la   póngase   larga   de   camisa
6. chica   al   era   compañía   principio   la

B. In Spanish:

1. Name three articles of clothing needed for work in cold weather.

_____   _____   _____

2. Name three clothing items that are commonly worn by women.

_____   _____   _____

3. Name three well-known pieces of safety equipment.

_____   _____   _____

Action Words!

As you have learned, the best way to provide training in Spanish is to insert verb infinitives into short, practical phrases:

You need to begin.   **Necesita** comenzar. *(neh-seh-'see-tah koh-mehn-'sahr)*
You have to finish.   **Tiene que** terminar. *(tee-'eh-neh keh tehr-mee-'nahr)*

However, it's easier if you break your phrases into sets of three. Simply add to each phrase any word from the list below and go on making your own sentences:

I want (to) ...   **Quiero ...** *(kee-'eh-roh)*
I'm able (to)...   **Puedo...** *('pweh-doh)*
I'm going to ...   **Voy a ...** *('voh-ee ah)*

It's important (to)...   **Es importante...** *(ehs eem-pohr-'tahn-teh)*
It's dangerous (to)...   **Es peligroso...** *(ehs peh-lee-'groh-soh)*
It's easy (to)...   **Es fácil...** *(ehs 'fah-seel)*

to allow	**dejar** *(deh-'hahr)*
	Quiero dejar el trabajo para mañana.
to arrive	**llegar** *(yeh-'gahr)*
	Es importante llegar a las ocho.
to ask for	**pedir** *(peh-'deer)*
to assemble	**ensamblar** *(ehn-sahm-'blahr)*
to attach	**sujetar** *(soo-heh-'tahr)*
to bend	**doblar** *(doh-'blahr)*
to check	**verificar** *(veh-ree-fee-'kahr)*
to climb	**subir** *(soo-'beer)*

to connect	**conectar** *(koh-nehk-'tahr)*
to cut	**cortar** *(kohr-'tahr)*
to dig	**excavar** *(ex-kah-'vahr)*
to drill	**taladrar** *(tah-lah-'drahr)*
to explain	**explicar** *(ex-plee-'kahr)*
to glue	**pegar** *(peh-'gahr)*
to grind	**moler** *(moh-'lehr)*
to hang	**colgar** *(kohl-'gahr)*
to heat	**calentar** *(kah-lehn-'tahr)*
to learn	**aprender** *(ah-prehn-'dehr)*
to load	**cargar** *(kahr-'gahr)*
to lock	**cerrar con llave** *(sehr-'rahr kohn 'yah-veh)*
to lose	**perder** *(pehr-'dehr)*
to mark	**marcar** *(mahr-'kahr)*
to measure	**medir** *(meh-'deer)*
to mix	**mezclar** *(mehs-'klahr)*
to paint	**pintar** *(peen-'tahr)*

to pile	**apilar** *(ah-pee-'lahr)*
to repair	**reparar** *(reh-pah-'rahr)*
to replace	**reemplazar** *(reh-ehm-plah-'zahr)*
to rest	**descansar** *(dehs-kahn-'sahr)*
to review	**repasar** *(reh-pah-'sahr)*
to sand	**lijar** *(lee-'hahr)*
to scrub	**fregar** *(freh-'gahr)*
to stamp	**estampar** *(ehs-tahm-'pahr)*
to study	**estudiar** *(ehs-too-dee-'ahr)*
to sweep	**barrer** *(bahr-'rehr)*
to teach	**enseñar** *(ehn-sehn-'yahr)*
to tighten	**apretar** *(ah-preh-'tahr)*
to touch	**tocar** *(toh-'kahr)*
to train	**entrenar** *(ehn-treh-'nahr)*
to try	**tratar** *(trah-'tahr)*
to unload	**descargar** *(dehs-kahr-'gahr)*
to weld	**soldar** *(sohl-'dahr)*

Verbs: The Past (Preterit)
Los verbos: el pasado (pretérito)

 (lohs 'vehr-bohs ehl pah-'sah-do preh-'teh-ree-toh)

So far we have seen actions taking place in the present and in the future. Let's review:

BASIC VERB: TO WORK **TRABAJAR** *(trah-bah-'hahr)*

Right now: I'm working. **Estoy trabajando.**
(ehs-'toh-ee trah-bah-'hahn-doh)

Every day: I work. **Trabajo.** *(trah-'bah-hoh)*

Tomorrow: I'm going to work. **Voy a trabajar.**
('voh-ee ah trah-bah-'hahr)

Now let's take a look at one of the ways to express past actions in Spanish. Read the following conjugations of **-ar, -er,** and **-ir** verbs in the PRETERIT:

-AR verbs: e.g., TO SPEAK **HABLAR** *(ah-'blahr)*
I spoke with the boss.
Hablé con el jefe. *(ah-'bleh kohn ehl 'heh-feh)*

You, He, She spoke a lot.
Habló mucho. *(ah-'bloh 'moo-choh)*

You (pl.), They spoke English.
Hablaron inglés. *(ah-'blah-rohn een-'glehs)*

We spoke a little.
Hablamos un poco. *(ah-'blah-mohs oon 'poh-koh)*

-ER/-IR verbs: e.g., TO LEAVE **SALIR** *(sah-'leer)*
I left at 5:00.
Salí a las cinco. *(sah-'lee ah lahs 'seen-koh)*

You, He, She left late.
Salió tarde. *(sah-lee-'oh 'tahr-deh)*

You (pl.), They left early.
Salieron temprano. *(sah-lee-'eh-rohn tehm-'prah-noh)*

We left on Friday.
Salimos el viernes. *(sah-'lee-mohs ehl vee-'ehr-nehs)*

Unfortunately, some verbs have irregular past tenses. These three are pretty common and should be practiced first. Don't forget to create your own examples on the line:

TO GO	**IR** *(eer)*	
I went	**Fui** *(fwee)*	<u>**Fui** a la oficina.</u>
You, He, She went	**Fue** *(fweh)*	_____
You (pl.), They went	**Fueron** *('fweh-rohn)*	_____
We went	**Fuimos** *('fwee-mohs)*	_____

Very important: The verb **Ser** *(sehr—*to be*)* has the same preterit forms as the verb **Ir** *(eer—*to go*)*.

TO HAVE	**TENER** *(teh-'nehr)*	
I had	**Tuve** *('too-veh)*	<u>**Tuve** un problema.</u>
You, He, She had	**Tuvo** *('too-voh)*	_____
You (pl.), They had	**Tuvieron** *(too-vee-'eh-rohn)*	_____
We had	**Tuvimos** *(too-'vee-mohs)*	_____

TO SAY	**DECIR** *(deh-seer)*	
I said	**Dije** *('dee-heh)*	<u>**Dije** la verdad.</u>
You, He, She said	**Dijo** *('dee-hoh)*	_____
You (pl.), They said	**Dijeron** *(dee-'heh-rohn)*	_____
We said	**Dijimos** *(dee-'hee-mohs)*	_____

 ## The Culture

> Once an employee establishes a friendly relationship, it's not uncommon for native Hispanics to use nicknames when referring to others. It is meant to show intimacy, and not disrespect.

Let's Practice (25)

A. Translate into English:

1. Es peligroso tocar la máquina.

_____

2. Puedo mezclar los dos materiales.

_____

3. Es importante cerrar la puerta con llave.

_____

4. Debe usted repasar la lección.

_____

5. Quiero aprender más español.

_____

B. Using what you've learned, follow the examples and fill in the blanks below:

1. ¿Trató usted?   Sí, yo traté.
2. ¿Comió usted?   Sí, yo comí.
1. ¿Estudió usted?   _____
2. ¿Subió usted?   _____
3. ¿Taladró usted?   _____
4. ¿Aprendió usted? _____
5. ¿Fue usted?   _____

Chapter Five

Capítulo Cinco
(kah-'pee-too-loh 'seen-koh)

The Difficulties
Las dificultades
(lahs dee-fee-kool-'tah-dehs)

What Happened?
¿Qué pasó?
(keh pah-'soh)

Things don't always go smoothly at work, so learn those descriptive words and phrases that refer to potential difficulties, problems, and concerns. Begin by finding out what's wrong with the tools or equipment. Note how :

Why such ...?	**¿Por qué ...?** *(pohr keh)*
concern	**tal apuro** *(tahl ah-'poo-roh)*
explosion	**tal explosión** *(tahl ex-ploh-see-'ohn)*
noise	**tal ruido** *(tahl 'rwee-doh)*
smell	**tal olor** *(tahl oh-'lohr)*
sound	**tal sonido** *(tahl soh-'nee-doh)*
trouble	**tal problema** *(tahl proh-'bleh-mah)*
urgency	**tal urgencia** *(tahl oor-'hehn-see-ah)*
vibration	**tal vibración** *(tahl vee-brah-see-'ohn)*
Is there ...?	**¿Hay...?** *('ah-ee)*
flames	*llamas ('yah-mahs)*
fumes	*vapores (vah-'poh-rehs)*
leaks	*escapes (ehs-'kah-pehs)*
smoke	*humo ('oo-moh)*
sparks	*chispas ('chees-pahs)*

131

Can you see (the)…?	**¿Puede ver…?** *('pweh-deh vehr)*
break	**la rotura** *(lah roh-'too-rah)*
bump	**el bulto** *(ehl 'bool-toh)*
crinkle	**la arruga** *(lah ahr-'roo-gah)*
damage	**el daño** *(ehl 'dahn-yoh)*
gap	**el hueco** *(ehl 'hweh-koh)*
hole	**el hoyo** *(ehl 'oh-yoh)*
tear	**el rasgón** *(ehl rahs-'gohn)*
Is it …?	**¿Está …?** *(ehs-'tah)*
bent	**doblado** *(doh-'blah-doh)*
broken	**roto** *('roh-toh)*
burned	**quemado** *(keh-'mah-doh)*
chipped	**astillado** *(ahs-tee-'yah-doh)*
crushed	**aplastado** *(ah-plahs-'tah-doh)*
cut	**cortado** *(kohr-'tah-doh)*
damaged	**dañado** *(dahn-'yah-doh)*
defective	**defectuoso** *(deh-fehk-too-'oh-soh)*
destroyed	**destruido** *(dehs-troo-'ee-doh)*
inoperative	**inoperable** *(ee-noh-peh-'rah-bleh)*
lost	**perdido** *(pehr-'dee-doh)*
malfunctioning	**funcionando mal** *(foon-see-oh-'nahn-doh mahl)*
missing parts	**faltando partes** *(fahl-'tahn-doh 'pahr-tehs)*
out of service	**fuera de servicio** *('fweh-rah deh sehr-'vee-see-oh)*
rotten	**podrido** *(poh-'dree-doh)*
ruined	**arruinado** *(ahr-roo-ee-'nah-doh)*
stained	**manchado** *(mahn-'chah-doh)*
stuck	**pegado** *(peh-'gah-doh)*
torn	**rasgado** *(rahs-'gah-doh)*
worthless	**sin valor** *(seen vah-'lohr)*

Next, try to gather as much information as you can:

Is there a problem with (the)…?	**¿Hay algún problema con…?** *('ah-ee ahl-'goon proh-'bleh-mah kohn)*
control	**el control** *(ehl kohn-'trohl)*
current	**la corriente** *(lah kohr-ree-'ehn-teh)*
cycle	**el ciclo** *(ehl 'seek-loh)*

flow	**el flujo** *(ehl 'floo-hoh)*
force	**la fuerza** *(lah 'fwehr-sah)*
horsepower	**el caballaje** *(ehl kah-bah-'yah-heh)*
level	**el nivel** *(ehl nee-'vehl)*
load	**la carga** *(lah 'kahr-gah)*
power	**la potencia** *(lah poh-'tehn-see-ah)*
pressure	**la presión** *(lah preh-see-'ohn)*
propulsion	**la propulsión** *(lah proh-pool-see-'ohn)*
resistance	**la resistencia** *(lah reh-sees-'tehn-see-ah)*
speed	**la velocidad** *(lah veh-loh-see-'dahd)*
temperature	**la temperatura** *(lah tehm-peh-rah-'too-rah)*
torque	**el par de torsión** *(ehl pahr deh tohr-see-'ohn)*
voltage	**el voltaje** *(ehl vohl-'tah-heh)*

Did you check (the)…?	**¿Revisó…?** *(reh-vee-'soh)*

amount	**la cantidad** *(lah kahn-tee-'dahd)*
connection	**la conexión** *(lah koh-nehk-see-'ohn)*
depth	**la profundidad** *(lah proh-foon-dee-'dahd)*
distance	**la distancia** *(lah dees-'tahn-see-ah)*
height	**la altura** *(lah ahl-'too-rah)*
measurement	**la medida** *(lah meh-'dee-dah)*
position	**la posición** *(lah poh-see-see-'ohn)*
shape	**la forma** *(lah 'fohr-mah)*
size	**el tamaño** *(ehl tah-'mahn-yoh)*
time	**la hora** *(lah 'oh-rah)*
weight	**el peso** *(ehl 'peh-soh)*

Are you going (to) … it?	**¿Lo va a …?** *(loh vah ah)*

cancel	**cancelar** *(kahn-seh-'lahr)*
deactivate	**desactivar** *(dehs-ahk-tee-'vahr)*
disconnect	**desconectar** *(dehs-koh-nehk-'tahr)*
pause	**pausar** *(pah-oo-'sahr)*
stop	**parar** *(pah-'rahr)*
switch off	**apagar** *(ah-pah-'gahr)*
unplug	**desenchufar** *(dehs-ehn-choo-'fahr)*

Extra Info!

Are you still practicing descriptions in pairs of opposites?

It looks...	Se ve... *(seh veh)*
twisted	**torcido** *(tohr-'see-doh)*
straight	**recto** *('rehk-toh)*
loose	**suelto** *('swehl-toh)*
tight	**apretado** *(ah-preh-'tah-doh)*
heavy	**pesado** *(peh-'sah-doh)*
light	**ligero** *(lee-'heh-roh)*
sloppy	**desaliñado** *(deh-sah-leen-'yah-doh)*
neat	**limpio** *('leem-pee-oh)*
even	**llano** *('yah-noh)*
uneven	**desigual** *(desh-see-'gwahl)*

Repairs
Las reparaciones
(lahs reh-pah-rah-see-'oh-nehs)

When machinery breaks down, you'll have to point out the spare parts in Spanish.

Bring (the)...	**Traiga...** *('trah-ee-gah)*
Change (the)...	**Cambie...** *('kahm-bee-eh)*
Look for (the)...	**Busque...** *('boos-keh)*
Remove (the)...	**Saque...** *('sah-keh)*
Use (the)...	**Use...** *('oo-seh)*
bar	**la barra** *(lah 'bahr-rah)*
bearing	**el cojinete** *(ehl koh-ee-'neh-teh)*
board	**la tabla** *(lah 'tah-blah)*
bolt	**el perno** *(ehl 'pehr-noh)*
bracket	**la ménsula** *(lah 'mehn-soo-lah)*
cap	**la tapa** *(lah 'tah-pah)*

cartridge	**el cartucho** *(ehl kahr-'too-choh)*
case	**la caja** *(lah 'kah-hah)*
casing	**la cubierta** *(lah koo-bee-'ehr-tah)*
cell	**la célula** *(lah 'seh-loo-lah)*
chassis	**el bastidor** *(ehl bahs-tee-'dohr)*
clip	**la sujetadora** *(lah soo-heh-tah-'doh-rah)*
coil	**el rollo** *(ehl 'roh-yoh)*
crank	**la manivela** *(lah mah-nee-'veh-lah)*
fitting	**el acoplamiento** *(ehl ah-koh-plah-mee-'ehn-toh)*
gear	**el embrague** *(ehl ehm-'brah-geh)*
handle	**la perilla** *(lah peh-'ree-yah)*
hinge	**la bisagra** *(lah bee-'sah-grah)*
lever	**la palanca** *(lah pah-'lahn-kah)*
lightbulb	**el foco** *(ehl 'foh-koh)*
lining	**el forro** *(ehl 'fohr-roh)*
nail	**el clavo** *(ehl 'klah-voh)*
nozzle	**el pitón** *(ehl pee-'tohn)*
nut	**la tuerca** *(lah 'twehr-kah)*
panel	**el panel** *(ehl pah-'nehl)*
peg	**la clavija** *(lah klah-'vee-hah)*
piston	**el émbolo** *(ehl 'ehm-boh-loh)*
plate	**la placa** *(lah 'plah-kah)*
propeller	**la hélice** *(lah 'eh-lee-seh)*
ratchet	**el trinquete** *(ehl treen-'keh-teh)*
rivet	**el remache** *(ehl reh-'mah-cheh)*
rod	**la varilla** *(lah vah-'ree-yah)*
roller	**el rodillo** *(ehl roh-'dee-yoh)*
screw	**el tornillo** *(ehl tohr-'nee-yoh)*
shaft	**el astil** *(ehl ahs-'teel)*
spool	**el carrete** *(ehl kahr-'reh-teh)*
spring	**el resorte** *(ehl reh-'sohr-teh)*
tire	**el neumático** *(ehl neh-oo-'mah-tee-koh)*
washer	**la arandela** *(lah ah-rahn-'deh-lah)*
wheel	**la rueda** *(lah 'rweh-dah)*

Then somebody has to clean up after the repair work:

Clean up (the)…	**Limpie…** *('leem-pee-eh)*
dirt	**la tierra** *(lah tee-'ehr-rah)*
dust	**el polvo** *(ehl 'pohl-voh)*
refuse	**los desperdicios** *(lohs dehs-pehr-'dee-see-ohs)*
scrap	**el desecho** *(ehl dehs-'eh-choh)*
trash	**la basura** *(lah bah-'soo-rah)*
waste	**los residuos** *(lohs reh-'see-doo-ohs)*

Wash it with (the)…	**Lávelo con…** *('lah-veh-loh kohn)*
acid	**el ácido** *(ehl 'ah-see-doh)*
bleach	**el cloro** *(ehl 'kloh-roh)*
chemicals	**los productos químicos** *(lohs proh-'dook-tohs 'kee-mee-kohs)*
cleanser	**el limpiador** *(ehl leem-pee-ah-'dohr)*
compound	**el compuesto** *(ehl kohm-'pwehs-toh)*
detergent	**el detergente** *(ehl deh-tehr-'hehn-teh)*
soap	**el jabón** *(ehl hah-'bohn)*

When There's a Problem
Cuando hay un problema
('kwahn-doh 'ah-ee oon proh-'bleh-mah)

Something's wrong!	**¡Algo está mal!** *('ahl-goh ehs-'tah mahl)*
It looks strange!	**¡Esto se ve raro!** *('ehs-toh seh veh 'rah-roh)*
Let's fix it!	**¡Vamos a repararlo!** *('vah-mohs ah reh-pah-'rahr-loh)*

And here's a way to keep your messages clear and simple:

Where's (the)…?	**¿Dónde está…?** *('dohn-deh ehs-'tah)*
thing	**la cosa** *(lah 'koh-sah)*
piece	**la pieza** *(lah pee-'eh-sah)*
part	**la parte** *(lah 'pahr-teh)*

Let's Practice

A. Connect the words that belong together best:

1. la fuerza	la tierra
2. el perno	el sonido
3. el rasgón	la medida
4. el ruido	la llama
5. el jabón	la tuerca
6. la chispa	la rotura
7. el tamaño	la potencia
8. el polvo	el detergente

B. Translate, then give the opposite of each infinitive:

1. desconectar _____ _____
2. desactivar _____ _____
3. desenchufar _____ _____

Personal Problems
Los problemas personales
(lohs proh-'bleh-mahs pehr-soh-'nah-lehs)

Things do go wrong with employees, so let's look over a list of personal problems that employers deal with all the time. And remember, it might be wise to have a bilingual speaker around:

Let's talk in my office.
Vamos a hablar en mi oficina. *('vah-mohs ah ah-'blahr ehn mee oh-fee-'see-nah)*

Everything is confidential.
Todo es confidencial. *('toh-doh ehs kohn-fee-dehn-see-'ahl)*

I want to help you.
Quiero ayudarle. *(kee-'eh-roh ah-yoo-'dahr-leh)*

Ask questions that require a brief but meaningful response:

Did you hear about (the)…	**¿Escuchó algo de…?** *(ehs-koo-'choh 'ahl-goh deh)*
subject	**el tema** *(ehl 'teh-mah)*
issue	**el asunto** *(ehl ah-'soon-toh)*

Is there a concern?
¿Hay un problema? *('ah-ee oon proh-'bleh-mah)*

Do you wish to talk to me?
¿Desea hablar conmigo? *(deh-'seh-ah ah-'blahr kohn-'mee-goh)*

Do you have something to say?
¿Tiene algo que decir? *(tee-'eh-neh 'ahl-goh keh deh-'seer)*

Can you tell me what happened?
¿Puede decirme qué pasó? *('pweh-deh deh-'seer-meh keh pah-'soh)*

Where did it happen?
¿Dónde pasó eso? *('dohn-deh pah-'soh 'eh-soh)*

Who saw what happened?
¿Quién vio lo que pasó? *(kee-'ehn vee-'oh loh keh pah-'soh)*

When did it happen?
¿Cuándo pasó eso? *('kwahn-doh pah-'soh 'eh-soh)*

Can you write down what happened?
¿Puede escribir lo que pasó? *('pweh-deh ehs-kree-'beer loh keh pah-'soh)*

Do you have problems with (the)…?	**¿Tiene problemas con…?** *(tee-'eh-neh proh-'bleh-mahs kohn)*
job	**el trabajo** *(ehl trah-'bah-hoh)*
other employee	**el otro empleado/la otra empleada** *(ehl 'oh-troh ehm-pleh-'ah-doh/lah 'oh-trah ehm-pleh-'ah-dah)*
regulations	**los reglamentos** *(lohs reh-glah-'mehn-tohs)*
schedule	**el horario** *(ehl oh-'rah-ree-oh)*
supervisor	**el supervisor/la supervisora** *(ehl soo-pehr-vee-'sohr/lah soo-pehr-vee-'soh-rah)*

Do you want to talk about (the)..?	**¿Quiere hablar sobre..?** *(kee-'eh-reh ah-'blahr 'soh-breh)*

absences	**las ausencias** *(lahs ah-oo-'sehn-see-ahs)*
accident	**el accidente** *(ehl ahk-see-'dehn-teh)*
alcohol	**el alcohol** *(ehl ahl-koh-'ohl)*
argument	**la discusión** *(lah dees-koo-see-'ohn)*
complaint	**la queja** *(lah 'keh-hah)*
conditions	**las condiciones** *(lahs kohn-dee-see-'oh-nehs)*
conflict	**el conflicto** *(ehl kohn-'fleek-toh)*
disturbance	**el disturbio** *(ehl dees-'toor-bee-oh)*
drugs	**las drogas** *(lahs 'droh-gahs)*
errors	**los errores** *(lohs ehr-'roh-rehs)*
fight	**la pelea** *(lah peh-'leh-ah)*
illness	**la enfermedad** *(lah ehn-fehr-meh-'dahd)*
injury	**la herida** *(lah eh-'ree-dah)*
poor decisions	**las malas decisiones** *(lahs 'mah-lahs deh-see-see-'oh-nehs)*
tardiness	**las tardanzas** *(lahs tahr-'dahn-sahs)*
threat	**la amenaza** *(lah ah-meh-'nah-sah)*

Now focus on a specific area of concern:

The work is...	**El trabajo está...** *(ehl trah-'bah-hoh ehs-'tah)*

incomplete	**incompleto** *(een-kohm-'pleh-toh)*
late	**retrasado** *(reh-trah-'sah-doh)*
missing	**perdido** *(pehr-'dee-doh)*

Let's chat about (the)…	**Hablemos de...** *(ah-'bleh-mohs deh)*

cultural differences	**las diferencias culturales** *(lahs dee-feh-'rehn-see-ahs kool-too-'rah-lehs)*
lack of transportation	**la falta de transporte** *(lah 'fahl-tah deh trahns-'pohr-teh)*
language proficiency	**la competencia en el lenguaje** *(lah kohm-peh-'tehn-see-ah ehn ehl lehn-'gwah-heh)*
personal hygiene	**la higiene personal** *(lah ee-hee-'eh-neh pehr-soh-'nahl)*
safety standards	**los estándares de seguridad** *(lohs ehs-'tahn-dah-rehs deh seh-goo-ree-'dahd)*
style of clothing	**el estilo de su ropa** *(ehl ehs-'tee-loh deh soo 'roh-pah)*

I'm hearing complaints about (the) ...	**Estoy escuchando quejas sobre...** *(ehs-'toh-ee ehs-koo-'chahn-doh 'keh-hahs 'soh-breh)*
foul language	**el lenguaje sucio** *(ehl lehn-'gwah-heh 'soo-see-oh)*
poor attitude	**la actitud negativa** *(lah ahk-tee-'tood neh-gah-'tee-vah)*
physical abuse	**el abuso físico** *(ehl ah-'boo-soh 'fee-see-koh)*
racial discrimination	**la discriminación racial** *(lah dees-kree-mee-nah-see-'ohn rah-see-'ahl)*
sexual harassment	**el acosamiento sexual** *(ehl ah-koh-sah-mee-'ehn-toh sehk-soo-'ahl)*

Check these questions related to attendance and punctuality:

Are you going to miss work?
¿Va a faltar del trabajo? *(va ah fahl-'tahr ahl trah-'bah-hoh)*

Are you going to be late?
¿Va a llegar tarde? *(vah ah yeh-'gahr 'tahr-deh)*

Did you call the office?
¿Llamó a la oficina? *(yah-'moh ah lah oh-fee-'see-nah)*

Do you have an excuse?
¿Tiene una excusa? *(tee-'eh-neh 'oo-nah ex-'koo-sah)*

What's the reason?
¿Cuál es la razón? *(kwahl ehs lah rah-'sohn)*

Contact me if you have a problem.
Comuníquese conmigo si tiene un problema.
(koh-moo-'nee-keh-seh kohn-'mee-goh see tee-'eh-neh oon proh-'bleh-mah)

 ## The Culture

One of the most difficult things to discuss in a foreign language concerns social ethics and values. Your personal feelings, attitudes, and beliefs cannot be communicated in a few short sentences. Therefore, the best way to express any personal matter is either through an interpreter or by having a prepared written note. Be sure that your employee knows exactly what you consider to be right or wrong at the workplace.

Critical Concerns
Asuntos de gravedad
(ah-'soon-tohs deh grah-veh-dahd)

When personal problems get more serious, you may have to confront employees directly:

It was your fault.	**Usted tenía la culpa.** *(oos-'tehd teh-nee-ah lah 'kool-pah)*
You did it.	**Lo hizo usted.** *(loh 'ee-soh oos-tehd)*
You're guilty.	**Usted es culpable.** *(oos-'tehd ehs kool-'pah-bleh)*

It seems that you were...	**Parece que usted fue...** *(pah-'reh-seh keh oos-'tehd fweh)*

careless	**descuidado** *(dehs-kwee-'dah-doh)*
dishonest	**deshonesto** *(dehs-oh-'nehs-toh)*
disrespectful	**irrespetuoso** *(eer-rehs-peh-too-'oh-soh)*
incompetent	**incompetente** *(een-kohm-peh-'tehn-teh)*
irresponsible	**irresponsable** *(eer-rehs-pohn-'sah-bleh)*
mean	**cruel** *(kroo-'ehl)*
negligent	**negligente** *(neh-glee-'gehn-teh)*
rude	**grosero** *(groh-'seh-roh)*
sarcastic	**sarcástico** *(sahr-'kahs-tee-koh)*

If a crime is committed, all sorts of terminology will be required:

It's a crime.	**Es un crimen.** *(ehs oon 'kree-mehn)*
We have witnesses.	**Tenemos testigos.** *(teh-'neh-mohs tehs-'tee-gohs)*
There is proof.	**Hay pruebas.** *('ah-ee proo-'eh-bahs)*
We have surveillance.	**Tenemos vigilancia.** *(teh-'neh-mohs vee-hee-'lahn-see-ah)*
There will be an investigation.	**Habrá una investigación.** *(ah-'brah 'oo-nah een-vehs-tee-gah-see-'ohn)*

We're aware of (the)...	**Sabemos de...** *(sah-'beh-mohs deh)*

drug use	**el uso de drogas** *(ehl 'oo-soh deh 'droh-gahs)*
embezzling	**el desfalco** *(ehl dehs-'fahl-koh)*
felony	**el delito mayor** *(ehl deh-'lee-toh mah-'yohr)*
firearm	**el arma de fuego** *(ehl 'ahr-mah deh 'fweh-goh)*
fraudulent document	**el documento fraudulento** *(ehl doh-koo-'mehn-toh frah-oo-doo-'lehn-toh)*

gambling   **los juegos de apuestas**
(lohs 'hweh-gohs deh ah-'pwehs-tahs)

lawsuit   **el pleito** *(ehl 'pleh-ee-toh)*

stealing   **los robos** *(lohs 'roh-bohs)*

vandalism   **el vandalismo** *(ehl vahn-dah-'lees-moh)*

warrant   **la orden de la corte** *(lah 'ohr-dehn deh lah 'kohr-teh)*

I called the police.   **Llamé a la policía.** *(yah-'meh ah lah poh-lee-'see-ah)*

It's very serious.   **Es muy serio.** *(ehs 'moo-ee 'seh-ree-oh)*

It's a shame.   **Es una lástima.** *(ehs 'oo-nah 'lahs-tee-mah)*

When inappropriate behavior leads to severe consequences:

This is a warning.
Esta es una advertencia.
('ehs-tah ehs 'oo-nah ahd-vehr-'tehn-see-ah)

This is going in your file.
Esto va en su archivo personal.
('ehs-toh vah ehn soo ahr-'chee-voh pehr-soh-'nahl)

This is the last time.
Esta es la última vez.
('ehs-tah ehs lah 'ool-tee-mah vehs)

You will be suspended.
Será suspendido/suspendida.
(seh-'rah soos-pehn-'dee-doh/soos-pehn-'dee-dah)

You will be demoted.
Será degradado/degradada.
(seh-'rah deh-grah-'dah-doh/deh-grah-'dah-dah)

You will have to resign.
Tendrá que renunciar.
(tehn-'drah keh reh-noon-see-'ahr)

You are fired.
Está despedido/depedida.
(ehs-'tah dehs-peh-'dee-doh/dehs-peh-'dee-dah)

Extra Info!

The trade union is **el sindicato** *(ehl seen-dee-'kah-toh)*. Depending on the job, it may surface as a topic of discussion when problems arise. These are the basic words every employer should know:

Do you want to talk about (the) ...?	**¿Quiere hablar sobre ...?** *('kee-'eh-reh ah-'blahr 'soh-breh)*
agreement	**el acuerdo** *(ehl ah-'kwehr-doh)*
arbitration	**el arbitraje** *(ehl ahr-bee-'trah-heh)*
benefits	**los beneficios** *(lohs beh-neh-'fee-see-ohs)*
conditions	**las condiciones** *(lahs kohn-dee-see-'oh-nehs)*
contract	**el contrato** *(ehl kohn-'trah-toh)*
demands	**las demandas** *(lahs deh-'mahn-dahs)*
dispute	**la disputa** *(lah dees-'poo-tah)*
grievances	**las quejas** *(lahs 'keh-hahs)*
laws	**las leyes** *(lahs 'leh-yehs)*
lawyer	**el abogado** *(ehl ah-boh-'gah-doh)*
march	**la manifestación** *(lah mah-nee-fehs-tah-see-'ohn)*
membership	**la afiliación** *(lah ah-fee-lee-ah-see-'ohn)*
negotiations	**las negociaciones** *(lahs neh-goh-see-ah-see-'oh-nehs)*
protest	**la protesta** *(lah proh-'tehs-tah)*
representative	**el representante** *(ehl reh-preh-sehn-'tahn-teh)*
rights	**los derechos** *(lohs deh-'reh-chohs)*
seniority	**la categoría según precedencia** *(lah kah-teh-goh-'ree-ah seh-'goon preh-seh-'dehn-see-ah)*
strike	**la huelga** *(lah oo-'ehl-gah)*
work stoppage	**el paro de trabajo** *(ehl 'pah-roh deh trah-'bah-hoh)*

Let's Practice

A. Complete each phrase with an appropriate vocabulary word:

Hablamos de… _____

Parece que usted fue… _____

¿Tiene problemas con…? _____

B. Change these descriptions to the negative. Here's an example:

ordenado   <u>desordenado</u>

1. completo   _____
2. responsable   _____
3. capaz   _____
4. honesto   _____
5. respetuoso   _____

C. Fill in the blanks with the missing word:

1. foul language   el _____ sucio
2. firearm   el arma de _____
3. warrant   la _____ de corte

Suggestions and Advice
Sugerencias y consejos
(soo-heh-'rehn-see-ahs ee kohn-'seh-hohs)

If there is need for further counsel or guidance, offer whatever advice you can. Simply take a verb and create a phrase on your own:

I think you should …	**Creo que debe …** *('kreh-oh keh 'deh-beh)*
call your lawyer	**llamar a su abogado** *(yah-'mahr ah soo ah-boh-'gah-doh)*
cooperate with the others	**cooperar con los otros** *(koh-oh-peh-'rahr kohn lohs 'oh-trohs)*
follow the instructions	**seguir las instrucciones** *(seh-'geer lahs eens-trook-see-'oh-nehs)*

look for help	**buscar ayuda** *(boos-'kahr ah-'yoo-dah)*
manage your time	**administrar su tiempo**
	(ahd-mee-nees-'trahr soo tee-'ehm-poh)
recognize the problem	**reconocer el problema**
	(reh-koh-noh-'sehr ehl proh-'bleh-mah)
review the material	**repasar el material** *(reh-pah-'sahr ehl mah-'teh-ree-ahl)*
see a doctor	**ver a un médico** *(vehr ah oon 'meh-dee-koh)*
share the information	**compartir la información**
	(kohm-pahr-'teer lah een-fohr-mah-see-'ohn)
study the regulations	**estudiar los reglamentos**
	(ehs-too-dee-'ahr lohs reh-glah-'mehn-tohs)
try to do the job	**tratar de hacer el trabajo**
	(trah-'tahr deh ah-'sehr ehl trah-'bah-hoh)

You should attend (the) ...	**Debe asistir a ...**
	('deh-beh ah-sees-'teer ah)
conference	**la conferencia** *(lah kohn-feh-'rehn-see-ah)*
class	**la clase** *(lah 'klah-seh)*
meeting	**la reunion** *(lah reh-oo-nee-'ohn)*

You should read (the)...	**Debe leer...** *('deh-beh leh-'ehr)*
recommendations	**las recomendaciones**
	(lahs reh-koh-mehn-dah-see-'oh-nehs)
suggestions	**las sugerencias** *(lahs soo-heh-'rehn-see-ahs)*
proposals	**las propuestas** *(lahs proh-'pwehs-tahs)*

Address the worker privately:

You need ...	**Necesita ...** *(neh-seh-'see-tah)*
to calm down	**calmarse** *(kahl-'mahr-seh)*
to control yourself	**controlarse** *(kohn-troh-'lahr-seh)*
to lower your voice	**bajar la voz** *(bah-'hahr lah vohs)*
to relax	**relajarse** *(reh-lah-'hahr-seh)*
to sit down	**sentarse** *(sehn-'tahr-seh)*

Please do not...	**Favor de no...** *(fah-'vohr deh noh)*
argue	**argumentar** *(ahr-goo-mehn-'tahr)*
antagonize	**antagonizar** *(ahn-tah-goh-nee-'sahr)*

gossip	**chismear** *(chees-meh-'ahr)*
curse	**maldecir** *(mahl-deh-'seer)*
yell	**gritar** *(gree-'tahr)*

Close out by explaining the reasons for your concern:

We're trying to improve (the) ...	**Estamos tratando de mejorar ...** *(ehs-'tah-mohs trah-'tahn-doh deh meh-hoh-'rahr)*
business	**el negocio** *(ehl neh-'goh-see-oh)*
morale	**la moral** *(lah moh-'rahl)*
production	**la producción** *(lah proh-dook-see-'ohn)*
quality	**la calidad** *(lah kah-lee-'dahd)*
service	**el servicio** *(ehl sehr-'vee-see-oh)*

Encouraging Words
Palabras alentadoras
(pah-'lah-brahs ah-lehn-tah-'doh-rahs)

Employers must also be helpful and supportive, especially when difficult situations arise. The following sentences stress the positive:

Good work!	**¡Bien hecho!** *(bee-'ehn 'eh-choh)*
I like what you did!	**¡Me gusta lo que hizo!** *(meh 'goos-tah loh keh 'ee-soh)*
Very good!	**¡Muy bien!** *('moo-ee bee-'ehn)*
What a great job!	**¡Qué buen trabajo!** *(keh bwehn trah-'bah-hoh)*
You learn quickly!	**¡Aprende rápido!** *(ah-'prehn-deh 'rah-pee-doh)*

How...!	**¡Qué...!** *(keh)*
excellent	**excelente** *(ex-seh-'lehn-teh)*
good	**bueno** *('bweh-noh)*
fabulous	**fabuloso** *(fah-boo-'loh-soh)*
incredible	**increíble** *(een-kreh-'ee-bleh)*
remarkable	**extraordinario** *(ex-trah-ohr-dee-'nah-ree-oh)*

I see...	**Veo...** *('veh-oh)*
fast development	**desarrollo rápido** *(deh-sahr-'roh-yoh 'rah-pee-doh)*
good effort	**buen esfuerzo** *(bwehn ehs-foo-'ehr-soh)*
lots of desire	**mucho deseo** *('moo-choh deh-'seh-oh)*

more progress	**más progreso** *(mahs proh-'greh-soh)*
professionalism	**profesionalismo** *(proh-feh-see-oh-nah-'lees-moh)*

Keep passing out the compliments:

You have (the)...	**Usted tiene...** *(oos-'tehd tee-'eh-neh)*
confidence	**la confianza** *(lah kohn-fee-'ahn-sah)*
creativity	**la creatividad** *(lah kreh-ah-tee-vee-'dahd)*
enthusiasm	**el entusiasmo** *(ehl ehn-too-see-'ahs-moh)*
honesty	**la honradez** *(lah ohn-rah-'dehs)*
initiative	**la iniciativa** *(lah ee-nee-see-ah-'tee-vah)*
patience	**la paciencia** *(lah pah-see-'ehn-see-ah)*
respect	**el respeto** *(ehl rehs-'peh-toh)*
responsibility	**la responsabilidad** *(lah rehs-pohn-sah-bee-lee-'dahd)*
sincerity	**la sinceridad** *(lah seen-seh-ree-'dahd)*

I see you are...	**Veo que usted es...** *('veh-oh keh oos-'tehd ehs)*
ambitious	**ambicioso** *(ahm-bee-see-'oh-soh)*
competent	**competente** *(kohm-peh-'tehn-teh)*
efficient	**eficiente** *(eh-fee-see-'ehn-teh)*
independent	**independiente** *(een-deh-pehn-dee-'ehn-teh)*
organized	**organizado** *(ohr-gah-nee-'sah-doh)*
punctual	**puntual** *(poon-too-'ahl)*

Nothing works better than encouraging remarks!

You're part of the team!
¡Usted es parte de nuestro equipo!
(oos-'tehd ehs 'pahr-teh deh noo-'ehs-troh eh-'kee-poh)

We can't do it without you!
¡No podemos hacerlo sin usted!
(noh poh-'deh-mohs ah-'sehr-loh seen oos-'tehd)

Everyone must work together!
¡Todos tienen que trabajar juntos!
('toh-dohs tee-'eh-nehn keh trah-bah-'hahr 'hoon-tohs)

Extra Info!

Cognates are words that look the same or are similar in two languages. You already know this word pattern in English and Spanish:

complication	**la complicación** *(lah kohm-plee-kah-see-'ohn)*
initiation	**la iniciación** *(lah ee-nee-see-ah-see-'ohn)*
interruption	**la interrupción** *(lah een-tehr-roop-see-'ohn)*
observation	**la observación** *(lah ohb-sehr-vah-see-'ohn)*
operation	**la operación** *(lah oh-peh-rah-see-'ohn)*
preparation	**la preparación** *(lah preh-pah-rah-see-'ohn)*
satisfaction	**la satisfacción** *(lah sah-tees-fahk-see-'ohn)*

Now work on this other pattern in Spanish:

flexibility	**flexibilidad** *(flehk-see-bee-lee-'dahd)*
durability	**durabilidad** *(doo-rah-bee-lee-'dahd)*
priority	**prioridad** *(pree-oh-ree-'dahd)*
responsibility	**responsabilidad** *(rehs-pohs-sah-bee-lee-'dahd)*
stability	**estabilidad** *(ehs-tah-bee-lee-'dahd)*

Let's Practice ⓐ

A. Say each word aloud, and then translate it into English:

1. prioridad _____
2. corrección _____
3. puntual _____
4. limitación _____
5. apático _____
6. diarrea _____
7. ambulancia _____
8. náuseas _____

B. Underline the verbs that have negative meanings:

relajarse, blasfemar, reconocer, chismear, repasar, mentir, compartir

Let's Practice (28)

C. List three exclamatory remarks that employers use to encourage their employees:

_____   _____   _____

D. Translate into Spanish:

1. Everyone must work together!   _____
2. There is good effort.   _____
3. I think you should look for help.   _____

Health Concerns
Los problemas de salud
(lohs proh-'bleh-mahs deh sah-'lood)

Don't forget about your employee's emotional and physical well-being.

| How do you feel? | **¿Cómo se siente?** *('koh-moh seh see-'ehn-teh)* |
| Are you...? | **¿Está...?** *(ehs-'tah)* |

afraid	**asustado/asustada** *(ah-soos-'tah-doh/ah-soos-'tah-dah)*
angry	**enojado/enojada** *(eh-noh-'hah-doh/eh-noh-'hah-dah)*
anxious	**ansioso/ansiosa** *(ahn-see-'oh-soh/ahn-see-'oh-sah)*
apathetic	**apático/apática** *(ah-'pah-tee-koh/ah-'pah-tee-kah)*
bored	**aburrido/aburrida** *(ah-boor-'ree-doh/ah-boor-'ree-dah)*
bothered	**molesto/molesta** *(moh-'lehs-toh/moh-'lehs-tah)*
confused	**confundido/confundida** *(kohn-foon-'dee-doh/kohn-foon-'dee-dah)*
disgusted	**hastiado/hastiada** *(ahs-tee-'ah-doh/ahs-tee-'ah-dah)*
distracted	**distraído/distraída** *(dees-trah-'ee-doh/dees-trah-'ee-dah)*
embarrassed	**avergonzado/avergonzada** *(ah-vehr-gohn-'sah-doh/ah-vehr-gohn-'sah-dah)*
exhausted	**agotado/agotada** *(ah-goh-'tah-doh/ah-goh-'tah-dah)*
frustrated	**frustrado/frustrada** *(froos-'trah-doh/froos-'trah-dah)*

jealous	**celoso/celosa** *(seh-'loh-soh/seh-'loh-sah)*
nervous	**nervioso/nerviosa** *(nehr-vee-'oh-soh/nehr-vee-'oh-sah)*
overloaded	**sobrecargado/sobrecargada** *(soh-breh-kahr-'gah-doh/soh-breh-kahr-'gah-dah)*
resentful	**resentido/resentida** *(reh-sehn-'tee-doh/reh-sehn-'tee-dah)*
sad	**triste** *('trees-teh)*
tired	**cansado/cansada** *(kahn-'sah-doh/kahn-'sah-dah)*
uncomfortable	**incómodo/incómoda** *(een-'koh-moh-doh/een-'koh-moh-dah)*
unhappy	**descontento/descontenta** *(dehs-kohn-'tehn-toh/dehs-kohn-'tehn-tah)*
upset	**perturbado/perturbada** *(pehr-toor-'bah-doh/pehr-toor-'bah-dah)*
worried	**preocupado/preocupada** *(preh-oh-koo-'pah-doh/preh-oh-koo-'pah-dah)*

Move on to more questions about physical health. Again, listen for **sí** or **no**:

Do you feel _____?	**¿Se siente** _____? *(seh see-'ehn-teh)*
dizzy	**mareado/mareada** *(mah-reh-'ah-doh/mah-reh-'ah-dah)*
faint	**desmayado/desmayada** *(dehs-mah-'yah-doh/dehs-mah-'yah-dah)*
ill	**enfermo/enferma** *(ehn-'fehr-moh/ehn-'fehr-mah)*
poorly	**mal** *(mahl)*
sleepy	**soñoliento/soñolienta** *(sohn-yoh-lee-'ehn-toh/sohn-yoh-lee-'ehn-tah)*
sore	**dolorido/dolorida** *(doh-loh-'ree-doh/doh-loh-'ree-dah)*
tired	**cansado/cansada** *(kahn-'sah-doh/kahn-'sah-dah)*

Do you have (the)...?	**¿Tiene...?** *(tee-'eh-neh)*
allergies	**alergia** *(ah-'lehr-hee-ah)*
chill	**escalofríos** *(ehs-kah-loh-'free-ohs)*
cold	**resfriado** *(rehs-free-'ah-doh)*
constipation	**estreñimiento** *(eh-streh-nee-mee-'ehn-toh)*
cough	**tos** *(tohs)*
diarrhea	**diarrea** *(dee-ahr-'reh-ah)*
fever	**fiebre** *(fee-'eh-breh)*
flu	**influenza** *(een-floo-'ehn-sah)*
nausea	**náuseas** *('now-seh-ahs)*

pain	**dolor** *(doh-'lohr)*
rash	**erupción** *(eh-roop-see-'ohn)*
sneezing	**estornudos** *(eh-stohr-'noo-dohs)*

Check out the pattern here:

Is it (the)...	**Es...?** *(ehs)*
toothache	**el dolor de muela** *(ehl doh-'lohr deh 'mweh-lah)*
headache	**el dolor de cabeza** *(ehl doh-'lohr deh kah-'beh-sah)*
stomachache	**el dolor de estómago** *(ehl doh-'lohr deh eh-'stoh-mah-goh)*

Extra Info!

If the person is injured, approach him or her directly:

Did you lose consciousness?	**¿Perdió el conocimiento?** *(pehr-dee-'oh ehl koh-noh-see-mee-'ehn-toh)*
Does it hurt much?	**¿Le duele mucho?** *(leh doo-'eh-leh 'moo-choh)*
Did you injure your head?	**¿Se hizo daño a la cabeza?** *(seh 'ee-soh 'dahn-yoh ah lah kah-'beh-sah)*

Medical Emergency
La emergencia médica
(lah eh-mehr-'hehn-see-ah 'meh-dee-kah)

For medical emergencies, it will be necessary to use a different set of vocabulary items. Try calling for help first:

Call (the) ...	**Llame a ...** *('yah-meh ah)*
911	**nueve-uno-uno** *(noo-'eh-veh 'oo-noh 'oo-noh)*
ambulance	**la ambulancia** *(lah ahm-boo-'lahn-see-ah)*
doctor	**el doctor** *(ehl dohk-'tohr)*
family	**la familia** *(lah fah-'mee-lee-ah)*
fire department	**el departamento de bomberos** *(ehl deh-pahr-tah-'mehn-toh deh bohm-'beh-rohs)*

HAZMAT   **hasmat** *('hahs-maht)*
hospital   **el hospital** *(ehl ohs-pee-'tahl)*
paramedic   **el paramédico** *(ehl pah-rah-'meh-dee-koh)*
police   **la policía** *(lah poh-lee-'see-ah)*

Show me (the)…   **Muéstreme…** *(moo-'ehs-treh-meh)*

bruise   **la contusión** *(lah kohn-too-see-'ohn)*
burn   **la quemadura** *(lah keh-mah-'doo-rah)*
cut   **la cortada** *(lah kohr-'tah-dah)*
puncture   **la punción** *(lah poon-see-'ohn)*
scratch   **el rasguño** *(ehl rahs-'goon-yoh)*

Now add descriptions to the body parts as you create more sentences:

broken	**roto** *('roh-toh)*	¿Está roto **el brazo**?
burned	**quemado** *(keh-'mah-doh)*	¿Tiene **el pie** quemado?
infected	**infectado** *(een-fehk-'tah-doh)*	_____
swollen	**hinchado** *(een-'chah-doh)*	_____
twisted	**torcido** *(tohr-'see-doh)*	_____

You never know what can happen, so keep on pronouncing!

Did you have (a/an)…   **Tenía …** *(teh-'nee-ah)*

accident   **un accidente** *(oon ahk-see-'dehn-teh)*
bad fall   **una mala caída** *('oo-nah 'mah-lah kah-'ee-dah)*
convulsion   **una convulsión** *('oo-nah kohn-vool-see-'ohn)*
heart attack   **un infarto** *(oon een-'fahr-toh)*
seizure   **un ataque** *(oon ah-'tah-keh)*

Are you suffering from…   **Sufre de…** *('soo-freh deh)*

sunstroke   **insolación** *(een-soh-lah-see-'ohn)*
dehydration   **deshidratación** *(dehs-ee-drah-tah-see-'ohn)*
frostbite   **congelamiento** *(kohn-heh-lah-mee-'ehn-toh)*
contagious disease   **enfermedad contagiosa**
    (ehn-fehr-meh-'dahd kohn-tah-hee-'oh-sah)

While waiting for medical help, suggest the following:

He/She needs (the)...	**Necesita...** *(neh-seh-'see-tah)*
bandage	**un vendaje** *(oon vehn-'dah-heh)*
CPR	**respiración artificial** *(rehs-pee-rah-see-'ohn ahr-tee-fee-see-'ahl)*
crutches	**unas muletas** *('oo-nahs moo-'leh-tahs)*
first aid	**primeros auxilios** *(pree-'meh-rohs ah-ooks-'ee-lee-ohs)*
medicine	**una medicina** *('oo-nah meh-deh-'see-nah)*
oxygen	**oxígeno** *(ohk-'see-heh-noh)*
sling	**un cabestrillo** *(oon kah-behs-'tree-yoh)*
splint	**una tablilla** *('oo-nah tah-'blee-yah)*
tourniquet	**un torniquete** *(oon tohr-nee-'keh-teh)*
wheelchair	**una silla de ruedas** *('oo-nah 'see-yah deh roo-'eh-dahs)*

Extra Info!

To play it safe, memorize these:

Fire!	**¡Fuego!** *(foo-'eh-goh)*
Help!	**¡Socorro!** *(soh-'kohr-roh)*
Run!	**¡Corra!** *('kohr-rah)*

The Culture

In Latin America, the practice of home remedies—**los remedios caseros** *(lohs reh-'meh-dee-ohs kah-'seh-rohs)* is quite popular, so don't be surprised if your Hispanic employee offers to prepare something when a fellow worker gets sick or injured.

Prevention
La prevención
(lah preh-vehn-see-'ohn)

The best way to avoid accidents at the workplace is to talk about preventing them.

Be careful with (the)...!	**¡Tenga cuidado con...!** *('tehn-gah koo-ee-'dah-doh kohn)*
chemicals	**los químicos** *(lohs 'kee-mee-kohs)*
electricity	**la electricidad** *(lah eh-lehk-tree-see-'dahd)*
fuel	**el combustible** *(ehl kohm-boos-'tee-bleh)*
gas	**el gas** *(ehl gahs)*
grease	**la grasa** *(lah 'grah-sah)*
hot water	**el agua caliente** *(ehl 'ah-gwah kah-lee-'ehn-teh)*
oil	**el aceite** *(ehl ah-'seh-ee-teh)*
Don't touch (the)...!	**¡No toque...!** *(noh 'toh-keh)*
liquid	**el líquido** *(ehl 'lee-kee-doh)*
materials	**los materiales** *(lohs mah-teh-ree-'ah-lehs)*
scraps	**los residuos** *(lohs reh-'see-doo-ohs)*
spillage	**el derrame** *(ehl dehr-'rah-meh)*
It's...	**Es...** *(ehs)*
combustible	**combustible** *(kohm-boos-'tee-bleh)*
contaminated	**contaminado** *(kohn-tah-mee-'nah-doh)*
corrosive	**corrosivo** *(kohr-roh-'see-voh)*
dangerous	**peligroso** *(peh-lee-'groh-soh)*
explosive	**explosivo** *(ex-ploh-'see-voh)*
flammable	**inflamable** *(een-flah-'mah-bleh)*
illegal	**ilegal** *(ee-leh-'gahl)*
lethal	**letal** *(leh-'tahl)*
poisonous	**venenoso** *(veh-neh-'noh-soh)*
prohibited	**prohibido** *(proh-ee-'bee-doh)*
radioactive	**radioactivo** *(rah-dee-oh-ahk-'tee-voh)*
risky	**arriesgado** *(ahr-ree-'ehs-'gah-doh)*
toxic	**tóxico** *('tohk-see-koh)*

You must know about (the)…	**Tiene que saber sobre…** *(tee-'eh-neh keh sah-'behr 'soh-breh)*
environmental protection	**la protección del medio ambiente** *(lah proh-tehk-see-'ohn dehl 'meh-dee-oh ahm-bee-'ehn-teh)*
fire drill	**el simulacro de incendio** *(ehl see-moo-'lahk-roh deh een-'sehn-dee-oh)*
preventive maintenance	**el mantenimiento preventivo** *(ehl mahn-teh-nee-mee-'ehn-toh preh-vehn-'tee-voh)*
rescue procedure	**el plan de rescate** *(ehl plahn deh rehs-'kah-teh)*
room capacity	**la capacidad del recinto** *(lah kah-pah-see-'dahd dehl reh-'seen-toh)*
safety manual	**el manual de seguridad** *(ehl mah-noo-'ahl deh seh-goo-ree-'dahd)*

Always use (the)…	**Siempre use…** *(see-'ehm-preh 'oo-seh)*
alarm	**la alarma** *(lah ah-'lahr-mah)*
chain	**la cadena** *(lah kah-'deh-nah)*
deadbolt	**el pestillo** *(ehl pehs-'tee-yoh)*
key	**la llave** *(lah 'yah-veh)*
latch	**el cerrojo** *(ehl sehr-'roh-hoh)*
lock	**la cerradura** *(lah sehr-rah-'doo-rah)*
padlock	**el candado** *(ehl kahn-'dah-doh)*
safe	**la caja fuerte** *(lah 'kah-hah 'fwehr-teh)*

The Signs
Los letreros
(lohs leh-'treh-rohs)

Still another way to avoid medical emergencies is to check all the warning signs posted around the workplace. To clear up any confusion, print the following in both languages:

Caution	**Precaución** *(preh-kah-oo-see-'ohn)*
Danger	**Peligro** *(peh-'lee-groh)*
Do Not Block Entrance	**No Obstruir la Entrada** *(noh ohbs-troo-'eer lah ehn-'trah-dah)*
Emergency Exit	**Salida de Emergencia** *(sah-'lee-dah deh eh-mehr-'hehn-see-ah)*
High Power Cables	**Cables de Alto Voltaje** *('kah-blehs deh 'ahl-toh vohl-'tah-heh)*

No Exit	**Sin Salida** *(seen sah-'lee-dah)*
Stairway	**Escaleras** *(ehs-kah-'leh-rahs)*
Watch Your Step	**Mire por Donde Camina**
	('mee-reh pohr 'dohn-deh kah-'mee-nah)
Water Not Fit for	**Agua No Potable**
Drinking	*('ah-gwah noh poh-'tah-bleh)*
Wet Floor	**Piso Mojado** *('pee-soh moh-'hah-doh)*

Also don't forget to hang signs around the heavy machinery:

Do Not Operate
No Hacer Funcionar *(noh ah-'sehr foon-see-oh-'nahr)*

Hard Hat Area
Usar Casco Protector *(oo-'sahr 'kahs-koh proh-tehk-'tohr)*

This Equipment Starts Automatically
Este Equipo se Enciende Automáticamente
('ehs-teh eh-'kee-poh seh ehn-see-'ehn-deh aw-toh-'mah-tee-kah-mehn-teh)

Eye Protection Required
Utilizar Protección para los Ojos
(oo-tee-lee-'sahr proh-tehk-see-'ohn 'pah-rah lohs 'oh-hohs)

Keep Clear
Manténgase Alejado *(mahn-'tehn-gah-seh ah-leh-'hah-doh)*

Signs
Avisos
(ah-'vee-sohs)

Be sure that your employees understand signs in English:

Closed	**CERRADO** *(sehr-'rah-doh)*
Employees Only	**SÓLO PARA EMPLEADOS**
	('soh-loh 'pah-rah ehm-pleh-'ah-dohs)
Entrance	**ENTRADA** *(ehn-'trah-dah)*
Exit	**SALIDA** *(sah-'lee-dah)*
No Smoking	**NO FUMAR** *(noh foo-'mahr)*
No Trespassing	**PROHIBIDO EL PASO** *(proh-ee-'bee-doh ehl 'pah-soh)*
Open	**ABIERTO** *(ah-bee-'ehr-toh)*
Out of Order	**DESCOMPUESTO** *(dehs-kohm-'pwehs-toh)*

Pull	**JALE** *('hah-leh)*
Push	**EMPUJE** *(ehm-'poo-heh)*
Restrooms	**SANITARIOS** *(sah-nee-'tah-ree-ohs)*

Let's Practice

A. In Spanish…name three words that express how people feel:

_____ _____ _____

Name three signs found at a typical workplace:

_____ _____ _____

Name three common ailments or illnesses:

_____ _____ _____

B. Circle one word in each group that doesn't belong:

1. torcido, pestillo, cerrojo
2. cortada, cadena, ampolla
3. fiebre, escalofrío, celoso

C. Answer these questions about your health:

¿Se siente mal hoy?
¿Tiene dolor de espalda?
¿Está preocupado?

Natural Disasters
Los desastres naturales
(lohs deh-'sahs-trehs nah-too-'rah-lehs)

Natural disasters may also occur. Outline the steps to be taken, in Spanish, if trouble strikes.

Was it (the)…?	**¿Fue…?** *(foo-'eh)*
earthquake	**el terremoto** *(ehl tehr-reh-'moh-toh)*
flood	**la inundación** *(lah ee-noon-dah-see-'ohn)*

hurricane	**el huracán** *(ehl oo-rah-'kahn)*
landslide	**el desprendimiento de tierra** *(ehl dehs-prehn-dee-mee-'ehn-toh deh tee-'ehr-rah)*
rain	**la lluvia** *(lah 'yoo-vee-ah)*
snow	**la nieve** *(lah nee-'eh-veh)*
storm	**la tormenta** *(lah tohr-'mehn-tah)*
tornado	**el tornado** *(ehl tohr-'nah-doh)*
wildfire	**el incendio de bosque** *(ehl een-'sehn-dee-oh deh 'bohs-keh)*

 ## Action Words!

Don't forget that a complete list of **Spanish Commands for Employers** can be found at the end of this book. However, if you'd like to create your own command words, simply remember the three infinitive endings:

-ar as in **mirar** *(mee-'rahr)* (to look)
-er as in **correr** *(kohr-'rehr)* (to run)
-ir as in **abrir** *(ahb-'reer)* (to open)

To make a command, drop the last two letters of the infinitive form, and replace them as follows:

-AR	→	**E**	
mir<u>ar</u>	Look!	¡Mir<u>e</u>!	**Mire aquí.**

-ER	→	**A**	
corr<u>er</u>	Run!	¡Corr<u>a</u>!	**Corra hacia afuera.**

-IR	→	**A**	
abr<u>ir</u>	Open!	¡Abr<u>a</u>!	**Abra la puerta.**

Bear in mind that some forms are irregular and have to be memorized:

ir *(eer)*	Go! **¡Vaya!** *('vah-yah)*
venir *(veh-'neer)*	Come! **¡Venga!** *('vehn-gah)*
decir *(deh-'seer)*	Tell! **¡Diga!** *('dee-gah)*

You can accelerate the learning process by grouping commands in pairs with opposite meanings:

Empty	**Vacíe** *(vah-'see-eh)*
Fill	**Llene** *('yeh-neh)*
Load	**Cargue** *('kahr-geh)*
Unload	**Descargue** *(dehs-'kahr-geh)*
Raise	**Levante** *(leh-'vahn-teh)*
Lower	**Baje** *('bah-heh)*

Another way to give an order is to use the expression "Let's" (**Vamos a...** *('vah-mohs ah)* before an infinitive:

Let's begin.	**Vamos a comenzar.** *('vah-mohs ah koh-mehn-'sahr)*
Let's call.	**Vamos a llamar.** *('vah-mohs ah yah-'mahr)*
Let's leave.	**Vamos a salir.** *('vah-mohs ah sah-'leer)*

Extra Info!

To give commands to more than one person in Spanish, you generally add an **n** to the command word:

Hurry up, you guys!	**¡Apúrense!** *(ah-'poo-rehn-seh)*
Run, you guys!	**¡Corran!** *('kohr-rahn)*

Negative commands are easy. Just say **no**:

Come!	**¡Venga!** *('vehn-gah)*
Don't come!	**¡No venga!** *(noh 'vehn-gah)*
Run, you guys!	**¡Corran!** *('kohr-rahn)*
Don't run, you guys!	**¡No corran!** *(noh 'kohr-rahn)*

Verbs: The Past (Imperfect)
Los verbos: el pasado (imperfecto)
(lohs 'vehr-bohs ehl pah-'sah-doh eem-pehr-'fehk-toh)

Unlike the preterit tense, which expresses a completed past action, the imperfect tense expresses a continued, customary, or repeated action in the past. In other words, it's used to express "what was happening" or "what used to happen." For regular **-ar** verbs, change the endings just like this example:

TO WORK	**TRABAJAR** *(trah-bah-'hahr)*
I was working	**trabaj<u>aba</u>** *(trah-bah-'hah-bah)*
You were working; He, She was working	**trabaj<u>aba</u>** *(trah-bah-'hah-bah)*
You (pl.), They were working	**trabaj<u>aban</u>** *(trah-bah-'hah-bahn)*
We were working	**trabaj<u>ábamos</u>** *(trah-bah-'hah-bah-mohs)*

And for regular **-er** and **-ir** verbs, the endings are formed differently:

TO EAT	**COMER** *(koh-'mehr)*
I was eating	**com<u>ía</u>** *(koh-'mee-ah)*
You were eating; He, She was eating	**com<u>ía</u>** *(koh-'mee-ah)*
You (pl.), They were eating	**com<u>ían</u>** *(koh-'mee-an)*
We were eating	**com<u>íamos</u>** *(koh-'mee-ah-mohs)*

TO WRITE	**ESCRIBIR** *(ehs-kree-'beer)*
I was writing	**escrib<u>ía</u>** *(ehs-kree-'bee-ah)*
You were writing; He, She was writing	**escrib<u>ía</u>** *(ehs-kree-'bee-ah)*
You (pl.), They were writing	**escrib<u>ían</u>** *(ehs-kree-'bee-ahn)*
We were writing	**escrib<u>íamos</u>** *(ehs-kree-'bee-ah-mohs)*

These are the only two irregular forms in the imperfect:

TO BE	**SER** *(sehr)*
I was	**era** *('eh-rah)*
You were; He, She was	**era** *('eh-rah)*
You (pl.), They were	**eran** *('eh-rahn)*
We were	**éramos** *('eh-rah-mohs)*

TO GO	**IR** *(eer)*
I went	**iba** *('ee-bah)*
You, He, She went	**iba** *('ee-bah)*
You (pl.), They went	**iban** *('ee-bahn)*
We went	**íbamos** *('ee-bah-mohs)*

Unlike the preterit, these imperfect actions were never really "started and then completed." Notice the difference between the two:

I called the office.
Llamé a la oficina. *(yah-'meh ah lah oh-fee-'see-nah)*   (preterit)
I used to call the office.
Llamaba a la oficina *(yah-'mah-bah ah lah oh-fee-'see-nah)*   (imperfect)

Did they learn English?
¿Aprendieron inglés? *(ah-prehn-dee-'eh-rohn een-'glehs)*   (preterit)
Were they learning English?
¿Aprendían inglés? *(ah-prehn-'dee-ahn een-'glehs)*   (imperfect)

She fell asleep at 2:00.
Se durmió a las dos. *(seh door-mee-'oh ah lahs dohs)*   (preterit)
She used to fall asleep at 2:00.
Se dormía a las dos. *(seh dohr-'mee-ah ah lahs dohs)*   (imperfect)

Speaking of verb forms, these are the verbs you'll need to discuss topics related to employee concerns:

to advise	**aconsejar** *(ah-kohn-seh-'hahr)*
to argue	**argumentar** *(ahr-goo-mehn-'tahr)*
to bother	**molestar** *(moh-lehs-'tahr)*
to break	**romper** *(rohm-'pehr)*
to burn	**quemar** *(keh-'mahr)*
to calm down	**calmarse** *(kahl-'mahr-seh)*
to consult	**consultar** *(kohn-sool-'tahr)*
to converse	**conversar** *(kohn-vehr-'sahr)*
to counsel	**aconsejar** *(ah-kohn-seh-'hahr)*
to deny	**negar** *(neh-'gahr)*
to faint	**desmayarse** *(dehs-mah-'yahr-seh)*
to feel	**sentir** *(sehn-'teer)*
to fight	**pelear** *(peh-leh-'ahr)*
to forget	**olvidar** *(ohl-vee-'dahr)*
to grab	**agarrar** *(ah-gahr-'rahr)*
to help	**ayudar** *(ah-yoo-'dahr)*
to hold	**sostener** *(sohs-teh-'nehr)*
to improve	**mejorar** *(meh-hoh-'rahr)*
to injure	**herir** *(eh-'reer)*

to insist	**insistir** *(een-sees-'teer)*
to investigate	**investigar** *(een-vehs-tee-'gahr)*
to lie	**mentir** *(mehn-'teer)*
to lose	**perder** *(pehr-'dehr)*
to obey	**obedecer** *(oh-beh-deh-'sehr)*
to refuse	**negarse** *(neh-'gahr-seh)*
to relax	**relajarse** *(reh-lah-'hahr-seh)*
to support	**apoyar** *(ah-poh-'yahr)*
to improve oneself	**mejorarse** *(meh-hoh-'rahr-seh)*
to make a commitment	**comprometerse** *(kohm-proh-meh-'tehr-seh)*

Verbs: The Past Progressive
Verbos: El pasado progresivo
('vehr-bohs ehl pah-'sah-doh proh-greh-'see-voh)

Here's another verb form that refers to past actions. You'll need to change the infinitive endings to either **-ando** or **-iendo**, and use the words **estaba**, **estaban**, and **estábamos**. See how the Past Progressive resembles the Present Progressive you learned in Chapter One:

TO WORK	**TRABAJAR** *(trah-bah-'hahr)*
WORKING	**TRABAJANDO** *(trah-bah-'hahn-doh)*

I, He, She was; You were working
    Estaba trabajando
    (ehs-'tah-bah trah-bah-'hahn-doh)

They, You (pl.) were working
    Estaban trabajando
    (ehs-'tah-bahn trah-bah-'hahn-doh)

We were working
    Estábamos trabajando
    (ehs-'tah-bah-mohs trah-bah-'hahn-doh)

 The Culture

Offensive or foul language leads nowhere, so make it clear that it won't be allowed around your workplace. Use this line:

Please don't use foul language.
No diga groserías, por favor. *(noh 'dee-gah groh-seh-'ree-ahs, pohr fah-'vohr)*

Let's Practice (30)

A. Change these infinitives to command forms. Be careful with the irregular ones:

to fill (llenar)   **Llene**
to describe (describir)   **Describa**
1. to come (venir)   _____
2. to throw away (tirar)   _____
3. to drink (beber)   _____
4. to bring (traer)   _____
5. to help (ayudar)   _____

B. Translate each sentence:

1. Lleve la caja, por favor.   _____
2. Haga el trabajo, por favor.   _____
3. Prenda la máquina, por favor.   _____

C. Connect each word with its correct translation:

1. Give   Diga
2. Send   Busque
3. Follow   Dé
4. Look for   Mande
5. Tell   Siga
6. Call   Llame

D. Study the example and practice the imperfect tense. Talk about what you used to do:

regresar (to return) at 8:00   Yo regresaba a las ocho.
1. contestar (to answer) in Spanish   _____
2. desenchufar (to unplug) the computer   _____
3. ir (to go) to work late   _____
4. aprender (to learn) a lot   _____
5. obedecer (to obey) the boss   _____

Chapter Six

The Business
El negocio
(ehl neh-'goh-see-oh)

The Company
La compañía
(lah kohm-pah-'nee-ah)

Regardless of your line of work, it would be wise to familiarize yourself with those Spanish words that define the business itself.

This business is a…	**Este negocio es una…**
	('ehs-teh neh-'goh-see-oh ehs 'oo-nah)
corporation	**corporación** *(kohr-poh-rah-see-'ohn)*
family business	**empresa familiar** *(ehm-'preh-sah fah-mee-lee-'ahr)*
limited liability corporation	**sociedad limitada** *(soh-see-eh-'dahd lee-mee-'tah-dah)*
major company	**gran empresa** *(grahn ehm-'preh-sah)*
nonprofit organization	**organización sin fines lucrativos**
	(ohr-gah-nee-sah-see-'ohn seen 'fee-nehs loo-krah-'tee-vohs)
small business	**pequeña empresa** *(peh-'kehn-yah ehm-'preh-sah)*
sole proprietorship	**empresa individual** *(ehm-'preh-sah een-dee-vee-doo-'ahl)*
We…	**Nosotros…** *(noh-'soh-trohs)*
arrange	**arreglamos** *(ahr-reh-'glah-mohs)*
build	**construimos** *(kohns-troo-'ee-mohs)*
buy	**compramos** *(kohm-'prah-mohs)*
develop	**desarrollamos** *(deh-sahr-roh-'yah-mohs)*
install	**instalamos** *(eens-tah-'lah-mohs)*

invest	**invertimos** *(een-vehr-'tee-mohs)*
lease	**arrendamos** *(ahr-rehn-'dah-mohs)*
make	**hacemos** *(ah-'seh-mohs)*
manage	**manejamos** *(mah-neh-'hah-mohs)*
offer	**ofrecemos** *(oh-freh-'seh-mohs)*
prepare	**preparamos** *(preh-pah-'rah-mohs)*
produce	**producimos** *(proh-doo-'see-mohs)*
provide	**proveemos** *(proh-veh-'eh-mohs)*
repair	**reparamos** *(reh-pah-'rah-mohs)*
sell	**vendemos** *(vehn-'deh-mohs)*
send	**enviamos** *(ehn-vee-'ah-mohs)*

It's ...	**Es ...** *(ehs)*
domestic	**nacional** *(nah-see-oh-'nahl)*
foreign	**extranjero** *(ex-trahn-'heh-roh)*
global	**mundial** *(moon-dee-'ahl)*
interim	**provisional** *(proh-vee-see-oh-'nahl)*
international	**internacional** *(een-tehr-nah-see-oh-'nahl)*
interstate	**interestatal** *(een-tehr-ehs-tah-'tahl)*
local	**local** *(loh-'kahl)*
national	**nacional** *(nah-see-oh-'nahl)*
private	**privado** *(pree-'vah-doh)*
public	**público** *('poo-blee-koh)*
seasonal	**estacional** *(ehs-tah-see-oh-'nahl)*

We work with...	**Trabajamos con...** *(trah-bah-'hah-mohs kohn)*
deliveries	**las entregas** *(lahs ehn-'treh-gahs)*
goods	**los bienes** *(lohs bee-'eh-nehs)*
merchandise	**las mercancías** *(lahs mehr-kahn-'see-ahs)*
products	**los productos** *(lohs proh-'dook-tohs)*
raw materials	**las materias primas** *(lahs mah-'teh-ree-ahs 'pree-mahs)*
services	**los servicios** *(lohs sehr-'vee-see-ohs)*

Extra Info!

Don't forget your command words around the business office!

Weigh...	**Pese...** *('peh-seh)*
Ship...	**Envíe...** *(ehn-'vee-eh)*
Unload...	**Descargue...** *(dehs-'kahr-geh)*
cargo	**la carga** *(lah 'kahr-gah)*
freight	**el flete** *(ehl 'fleh-teh)*
payload	**la carga útil** *(lah 'kahr-gah 'oo-teel)*

The Business Office
La oficina comercial
(lah oh-fee-'see-nah koh-mehr-see-'ahl)

All kinds of folks drop by the business office, so be sure to introduce everyone to the Spanish speakers:

Let me introduce (the)...	**Le presento a...** *(leh preh-'sehn-toh ah)*
accountant	**el contador/la contadora** *(ehl kohn-tah-'dohr/lah kohn-tah-'doh-rah)*
administrator	**el administrador/la administradora** *(ehl ahd-mee-nees-trah-'dohr/lah ahd-mee-nees-trah-'doh-rah)*
analyst	**el/la analista** *(ehl/lah ah-nah-'lees-tah)*
buyer	**el jefe/la jefa de compras** *(ehl 'heh-feh/lah 'heh-fah deh 'kohm-prahs)*
cashier	**el cajero/la cajera** *(ehl kah-'heh-roh/lah kah-'heh-rah)*
consultant	**el consultor/la consultora** *(ehl kohn-sool-'tohr/lah kohn-sool-'toh-rah)*
courier	**el mensajero/la mensajera** *(ehl mehn-sah-'heh-roh/lah mehn-sah-'heh-rah)*
dealer	**el concesionario/la concesionaria** *(ehl kohn-seh-see-oh-'nah-ree-oh/lah kohn-seh-see-oh-'nah-ree-ah)*
lawyer	**el abogado/la abogada** *(ehl ah-boh-'gah-doh/lah ah-boh-'gah-dah)*

manager	**el/la gerente** *(ehl/lah heh-'rehn-teh)*
manufacturer	**el/la fabricante** *(ehl/lah fah-bree-'kahn-teh)*
office clerk	**el/la oficinista** *(ehl/lah oh-fee-see-'nees-tah)*
owner	**el dueño/la dueña** *(ehl doo-'ehn-yoh/lah doo-'ehn-yah)*
recruiter	**el reclutador/la reclutadora**
	(ehl reh-kloo-tah-'dohr/lah reh-kloo-tah-'doh-rah)
salesperson	**el vendedor/la vendedora**
	(ehl vehn-deh-'dohr/lah vehn-deh-'doh-rah)
shipper	**el fletador/la fletadora**
	(ehl fleh-tah-'dohr/lah fleh-tah-'doh-rah)
supplier	**el abastecedor/la abastecedora**
	(ehl ah-bahs-teh-seh-'dohr/lah ah-bahs-teh-seh-'doh-rah)

Now, let's get down to work.

Do you need (the)...?	**¿Necesita...?** *(neh-seh-'see-tah)*
bill	**la cuenta** *(lah 'kwehn-tah)*
claim	**la reclamación** *(lah reh-klah-mah-see-'ohn)*
form	**el formulario** *(ehl fohr-moo-'lah-ree-oh)*
invoice	**la factura** *(lah fahk-'too-rah)*
order	**el pedido** *(ehl peh-'dee-doh)*
receipt	**el recibo** *(ehl reh-'see-boh)*
slip	**el papelito** *(ehl pah-peh-'lee-toh)*

Did you check (the)...?	**¿Revisó...?** *(reh-vee-'soh)*
inventory	**las existencias** *(lahs ex-ees-'tehn-see-ahs)*
shipment	**el envío** *(ehl ehn-'vee-oh)*
stock	**la reserva** *(lah reh-'sehr-vah)*
supplies	**los suministros** *(lohs soo-mee-'nees-trohs)*
surplus	**el exceso** *(ehl ex-'seh-soh)*

Do you know (the)...?	**¿Sabe...?** *('sah-beh)*
content	**el contenido** *(ehl kohn-teh-'nee-doh)*
number	**el número** *(ehl 'noo-meh-roh)*
quality	**la calidad** *(lah kah-lee-'dahd)*
quantity	**la cantidad** *(lah kahn-tee-'dahd)*
subtotal	**el subtotal** *(ehl soob-toh-'tahl)*

sum	**la suma** *(lah 'soo-mah)*
total	**el total** *(ehl toh-'tahl)*
weight	**el peso** *(ehl 'peh-soh)*

Does it have (the)...?	**¿Tiene...?** *(tee-'eh-neh)*
brand	**la marca** *(lah 'mahr-kah)*
code	**el código** *(ehl 'koh-dee-goh)*
label	**la etiqueta** *(lah eh-tee-'keh-tah)*
logo	**el logotipo** *(ehl loh-goh-'tee-poh)*
patent	**la patente** *(lah pah-'tehn-teh)*
stamp	**el sello** *(ehl 'seh-yoh)*
title	**el título** *(ehl 'tee-too-loh)*
trademark	**la marca registrada** *(lah 'mahr-kah reh-hees-'trah-dah)*

 Let's Practice

A. Link the words that belong together:

1. suma	gerente
2. etiqueta	carga
3. dueño	marca
4. flete	recibo
5. factura	cantidad

B. Follow the example and answer the questions with the correct verb form:

¿Producen Uds.?   <u>Sí, producimos.</u>
1. ¿Venden Uds.?   _____
2. ¿Instalan Uds.?   _____
3. ¿Compran Uds.?   _____
4. ¿Construyen Uds.?   _____
5. ¿Invierten Uds.?   _____

Extra Info!

Spanish gets easier once you understand how complete phrases are created. See how the descriptive word is added at the end:

shipping	**el transporte** *(ehl trahns-'pohr-teh)*
air shipping	**el transporte <u>aéreo</u>**
	(ehl trahns-'pohr-teh ah-'eh-reo-oh)
rail shipping	**el transporte <u>ferroviario</u>**
	(ehl trahns-'pohr-teh fehr-roh-vee-'ah-ree-oh)
boat shipping	**el transporte <u>naviero</u>**
	(ehl trahns-'pohr-teh nah-vee-'eh-roh)
overland shipping	**el transporte <u>terrestre</u>**
	(ehl trahns-'pohr-teh tehr-'rehs-treh)

The Sales Department
El departamento de ventas
(ehl deh-pahr-tah-'mehn-toh deh 'vehn-tahs)

Here are a few one-liners that every sales rep should know:

How may I help you?
¿En qué puedo servirle? *(ehn keh 'pweh-doh sehr-'veer-leh)*

What are you looking for?
¿Qué está buscando? *(keh ehs-'tah boos-kahn-doh)*

Do you want to see what we have?
¿Quiere ver lo que tenemos? *(kee-'eh-reh vehr loh keh teh-'neh-mohs)*

Which one would you like?
¿Cuál le gustaría? *(kwahl leh goos-tah-'ree-ah)*

How many do you want?
¿Cuántos quiere? *('kwahn-tohs kee-'eh-reh)*

Would you like to place an order?
¿Quisiera ordenar algo? *(kee-see-'eh-rah ohr-deh-'nahr 'ahl-goh)*

Something else?
¿Algo más? *('ahl-goh mahs)*

Is that all?
¿Es todo? *(ehs 'toh-doh)*

How would you like to pay?
¿Cómo prefiere pagar? *('koh-moh preh-fee-'eh-reh pah-'gahr)*

Your total is _____.
Su total es _____. *(soo toh-'tahl ehs)*

Slide your card here.
Pase la tarjeta aquí. *('pah-seh lah tahr-'heh-tah ah-'kee)*

May I see an ID please?
¿Puedo ver su identificación, por favor? *('pweh-doh vehr soo ee-dehn-tee-fee-kah-see-'ohn pohr fah-'vohr)*

Did you find everything?
¿Encontró todo? *(ehn-kohn-'troh 'toh-doh)*

Do you need a bag?
¿Necesita una bolsa? *(neh-seh-'see-tah oo-nah 'bohl-sah)*

Would you like me to help with this?
¿Quisiera ayuda con esto? *(kee-see-'eh-rah ah-'yoo-dah kohn 'ehs-toh)*

Thanks for shopping at _____.
Gracias por comprar en _____. *('grah-see-ahs pohr kohm-'prahr ehn)*

Come back and see us.
Vuelva a visitarnos. *(voo-'ehl-vah ah vee-see-'tahr-nohs)*

Have a great day!
¡Que tenga un buen día! *(keh 'tehn-gah oon boo-'ehn 'dee-ah)*

We accept (the)…	**Aceptamos…** *(ah-sehp-'tah-mohs)*
ATM	**el cajero automático** *(ehl kah-'heh-roh aw-toh-'mah-tee-koh)*
cash	**el efectivo** *(ehl eh-fehk-'tee-voh)*
cashier's check	**el cheque de caja** *(ehl 'cheh-keh deh 'kah-hah)*
check	**el cheque** *(ehl 'cheh-keh)*
credit card	**la tarjeta de crédito** *(lah tahr-'heh-tah deh 'kreh-dee-toh)*
money order	**el giro postal** *(ehl 'hee-roh pohs-'tahl)*

Did you see (the)…?	**¿Vió…?** *(vee-'oh)*
advertisement	**el anuncio** *(ehl ah-'noon-see-oh)*
article	**el artículo** *(ehl ahr-'tee-koo-loh)*
billboard	**la cartelera** *(lah kahr-teh-'leh-rah)*
commercial	**el comercial** *(ehl koh-mehr-see-'ahl)*
magazine	**la revista** *(lah reh-'vees-tah)*
newspaper	**el periódico** *(ehl peh-ree-'oh-dee-koh)*
web site	**el sitio web** *(ehl 'see-tee-oh ueb)*
yellow pages	**las páginas amarillas** *(lahs 'pah-hee-nahs ah-mah-'ree-yahs)*

Now work on the following words and phrases, so that your Spanish-speaking employee becomes familiar with sales procedures:

Do you know (the)…?	**¿Conoce…?** *(koh-'noh-seh)*
buyer	**al jefe/a la jefa de compras** *(ahl 'heh-feh/ah lah 'heh-fah deh 'kohm-prahs)*
competitor	**al competidor/a la competidora** *(ahl kohm-peh-tee-'dohr/ah lah kohm-peh-tee-'doh-rah)*
consumer	**al consumidor/a la consumidora** *(ahl kohn-soo-mee-'dohr/ah lah kohn-soo-mee-'doh-rah)*
customer	**al cliente/a la clienta** *(ahl klee-'ehn-teh/a lah klee-'ehn-tah)*
public	**al público** *(ahl 'poo-blee-koh)*
shopper	**al comprador/a la compradora** *(ahl kohm-prah-'dohr/ah lah kohm-prah-'doh-rah)*

Do you know (the)...?	¿Sabe...? *('sah-beh)*
balance	el **saldo** *(ehl 'sahl-doh)*
charge	el **cargo** *(ehl 'kahr-goh)*
cost	el **costo** *(ehl 'kohs-toh)*
down payment	la **entrega inicial** *(lah ehn-'treh-gah ee-nee-see-'ahl)*
payment	el **pago** *(ehl 'pah-goh)*
price	el **precio** *(ehl 'preh-see-oh)*
tax	el **impuesto** *(ehl eem-'pwehs-toh)*
value	el **valor** *(ehl vah-lohr)*

Do you understand (the)...?	¿Entiende...? *(ehn-tee-'ehn-deh)*
bargain	la **ganga** *(lah 'gahn-gah)*
sale	la **venta** *(lah 'vehn-tah)*
installment	el **plazo** *(ehl 'plah-soh)*
refund	el **reembolso** *(ehl reh-ehm-'bohl-soh)*
offer	la **oferta** *(lah oh-'fehr-tah)*
discount	el **descuento** *(ehl dehs-'kwehn-toh)*
rebate	la **rebaja** *(lah reh-'bah-hah)*
guarantee	la **garantía** *(lah gah-rahn-'tee-ah)*

Do you see (the)..?	¿Ve...? *(veh)*
approach	el **enfoque** *(ehl ehn-'foh-keh)*
campaign	la **campaña** *(lah kahm-'pahn-yah)*
criteria	los **criterios** *(lohs kree-'teh-ree-ohs)*
cycle	el **ciclo** *(ehl 'see-kloh)*
design	el **diseño** *(ehl dee-'sehn-yoh)*
forecast	el **pronóstico** *(ehl proh-'nohs-tee-koh)*
layout	la **organización** *(lah ohr-gah-nee-sah-see-'ohn)*
manner	la **manera** *(lah mah-'neh-rah)*
method	el **método** *(ehl 'meh-toh-doh)*
model	el **modelo** *(ehl moh-'deh-loh)*
pattern	el **patrón** *(ehl pah-'trohn)*
plan	el **plan** *(ehl plahn)*
principle	el **principio** *(ehl preen-'see-pee-oh)*
program	el **programa** *(ehl proh-'grah-mah)*
project	el **proyecto** *(ehl proh-'yehk-toh)*
purpose	el **propósito** *(ehl proh-'poh-see-toh)*

reason	la razón *(lah rah-'sohn)*
strategy	la estrategia *(lah ehs-trah-'teh-hee-ah)*
style	el estilo *(ehl ehs-'tee-loh)*
system	el sistema *(ehl sees-'teh-mah)*
technique	la técnica *(lah 'tehk-nee-kah)*
trend	la tendencia *(lah tehn-'dehn-see-ah)*
way	el modo *(ehl 'moh-doh)*

Address the employee with more questions, using verbs in both the present and past tenses:

How much…?	¿Cuánto …? *('kwahn-toh)*
does it cost	cuesta *('kwehs-tah)*
did you pay	pagó *(pah-'goh)*
is it worth	vale *('vah-leh)*

How many…?	¿Cuántos …? *('kwahn-tohs)*
did you order	pidió *(pee-dee-'oh)*
do you need	necesita *(neh-seh-'see-tah)*
did you buy	compró *(kohm-'proh)*

Now focus on more detail:

Is it …?

delayed	¿Está retrasado? *(ehs-'tah reh-trah-'sah-doh)*
duty free	¿Está libre de impuestos? *(ehs-'tah 'lee-breh deh eem-'pwehs-tohs)*
free	¿Es gratuito? *(ehs grah-too-'ee-toh)*
imported	¿Es importado? *(ehs eem-pohr-'tah-doh)*
included	¿Está incluído? *(ehs-'tah een-kloo-'ee-doh)*
overdue	¿Está vencido? *(ehs-'tah vehn-'see-doh)*
paid	¿Está pagado? *(ehs-'tah pah-'gah-doh)*
used	¿Está usado? *(ehs-'tah oo-'sah-doh)*
voided	¿Está cancelado? *(ehs-'tah kahn-seh-'lah-doh)*

Does it include (the)...?	**¿Incluye...?** *(een-'kloo-yeh)*
delivery	**la entrega** *(lah ehn-'treh-gah)*
express mail	**el correo expreso** *(ehl kohr-'reh-oh ex-'preh-soh)*
handling	**los gastos de tramitación** *(lohs 'gahs-tohs deh trah-mee-tah-see-'ohn)*
packaging	**el embalaje** *(ehl ehm-bah-'lah-heh)*
service	**el servicio** *(ehl sehr-'vee-see-oh)*
shipping	**el envío** *(ehl ehn-'vee-oh)*
taxes	**los impuestos** *(lohs eem-'pwehs-tohs)*
Which is (the) ...?	**¿Cuál es ...?** *(kwahl ehs)*
base price	**el precio base** *(ehl 'preh-see-oh 'bah-seh)*
fixed price	**el precio fijo** *(ehl 'preh-see-oh 'fee-hoh)*
list price	**el precio de catálogo** *(ehl 'preh-see-oh deh kah-'tah-loh-goh)*
price drop	**la baja de precio** *(lah 'bah-hah deh 'preh-see-oh)*
price increase	**el aumento de precio** *(ehl aw-'mehn-toh deh 'preh-see-oh)*
price range	**la variación del precio** *(lah vah-ree-ah-see-'ohn dehl 'preh-see-oh)*
retail price	**el precio al por menor** *(ehl 'preh-see-oh ahl pohr meh-'nohr)*
wholesale price	**el precio al por mayor** *(ehl 'preh-see-oh ahl pohr mah-'yohr)*
What is (the)...?	**¿Qué es...?** *(keh ehs)*
sales budget	**el presupuesto de ventas** *(ehl preh-soo-'pwehs-toh deh 'vehn-tahs)*
sales estimate	**la estimación de ventas** *(lah ehs-tee-mah-see-'ohn deh 'vehn-tahs)*
sales force	**el personal de ventas** *(ehl pehr-soh-'nahl deh 'vehn-tahs)*
sales pitch	**la labia de comerciante** *(lah 'lah-bee-ah deh koh-mehr-see-'ahn-teh)*
sales tax	**el impuesto de ventas** *(ehl eem-'pwehs-toh deh 'vehn-tahs)*
sales territory	**el territorio de ventas** *(ehl tehr-ree-'toh-ree-oh deh 'vehn-tahs)*

Continue to divide your business vocabulary into similar sets. Without worrying about spelling, write simple sentences using each new word below:

coupon	**el cupón** *(ehl koo-'pohn)*	**No tengo el cupón.**
catalogue	**el catálogo** *(ehl kah-'tah-loh-goh)*	_____
brochure	**el folleto** *(ehl foh-'yeh-toh)*	_____

dock charge — **el cargo de muelle** *(ehl 'kahr-goh deh 'mweh-yeh)*
¿Cuánto es el cargo de muelle? _____

flat rate — **la tarifa fija** *(lah tah-'ree-fah 'fee-hah)*
_____

service fee — **la tarifa del servicio** *(lah tah-'ree-fah dehl sehr-'vee-see-oh)*
_____

rush order — **el pedido urgente** *(ehl peh-'dee-doh oor-'hehn-teh)*
Terminé con el pedido urgente. _____

mail order — **el pedido por correo** *(ehl peh-'dee-doh pohr kor-'reh-oh)*
_____

back order — **el pedido atrasado** *(ehl peh-'dee-doh ah-trah-'sah-doh)*
_____

potential sales — **las ventas potenciales** *(lahs 'vehn-tahs poh-tehn-see-'ah-lehs)*
Mire las ventas potenciales. _____

net sales — **las ventas netas** *(lahs 'vehn-tahs 'neh-tahs)*
_____

Internet sales — **las ventas por la red** *(lahs 'vehn-tahs pohr lah rehd)*
_____

Extra Info!

Specialized vocabulary. As always, highlight only the ones you'll need:

Have you seen (the) ...?	**¿Ha visto...?** *(ah 'vees-toh)*
flow chart	**el cuadro sinóptico** *(ehl 'kwah-droh see-'nohp-tee-koh)*
sales report	**el informe de ventas** *(ehl een-'fohr-meh deh 'vehn-tahs)*
public opinion poll	**la encuesta de la opinión pública** *(lah ehn-'kwehs-tah deh lah oh-pee-nee-'ohn 'poo-blee-kah)*
network	**la red de contactos** *(lah rehd deh kohn-'tahk-tohs)*
mailing list	**la lista de direcciones** *(lah 'lees-tah deh dee-rehk-see-'oh-nehs)*
direct mail	**el correo directo** *(ehl kohr-'reh-oh dee-'rehk-toh)*
graph	**el gráfico** *(ehl 'grah-fee-koh)*
web site	**el sitio web** *(ehl 'see-tee-oh ueb)*
The problem is (the)...	**El problema es ...** *(ehl proh-'bleh-mah ehs)*
cash flow	**el flujo de caja** *(ehl 'floo-hoh deh 'kah-hah)*
downtime	**el tiempo improductivo** *(ehl tee-'ehm-poh eem-proh-dook-'tee-voh)*
manpower	**la fuerza de trabajo** *(lah 'fwehr-sah deh trah-'bah-hoh)*
mass production	**la fabricación en serie** *(lah fah-bree-kah-see-'ohn ehn 'she-ree-eh)*
overhead costs	**los costos generales** *(lohs 'kohs-tohs heh-neh-'rah-lehs)*
production rate	**el volumen de producción** *(ehl voh-'loo-mehn deh proh-dook-see-'ohn)*
quality control	**el control de calidad** *(ehl kohn-'trohl deh kah-lee-'dahd)*
time frame	**el período de tiempo** *(ehl peh-'ree-oh-doh deh tee-'ehm-poh)*
workload	**la cantidad de trabajo** *(lah kahn-tee-'dahd deh trah-'bah-hoh)*

Extra Info!

Our hyphenated expressions are translated below:

across-the-board	**general** *(heh-neh-'rahl)*
as-is	**tal como está** *(tahl 'koh-moh ehs-'tah)*
break-even	**sin ganancia ni pérdida** *(seen gah-'nahn-see-ah nee 'pehr-dee-dah)*
close-out	**la liquidación** *(lah lee-kee-dah-see-'ohn)*
door-to-door	**de puerta en puerta** *(deh 'pwehr-tah ehn 'pwehr-tah)*
in-the-red	**endeudado** *(ehn-deh-oo-'dah-doh)*
large-scale	**en gran escala** *(ehn grahn ehs-'kah-lah)*
mark-down	**la reducción de precio** *(lah reh-dook-see-'ohn deh 'preh-see-oh)*
mark-up	**el margen de ganancia** *(ehl 'mahr-hehn deh gah-'nahn-see-ah)*
on-the-job	**por rutina** *(pohr roo-'tee-nah)*
paid-in-full	**pagado en su totalidad** *(pah-'gah-doh ehn soo toh-tah-lee-'dahd)*
red-tape	**el trámite burocrático** *(ehl 'trah-mee-teh boo-roh-'krah-tee-koh)*
self-service	**el autoservicio** *(ehl aw-toh-sehr-'vee-see-oh)*

Let's Practice

(32)

Circle the three words that belong in each group:

1. principio, propósito, impuesto, razón
2. efectivo, gráfico, crédito, cheque
3. proyecto, correo, entrega, envío
4. pagado, prendido, gratuito, incluído
5. consumidora, compradora, cliente, contestadora
6. vencido, revista, periódico, artículo

The Business Meeting
La reunión de ventas
(lah reh-oo-nee-'ohn deh 'vehn-tahs)

Here are handy sentences to select as the occasion requires:

Come on this date.
Venga en esta fecha *('vehn-gah ehn 'ehs-tah 'feh-chah)*

It's a sales meeting.
Es una reunión de ventas *(ehs 'oo-nah reh-oo-nee-'ohn deh 'vehn-tahs)*

You must attend.
Tiene que asistir. *(tee-'eh-neh keh ah-sees-'teer)*

Take a seat.
Tome asiento. *('toh-meh ah-see-'ehn-toh)*

Quiet, please.
Silencio, por favor. *(see-'lehn-see-oh pohr fah-'vohr)*

Let's get started.
Vamos a comenzar. *('vah-mohs ah koh-mehn-'sahr)*

This is the agenda.
Esta es la orden del día. *('ehs-tah ehs lah 'ohr-dehn dehl 'dee-ah)*

Please read the report.
Lea el informe, por favor. *(leh-ah ehl een-'fohr-meh pohr fah-'vohr)*

Do you have any questions?
¿Tiene alguna pregunta? *(tee-'eh-neh ahl-'goo-nah preh-'goon-tah)*

Choose what you need from these key phrases:

Have you (pl.) seen (the)...?	**¿Han visto ustedes....?** *(ahn 'vees-toh oos-'teh-dehs)*
data	**los datos** *(lohs 'dah-tohs)*
earnings	**las ganancias** *(lahs gah-'nahn-see-ahs)*

facts	**los hechos** *(lohs 'eh-chohs)*
figures	**las cifras** *(las 'seef-rahs)*
income	**los ingresos** *(lohs een-'greh-sohs)*
results	**los resultados** *(lohs reh-sool-'tah-dohs)*

Let's look at (the) ...	**Miramos a ...** *(mee-'rah-mohs ah)*

account	**la cuenta** *(lah 'kwehn-tah)*
amount	**la cantidad** *(lah kahn-tee-'dahd)*
average	**el promedio** *(ehl proh-'meh-dee-oh)*
index	**el índice** *(ehl 'een-dee-seh)*
level	**el nivel** *(ehl nee-'vehl)*
loss	**la pérdida** *(lah 'pehr-dee-dah)*
margin	**el margen** *(ehl 'mahr-hehn)*
maximum	**el máximo** *(ehl 'mahk-see-moh)*
minimum	**el mínimo** *(ehl 'mee-nee-moh)*
percentage	**el porcentaje** *(ehl pohr-sehn-'tah-heh)*
profit	**la ganancia** *(lah gah-'nahn-see-ah)*
quota	**la cuota** *(lah 'kwoh-tah)*
rate	**la tasa** *(lah 'tah-sah)*
ratio	**la proporción** *(lah proh-pohr-see'ohn)*
reduction	**la reducción** *(lah reh-dook-see-'ohn)*
return	**la devolución** *(lah deh-voh-loo-see-'ohn)*
variance	**la variación** *(lah vah-ree-ah-see-'ohn)*

I'm going to...	**Voy a...** *('voh-ee ah)*

clarify	**aclarar** *(ah-klah-'rahr)*
confirm	**confirmar** *(kohn-feer-'mahr)*
explain	**explicar** *(ex-plee-'kahr)*
identify	**identificar** *(ee-dehn-tee-fee-'kahr)*
suggest	**sugerir** *(soo-heh-'reer)*

I think it's...	**Pienso que es...** *(pee-'ehn-soh keh ehs)*

acceptable	**aceptable** *(ah-sehp-'tah-bleh)*
adequate	**adecuado** *(ah-deh-'kwah-doh)*
appropriate	**apropiado** *(ah-proh-pee-'ah-doh)*
better	**mejor** *(meh-'hohr)*
correct	**correcto** *(kohr-'rehk-toh)*
excellent	**excelente** *(ex-seh-'lehn-teh)*

good	**bueno** *('bweh-noh)*
high	**alto** *('ahl-toh)*
more	**más** *(mahs)*
outstanding	**notable** *(noh-'tah-bleh)*
successful	**exitoso** *(ex-ee-'toh-soh)*
typical	**típico** *('tee-pee-koh)*

I don't believe it's…	**No creo que sea…** *(noh 'kreh-oh keh 'seh-ah)*
incorrect	**incorrecto** *(een-kohr-'rehk-toh)*
less	**menos** *('meh-nohs)*
low	**bajo** *('bah-hoh)*
poor	**malo** *('mah-loh)*
rare	**raro** *('rah-roh)*
terrible	**terrible** *(tehr-'ree-bleh)*
unacceptable	**inaceptable** *(een-ah-sehp-'tah-bleh)*
worse	**peor** *(peh-'ohr)*

I'd like to hear (the)…	**Quisiera escuchar…** *(kee-see-'eh-rah ehs-koo-'chahr)*
comments	**los comentarios** *(lohs koh-mehn-'tah-ree-ohs)*
example	**el ejemplo** *(ehl eh-'hehm-ploh)*
idea	**la idea** *(lah ee-'deh-ah)*
input	**la aportación** *(lah ah-pohr-tah-see-'ohn)*
interpretation	**la interpretación** *(lah een-tehr-preh-tah-see-'ohn)*
opinion	**la opinión** *(lah oh-pee-nee-'ohn)*
question	**la pregunta** *(lah preh-'goon-tah)*
reaction	**la reacción** *(lah reh-ahk-see-'ohn)*
response	**la respuesta** *(leh rehs-'pwehs-tah)*
thought	**el pensamiento** *(ehl pehn-sah-mee-'ehn-toh)*

This is (the)…	**Esta/Este es…** *('ehs-tah/'ehs-teh ehs)*
best way	**la mejor manera** *(lah meh-'hohr mah-'neh-rah)*
closing remark	**el comentario final** *(ehl koh-mehn-'tah-ree-oh fee-'nahl)*
final decision	**la decisión final** *(lah deh-see-see-'ohn fee-'nahl)*
last opportunity	**la última oportunidad** *(lah 'ool-tee-mah oh-pohr-too-nee-'dahd)*
top priority	**la prioridad máxima** *(lah pree-oh-ree-'dahd 'mahk-see-mah)*

Extra Info!

Here are some business activities where employees can relax, socialize, and have some fun together:

Please come to the...	**Por favor, venga ...** *(pohr fah-'vohr 'vehn-gah)*
banquet	**al banquete** *(ahl bahn-'keh-teh)*
celebration	**a la celebración** *(ah lah seh-leh-brah-see-'ohn)*
ceremony	**a la ceremonia** *(ah lah seh-reh-'moh-nee-ah)*
dinner	**a la cena** *(ah lah 'seh-nah)*
festival	**al festival** *(ahl fehs-tee-'vahl)*
party	**a la fiesta** *(ah lah fee-'ehs-tah)*
picnic	**al picnic** *(ahl 'peek-neek)*
show	**al espectáculo** *(ahl ehs-pehk-'tah-koo-loh)*
We have...	**Tenemos...** *(teh-'neh-mohs)*
certificates	**certificados** *(sehr-tee-fee-'kah-dohs)*
free food	**comida gratuita** *(koh-'mee-dah grah-too-'ee-tah)*
games	**juegos** *('hweh-gohs)*
gifts	**regalos** *(reh-'gah-lohs)*
medals	**medallas** *(meh-'dah-yahs)*
prizes	**premios** *('preh-mee-ohs)*
rewards	**recompensas** *(reh-kohm-'pehn-sahs)*
trophies	**trofeos** *(troh-'feh-ohs)*

The Culture

To build teamwork with an international staff, mark on a calendar all the important dates that American businesses tend to recognize, including national holidays, and other special events. By inviting all employees to participate, you will have an opportunity to mingle with employees in festive settings, while learning about traditional celebrations in other countries.

Using the Telephone
El uso del teléfono
(ehl 'oo-soh dehl teh-'leh-foh-noh)

Most employers still rely on the telephone to communicate with others. Practice each group of words using the sentence patterns below:

Use (the) ...	**Use ...** *('oo-seh)*
answering machine	**el contestador telefónico** *(ehl kohn-tehs-tah-'dohr teh-leh-'foh-nee-koh)*
cell phone	**el celular** *(ehl seh-loo-'lahr)*
headset	**los auriculares telefónicos** *(lohs aw-ree-koo-'lah-rehs teh-leh-'foh-nee-kohs)*
multi-line phone	**el teléfono de multilínea** *(ehl teh-'leh-foh-noh deh mool-tee-'lee-neh-ah)*
other line	**la otra línea** *(lah 'oh-trah 'lee-neh-ah)*
PDA	**la computadora de bolsillo** *(lah kohm-poo-tah-'doh-rah deh bohl-'see-yoh)*
phone service	**el servicio telefónico** *(ehl sehr-'vee-see-oh teh-leh-foh-nee-koh)*
switchboard	**el conmutador** *(ehl kohn-moo-tah-'dohr)*
two-way radio	**el radioteléfono portátil** *(ehl rah-dee-oh-teh-'leh-foh-noh pohr-'tah-teel)*

It has ...	**Tiene...** *(tee-'eh-neh)*
an alarm	**una alarma** *('oo-nah ah-'lahr-mah)*
caller ID	**identificación de llamada** *(ee-dehn-tee-fee-kah-see-'ohn deh yah-'mah-dah)*
call-waiting	**llamada en espera** *(yah-'mah-dah ehn ehs-'peh-rah)*
a camera	**una cámara** *('oo-nah 'kah-mah-rah)*
e-mail	**correo electrónico** *(kohr-'reh-oh eh-lehk-'troh-nee-koh)*
Internet	**internet** *(een-tehr-'neht)*
voice mail	**telemensaje** *(teh-leh-mehn-'sah-heh)*

Do you know (the)...?	**¿Sabe...?** *('sah-beh)*
800 number	**el número de ochocientos** *(ehl 'noo-meh-roh deh oh-choh-see-'ehn-tohs)*

area code	**el código de area** *(ehl 'koh-dee-goh deh 'ah-reh-ah)*
extension	**la extensión** *(lah ex-tehn-see'ohn)*
number	**el número** *(ehl 'noo-meh-roh)*
password	**la contraseña** *(lah kohn-trah-'sehn-yah)*

When You Call
Cuando usted llama
('kwahn-doh oos-'tehd 'yah-mah)

Place this next set of phrases near the business phone, and then wait for the chance to practice:

Hello, is _____ there?
¿Aló, está _____? *(ah-'loh ehs-'tah)*

May I speak to _____?
Puedo hablar con _____. *('pweh-doh ah-'blahr kohn)*

Please, it's very urgent.
Por favor, es muy urgente. *(pohr fah-'vohr ehs 'moo-ee oor-'hehn-teh)*

We have a bad connection.
La conexión está mala. *(lah cohn-ehk-see-'ohn ehs-'tah 'mah-lah)*

I'm calling about _____.
Estoy llamando sobre _____. *(ehs-'toh-ee yah-'mahn-doh 'soh-breh)*

I'd like to leave a message.
Quisiera dejar un recado. *(kee-see-'eh-rah deh-'hahr oon reh-'kah-doh)*

Tell him/her that _____.
Dígale que _____. *('dee-gah-leh keh)*

I'll call back later.
Llamaré más tarde. *(yah-mah-'reh mahs 'tahr-deh)*

When You Get a Call
Cuando recibe una llamada
('kwahn-doh reh-'see-beh 'oo-nah yah-'mah-dah)

Who are you calling, please?
¿A quién está llamando, por favor?
(ah kee-'ehn ehs-'tah yah-'mahn-doh pohr fah-'vohr)

You have a wrong number.
Tiene un número equivocado. *(tee-'eh-neh oon 'noo-meh-roh eh-kee-voh-'kah-doh)*

The number has been changed.
El número ha cambiado. *(ehl 'noo-meh-roh ah kahm-bee-'ah-doh)*

He/She isn't here right now.
No está aquí en este momento. *(noh ehs-'tah ah-'kee ehn 'ehs-teh moh-'mehn-toh)*

He/She doesn't work here.
No trabaja aquí. *(noh trah-'bah-hah ah-'kee)*

He/She can't come to the phone.
No puede contestar su llamada. *(noh 'pweh-deh kohn-tehs-'tahr soo yah-'mah-dah)*

He/She is very busy.
Está muy ocupado/a. *(ehs-'tah 'moo-ee oh-koo-'pah-doh/ah)*

He/She is in a meeting.
Está en conferencia. *(ehs-'tah ehn kohn-feh-'rehn-see-ah)*

He/She is on the other line.
Está en la otra línea. *(ehs-'tah ehn lah 'oh-trah 'lee-neh-ah)*

More slowly, please.
Más despacio, por favor. *(mahs dehs-'pah-see-oh pohr fah-'vohr)*

Could you please repeat that?
¿Puede repetirlo, por favor? *('pweh-deh reh-peh-'teer-loh pohr fah-'vohr)*

Wait a moment, please.
Espere un momento, por favor. *(ehs-'peh-reh oon moh-'mehn-toh pohr fah-'vohr)*

I'll transfer you to his/her voicemail.
Lo/La voy a transferir a su telemensaje.
(loh/lah 'voh-ee ah trahns-feh-'reer ah soo teh-leh-mehn-'sah-heh)

Sorry, but he/she doesn't answer.
Lo siento, pero no contesta. *(loh see-'ehn-toh 'peh-roh noh kohn-'tehs-tah)*

Do you want to leave a message?
¿Quiere dejarle un recado? *(kee-'eh-reh deh-'hahr-leh oon reh-'kah-doh)*

Your cell number, please.
Su número del celular, por favor.
(soo 'noo-meh-roh dehl seh-loo-'lahr pohr fah-'vohr)

Your home number, please.
Su número de casa, por favor. *(soo 'noo-meh-roh deh 'kah-sah pohr fah-'vohr)*

Dial this number, please.
Marque este número, por favor *('mahr-keh 'ehs-teh 'noo-meh-roh pohr fah-'vohr)*

I will give him/her your message.
Le voy a dejar su mensaje. *(leh 'voh-ee ah deh-'hahr soo mehn-'sah-heh)*

Can you call back later?
¿Puede llamar más tarde? *('pweh-deh yah-'mahr mahs 'tahr-deh)*

He/She will return your call later.
Lo/la llamará más tarde. *(loh/lah yah-mah-'rah mahs 'tahr-deh)*

Extra Info!

Is it...?	¿Es...? *(ehs)*
a collect call	**una llamada a cobro revertido** *('oo-nah yah-'mah-dah ah 'koh-broh reh-vehr-'tee-doh)*
cordless	**sin cable** *(seen 'kah-bleh)*
digital	**digital** *(dee-hee-'tahl)*
a local call	**una llamada local** *('oo-nah yah-'mah-dah loh-'kahl)*
a long distance call	**una llamada de larga distancia** *('oo-nah yah-'mah-dah deh 'lahr-gah dees-'tahn-see-ah)*
portable	**portátil** *(pohr-'tah-teel)*
prepaid	**prepagado** *(preh-pah-'gah-doh)*
Is it...?	¿Está...? *(ehs-'tah)*
blocked	**bloqueado** *(bloh-keh-'ah-doh)*
restricted	**limitado** *(lee-mee-'tah-doh)*
disconnected	**desconectado** *(dehs-koh-nehk-'tah-doh)*

Let's Practice (33)

A. Translate this telephone conversation:

Hello, is Antonio there? It's very urgent.
No, I'm sorry. Do you want to leave a message?
Yes, thank you. My name is Mr. Miller, and I'm calling about the problem at the office.

B. Choose the best word from the list to fill in each blank below:

CENA, INFORME, EXPLICAR, PEOR, TRABAJA

1. Lea el _____, por favor.
2. No creo que sea _____.
3. ¡Venga a la _____!
4. Ella no _____ aquí.
5. Voy a _____ todo.

C. Put each group of words in correct order:

una ventas de es conferencia	Es una conferencia de ventas.
1. visto ganancias las han	_____
2. al cuenta en promedio miramos la	_____
3. clienta tiene llamada de la una	_____

City Businesses
Los negocios en la ciudad
(lohs neh-'goh-see-ohs ehn lah see-oo-'dahd)

If you involve Spanish-speaking employees in business around town, this vocabulary will be useful:

Here's (the)...	**Aquí tiene...** *(ah-'kee tee-'eh-neh)*
address	**la dirección** *(lah dee-rehk-see-'ohn)*
map	**el mapa** *(ehl 'mah-pah)*
schedule	**el horario** *(ehl oh-'rah-ree-oh)*

Look at (the)…	**Mire…** *('mee-reh)*
buildings	**los edificios** *(lohs eh-dee-'fee-see-ohs)*
signs	**los letreros** *(lohs leh-'treh-rohs)*
street names	**los nombres de las calles** *(lohs 'nohm-brehs deh lahs 'kah-yehs)*
It's in (the)…	**Está en…** *(ehs-'tah ehn)*
downtown area	**el centro** *(ehl 'sehn-troh)*
neighborhood	**el vecindario** *(ehl veh-seen-'dah-ree-oh)*
outskirts	**las afueras** *(lahs ah-'fweh-rahs)*
Go to the…	**Vaya…** *('vah-yah)*
apartment building	**al edificio de apartamentos** *(ahl eh-dee-'fee-see-oh deh ah-pahr-tah-'mehn-tohs)*
bank	**al banco** *(ahl 'bahn-koh)*
beauty salon	**al salón de belleza** *(ahl sah-'lohn deh beh-'yeh-sah)*
car lot	**al lote de carros** *(ahl 'loh-teh deh 'kahr-rohs)*
church	**a la iglesia** *(ah lah eeg-'leh-see-ah)*
city hall	**al municipio** *(ahl moo-nee-see-pee-'oh)*
clinic	**a la clínica** *(ah lah 'klee-nee-kah)*
coffee shop	**al café** *(ahl kah-'feh)*
department store	**al almacén** *(ahl ahl-mah-'sehn)*
factory	**a la fábrica** *(ah lah 'fah-bree-kah)*
gas station	**a la gasolinera** *(ah lah gah-soh-lee-'neh-rah)*
hospital	**al hospital** *(ahl ohs-pee-'tahl)*
hotel	**al hotel** *(ahl oh-'tehl)*
laundromat	**a la lavandería** *(ah lah lah-vahn-deh-'ree-ah)*
library	**a la biblioteca** *(ah lah beeb-lee-oh-'teh-kah)*
movie theater	**al cine** *(ahl 'see-neh)*
museum	**al museo** *(ahl moo-'seh-oh)*
park	**al parque** *(ahl 'pahr-keh)*
pharmacy	**a la farmacia** *(ah lah fahr-'mah-see-ah)*
post office	**a la oficina de correos** *(ah lah oh-fee-'see-nah deh kohr-'reh-ohs)*
restaurant	**al restaurante** *(ahl rehs-tah-oo-'rahn-teh)*
school	**a la escuela** *(ah lah ehs-'kweh-lah)*
shopping center	**al centro comercial** *(ahl 'sehn-troh koh-mehr-see-'ahl)*
store	**a la tienda** *(ah lah tee-'ehn-dah)*
supermarket	**al supermercado** *(ahl soo-pehr-mehr-'kah-doh)*

train station	**a la estación de tren** *(ah lah ehs-tah-see-'ohn deh trehn)*
university	**a la universidad** *(ah lah oo-nee-vehr-see-'dahd)*

It's near (the)…	**Está cerca…** *(ehs-'tah 'sehr-kah)*
bridge	**del puente** *(dehl 'pwehn-teh)*
fountain	**de la fuente** *(deh lah 'fwehn-teh)*
parking lot	**del estacionamiento** *(dehl ehs-tah-see-oh-nah-mee-'ehn-toh)*
statue	**de la estatua** *(deh lah ehs-'tah-twah)*
tunnel	**del túnel** *(dehl 'too-nehl)*

Let's meet at (the)…	**Nos encontramos en…** *(nohs ehn-kohn-'trah-mohs ehn)*
corner	**la esquina** *(lah ehs-'kee-nah)*
entrance	**la entrada** *(lah ehn-'trah-dah)*
exit	**la salida** *(lah sah-'lee-dah)*

We have to…	**Tenemos que…** *(teh-'neh-mohs keh)*
arrive	**llegar** *(yeh-'gahr)*
attend	**asistir** *(ah-sees-'teer)*
buy	**comprar** *(kohm-'prahr)*
carry	**llevar** *(yeh-'vahr)*
deliver	**entregar** *(ehn-treh-'gahr)*
distribute	**distribuir** *(dees-tree-boo-'eer)*
enter	**entrar** *(ehn-'trahr)*
follow	**seguir** *(seh-'geer)*
leave	**salir** *(sah-'leer)*
load	**cargar** *(kahr-'gahr)*
move	**mover** *(moh-'vehr)*
negotiate	**negociar** *(neh-goh-see-'ahr)*
order	**pedir** *(peh-'deer)*
package	**empaquetar** *(ehm-pah-keh-'tahr)*
park	**estacionar** *(ehs-tah-see-oh-'nahr)*
pick up	**recoger** *(reh-koh-'hehr)*
provide	**proveer** *(proh-veh-'ehr)*
sell	**vender** *(vehn-'dehr)*
ship	**enviar** *(ehn-vee-'ahr)*
spend	**gastar** *(gahs-'tahr)*
stop	**parar** *(pah-'rahr)*
transfer	**transferir** *(trahns-feh-'reer)*

transport	**transportar** *(trahns-pohr-'tahr)*
turn	**voltear** *(vohl-teh-'ahr)*
unload	**descargar** *(dehs-kahr-'gahr)*

Extra Info!

This is for the employer who uses Spanish while he/she is **de viaje** *(deh vee-'ah-heh,* traveling):

I need (the)...	**Necesito...** *(neh-seh-'see-toh)*
confirmation	**la confirmación** *(lah kohn-feer-mah-see-'ohn)*
gas	**la gasolina** *(lah gah-soh-'lee-nah)*
hotel	**el hotel** *(ehl oh-'tehl)*
receipt	**el recibo** *(ehl reh-'see-boh)*
rental car	**el carro de alquiler** *(ehl 'kahr-roh deh ahl-kee-'lehr)*
reservation	**la reserva** *(lah reh-'sehr-vah)*
restroom	**el servicio** *(ehl sehr-'vee-see-oh)*
room	**la habitación** *(lah ah-bee-tah-see-'ohn)*
suitcase	**la maleta** *(lah mah-'leh-tah)*
taxi	**el taxi** *(ehl 'tahk-see)*
traveler's checks	**los cheques de viajero** *(lohs 'cheh-kehs deh vee-'ah-heh-roh)*

Where's (the)...	**¿Dónde está...?** *('dohn-deh ehs-'tah)*
airport	**el aeropuerto** *(ehl ah-eh-roh-'pwehr-toh)*
boarding pass	**la tarjeta de embarque** *(lah tahr-'heh-tah deh ehm-'bahr-keh)*
customs	**la aduana** *(lah ah-'dwah-nah)*
flight	**el vuelo** *(ehl voo-'eh-loh)*
flight number	**el número del vuelo** *(ehl 'noo-meh-roh deh voo-'eh-loh)*
identification	**la identificación** *(lah ee-dehn-tee-fee-kah-see-'ohn)*
lost and found	**la oficina de objetos perdidos** *(lah oh-fee-'see-nah deh ohb-'heh-tohs pehr-'dee-dohs)*
luggage	**el equipaje** *(ehl eh-kee-'pah-heh)*
passport	**el pasaporte** *(ehl pah-sah-'pohr-teh)*
plane	**el avión** *(ehl ah-vee-'ohn)*
terminal	**el terminal** *(ehl tehr-mee-'nahl)*

Transportation
El transporte
(ehl trahns-'pohr-teh)

Let's take (the) ...	**Vayamos en ...** *(vah-'yah-mohs ehn)*
car	**el carro** *(ehl 'kahr-roh)*
bus	**el autobús** *(ehl aw-toh-'boos)*
commercial vehicle	**el vehículo comercial** *(ehl veh-'ee-koo-loh koh-mehr-see-'ahl)*
delivery truck	**el camión de reparto** *(ehl kah-mee-'ohn deh reh-'pahr-toh)*
flatbed truck	**el camión de plataforma** *(ehl kah-mee-'ohn deh plah-tah-'fohr-mah)*
SUV	**el vehículo deportivo utilitario** *(ehl veh-'ee-koo-loh deh-pohr-'tee-voh oo-tee-lee-'tah-ree-oh)*
pickup truck	**la camioneta** *(lah kah-mee-oh-'neh-tah)*
semi-trailer	**el semirremolque** *(ehl seh-mee-reh-'mohl-keh)*
subway	**el metro** *(ehl 'meh-troh)*
tractor trailer	**el camión tractor** *(ehl kah-mee-'ohn trahk-'tohr)*
train	**el tren** *(ehl trehn)*
truck	**el camión** *(ehl kah-mee-'ohn)*
van	**la furgoneta** *(lah foor-goh-'neh-tah)*

Use a simple sentence to get your message across:

There's a lot of traffic.
Hay mucho tráfico. *('ah-ee 'moo-choh 'trah-fee-koh)*

How many blocks?
¿Cuántas cuadras? *('kwahn-tahs 'kwah-drahs)*

It's the next exit.
Es la siguiente salida. *(ehs lah see-gee-'ehn-teh sah-'lee-dah)*

It's the main _____.	**Es _____ principal.** *(ehs ___ preen-see-'pahl)*
avenue	**la avenida** *(lah ah-veh-'nee-dah)*
highway	**la carretera** *(lah kahr-reh-'teh-rah)*
road	**el camino** *(ehl kah-'mee-noh)*
route	**la ruta** *(lah 'roo-tah)*
street	**la calle** *(lah 'kah-yeh)*

Did you see (the)…?	¿Vió…? *(vee-'oh)*
bus stop	**la parada de autobús** *(lah pah-'rah-dah deh aw-toh-'boos)*
crosswalk	**el cruce de peatones** *(ehl 'kroo-seh deh peh-ah-'toh-nehs)*
stop sign	**la señal de parada** *(lah sehn-'yahl deh pah-rah-dah)*
toll booth	**la cabina de peaje** *(lah kah-'bee-nah deh peh-'ah-heh)*
traffic signal	**el semáforo** *(ehl seh-'mah-foh-roh)*

If your Spanish-speaking employee is unfamiliar with key words posted on our roadways, here's help:

Pedestrian Crossing	**PASO DE PEATONES**
Speed Limit	**LÍMITE DE VELOCIDAD**
Railroad Crossing	**CRUCE DE VÍAS**
Detour	**DESVIACIÓN**
Do Not Cross	**NO CRUZAR**
Emergency	**EMERGENCIA**
No Passing	**NO PASAR**
One Way	**CIRCULACIÓN**
Slow	**DESPACIO**
Stop	**ALTO**
Traffic Circle	**GLORIETA**
Yield	**CEDA EL PASO**
Do Not Litter	**NO TIRE BASURA**
Narrow Road	**CAMINO ESTRECHO**
Wrong Way	**VÍA EQUIVOCADA**
Handicapped	**MINUSVÁLIDOS**
Curve	**CURVA**
No U Turn	**PROHIBIDA LA VUELTA EN "U"**
Tow Away Zone	**SE USARÁ GRÚA**

And don't forget—there are plenty of ways to travel:

I prefer (the)…	**Prefiero…** *(preh-fee-'eh-roh)*
motorcycle	**la motocicleta** *(lah moh-toh-see-'kleh-tah)*
bicycle	**la bicicleta** *(lah bee-see-'kleh-tah)*
boat	**el barco** *(ehl 'bahr-koh)*
helicopter	**el helicóptero** *(ehl eh-lee-'kohp-teh-roh)*
tow truck	**la grúa** *(lah 'groo-ah)*

Let's Practice ㉞

A. In Spanish:

Name five common buildings found in cities everywhere:

_____ _____ _____ _____ _____

Name three signs you might find posted on the side of a road:

_____ _____ _____

B. Fill in the blanks with words you just learned about the city:

¿Vió _____? Está en _____ principal.
Nos encontramos en _____. Está cerca de _____.
Tenemos que _____. Vayamos en _____.

The Culture

Do not translate names of businesses, brands, streets. All over the world, most formal titles in English remain the same.

More Pronouns
Más pronombres
(mahs proh-'nohm-brehs)

Notice how the pronoun **le** can refer to "you," "him," or "her." This pronoun usually goes before the verb in a sentence, but may also appear at the end of an infinitive:

I told you/him/her.   **Le dije.** *(leh 'dee-heh)*
I brought you/him/her.   **Le traje.** *(leh 'trah-heh)*

I would like to thank you.
Quisiera agadecerle. *(kee-see-'eh-rah ah-grah-deh-'sehr-leh)*

I'm going to assure him.
Voy a asegurarle. *('voh-ee ah ah-seh-goo-'rahr-leh)*

I need to pay her.
Necesito pagarle. *(neh-seh-'see-toh pah-'gahr-leh)*

Other pronouns in Spanish include the little words **me** *(meh,* me) **les** *(lehs,* them or you, plural), and **nos** *(nohs,* us). Notice how they can be used with commands:

Explain to me	**Explíqueme** *(ex-'plee-keh-meh)*
Answer them	**Contésteles** *(kohn-'tehs-teh-lehs)*
Listen to us	**Escúchenos** *(ehs-'koo-cheh-nohs)*

Again, the **le** refers to people, while the pronouns **lo**, **los**, **la**, and **las** generally refer to things. Be aware of the difference in gender:

I cleaned the floor. I cleaned it.
Limpié <u>el piso.</u> Lo limpié. *(leem-pee-'eh ehl 'pee-soh loh leem-pee-'eh)*

I opened the box. I opened it.
Abrí <u>la caja.</u> La abrí. *(ah-'bree lah 'kah-hah lah ah-'bree)*

Let's Practice (35)

Use a pronoun with each of the following verb infinitives. Follow the examples provided:

to invest	invertir	<u>Lo estoy invirtiendo.</u>
to owe	deber	<u>Le debo el dinero.</u>
to save	ahorrar	_____
to spend	gastar	_____
to buy	comprar	_____
to sell	vender	_____
to charge	cobrar	_____

Read through these other business-related infinitives:

to advertise	**anunciar** *(ah-noon-see-'ahr)*
to build	**construir** *(kohns-troo-'eer)*
to cancel	**cancelar** *(kahn-seh-'lahr)*
to collect	**colectar** *(koh-lehk-'tahr)*
to commit	**comprometer** *(kohm-proh-meh-'tehr)*
to deliver	**entregar** *(ehn-treh-'gahr)*
to demand	**reclamar** *(reh-klah-'mahr)*
to deposit	**depositar** *(deh-poh-see-'tahr)*
to develop	**desarrollar** *(deh-sahr-roh-'yahr)*
to export	**exportar** *(ex-pohr-tahr)*
to guarantee	**garantizar** *(gah-rahn-tee-'sahr)*
to import	**importar** *(eem-pohr-'tahr)*
to include	**incluir** *(een-kloo-'eer)*
to overcharge	**cobrar en exceso** *(koh-'brahr ehn ex-'seh-soh)*
to overspend	**gastar más de la cuenta** *(gahs-'tahr mahs deh lah 'kwehn-tah)*
to plan	**planear** *(plah-neh-'ahr)*
to postpone	**posponer** *(pohs-poh-'nehr)*
to process	**tramitar** *(trah-mee-'tahr)*
to produce	**producir** *(proh-doo-'seer)*
to return	**volver** *(vohl-'vehr)*
to serve	**servir** *(sehr-'veer)*
to share	**compartir** *(kohm-pahr-'teer)*
to ship	**transportar** *(trahns-pohr-'tahr)*
to transfer	**transferir** *(trahns-feh-'reer)*
to travel	**viajar** *(vee-ah-'hahr)*

Action Words!

Spanish infinitives can be used in a variety of ways. Look over these examples:

Off to work!
¡A <u>trabajar</u>! *(ah trah-bah-'hahr)*

Reading is important.
<u>Leer</u> es importante. *(leh-'ehr ehs eem-pohr-'tahn-teh)*

Shut the door when you leave.
Al <u>salir</u>, cierre la puerta. *(ahl sah-'leer see-'ehr-reh lah 'pwehr-tah)*

Verbs: The Present Perfect
Los verbos: el presente perfecto
(lohs 'vehr-bohs ehl preh-'sehn-teh pehr-'fehk-toh)

Review the verb forms we've studied. Note the spelling and pronunciation changes that take place when you shift from one time reference to the next:

I'm working there <u>now</u>.
Estoy trabajando ahí <u>ahora</u>. *(ehs-'toh-ee trah-bah-'hahn-doh ah-'ee ah-'oh-rah)*

I work there <u>every day</u>.
Trabajo ahí <u>todos los días</u>. *(trah-'bah-hoh ah-'ee 'toh-dohs lohs 'dee-ahs)*

I will work there <u>tomorrow</u>.
Voy a trabajar ahí <u>mañana</u>. *('voh-ee ah trah-bah-'hahr ah-'ee mahn-'yah-nah)*

I worked there <u>yesterday</u>.
Trabajé ahí <u>ayer</u>. *(trah-bah-'heh ah-'ee ah-'yehr)*

I worked there <u>a long time ago</u>.
Trabajaba ahí <u>hace muchos años</u>.
(trah-bah-'hah-bah ah-'ee 'ah-seh 'moo-chohs 'ahn-yohs)

Now, look at this next two-part verb form, which refers to actions that have already taken place.

The first part consists of forms of the verb **HABER** *(ah-'behr)*, whereas the second part consists of the past participle of the action word. Both parts must be used together.

I've left	**He salido** *(eh sah-'lee-doh)*
I've eaten	**He comido** *(eh koh-'mee-doh)*
You've, She's, He's arrived	**Ha llegado** *(ah yeh-'gah-doh)*
You've cleaned	**Ha limpiado** *(ah leem-pee-'ah-doh)*
You've (pl.), They've worked	**Han trabajado** *(ahn trah-bah-'hah-doh)*
You've (pl.), They've driven	**Han manejado** *(ahn mah-neh-'hah-doh)*
We've learned	**Hemos aprendido** *('eh-mohs ah-prehn-'dee-doh)*
We've flown	**Hemos volado** *('eh-mohs voh-'lah-doh)*

Here's how it is used in sentences:

I've parked here many times.
He estacionado aquí muchas veces.
(eh ehs-tah-see-oh-'nah-doh ah-'kee 'moo-chahs 'veh-sehs)

She's driven a truck.
Ella ha manejado un camión.
('eh-yah ah mah-neh-'hah-doh oon kah-mee-'ohn)

We've delivered machines before.
Hemos entregado máquinas antes.
('eh-mohs ehn-treh-'gah-doh 'mah-kee-nahs 'ahn-tehs)

 ## Action Words!

Many past participles in Spanish can be used as descriptive words:

They are <u>used</u> cars.
Son carros <u>usados</u>. *(sohn 'kahr-rohs oo-'sah-dohs)*

The doors are <u>painted</u>.
Las puertas están <u>pintadas</u>. *(lahs 'pwehr-tahs ehs-'tahn peen-'tah-dahs)*

They are <u>broken</u>.
Están <u>quebrados</u>. *(ehs-'tahn keh-'brah-dohs)*

Unfortunately, a few past participles are irregular. Here are three examples:

I've <u>done</u> the job. **(Hacer)**
He <u>hecho</u> el trabajo. *(eh 'eh-choh ehl trah-'bah-hoh)*

He's <u>put</u> the money here. **(Poner)**
Ha <u>puesto</u> el dinero aquí. *(ah 'pwehs-toh ehl dee-'neh-roh ah-'kee)*

We've <u>seen</u> the man. **(Ver)**
Hemos <u>visto</u> al hombre. *('eh-mohs 'vees-toh ahl 'ohm-breh)*

Let's Practice

A. Study this example and then fill in each blank below with the correct question:

Did you sell it?	(el carro)	<u>¿Lo vendió Ud.?</u>
1. Are you selling them?	(los libros)	_____
2. Have you sold it?	(la máquina)	_____
3. Will you sell it?	(el sombrero)	_____
4. Do you sell them?	(las sillas)	_____
5. Did you used to sell it?	(la leche)	_____

B. Write in the correct command:

<u>Yo</u> quiero saber. Tell me:	**Dígame.**
1. <u>Ella</u> quiere saber. Tell her:	_____
2. <u>Ellos</u> quieren saber. Tell them:	_____
3. <u>Nosotros</u> queremos saber. Tell us:	_____

C. Here's more verb review. Fill in the blanks with the correct forms. The first one is done for you:

TO BUY	COMPRAR
I'm buying	Estoy comprando
I buy	Compro
I will buy	Compraré
I bought	Compré
I used to buy	Compraba
I have bought	He comprado

1. TO SPEND	GASTAR
I'm spending	_____
I spend	_____
I will spend	_____
I spent	_____
I have spent	_____

2. TO SAVE	AHORRAR
I'm saving	_____
I save	_____
I will save	_____
I saved	_____
I used to save	_____
I have saved	_____

The Culture

The more trust that builds between you and your employee, the more comfortable you will feel around each other. Since hugging is a common form of greeting between friends, don't panic if someone leans forward to embrace you!

We're Done! Congratulations!
¡Hemos terminado! ¡Felicitaciones!
('eh-mohs tehr-mee-'nah-doh feh-lee-see-tah-see-'oh-nehs)

Good job, fellow employers! We've come to the end of our Spanish training in this guidebook. Hopefully, much of what you've read has already been put into practice, and you're excited about learning more. The vocabulary and grammar presentations, along with the language and culture tips, were specifically designed to get you started. So now, **mis amigos**, the rest is up to you.

Adiós y muy buena suerte,

Bill Harvey

English-Spanish Glossary

a, an **un, una** *(oon, 'oo-nah)*

A.M. **de la mañana** *(deh lah mahn-'yah-nah)*

above all **sobre todo** *('soh-breh 'toh-doh)*

above **encima** *(ehn-'see-mah)*

absences **las ausencias** *(lahs aw-'sehn-see-ahs)*

AC **la corriente alterna** *(lah kohr-ree-'ehn-teh ahl-'tehr-nah)*

acceptable **aceptable** *(ah-sehp-'tah-bleh)*

accessories **los accesorios** *(lohs ahk-seh-'soh-ree-ohs)*

accident **el accidente** *(ehl ahk-see-'dehn-teh)*

according to **según** *(seh-'goon)*

account **la cuenta** *(lah 'kwehn-tah)*

accountant **el contador/la contadora** *(ehl kohn-tah-'dohr/lah kohn-tah-'doh-rah)*

accounting **la contabilidad** *(lah kohn-tah-bee-lee-'dahd)*

adapter **el adaptador** *(ehl ah-dahp-'tah-'dohr)*

adding machine **la sumadora** *(lah soo-mah-'doh-rah)*

address **la dirección** *(la dee-rehk-see-'ohn)*

adequate **adecuado/adecuada** *(ah-deh-'kwah-doh/ah-deh-'kwah-dah)*

administration **la administración** *(lah ahd-mee-nees-trah-see-'ohn)*

administrator **el administrador/la administradora**
(ehl ahd-mee-nees-trah-'dohr/lah ahd-mee-nees-trah-'doh-rah)

advertisement **el anuncio** *(ehl ah-'noon-see-oh)*

advertising **la publicidad** *(lah poo-blee-see-'dahd)*

afraid **asustado/asustada** *(ah-soos-'tah-doh/ah-soos-'tah-dah)*

after **después** *(dehs-'pwehs)*

again **otra vez** *('oh-trah vehs)*

age **la edad** *(lah eh-'dahd)*

agency **la agencia** *(lah ah-'hehn-see-ah)*

agenda **la orden del día** *(lah 'ohr-dehn dehl 'dee-ah)*

agreement **el acuerdo** *(ehl ah-'kwehr-doh)*

air conditioning **el aire acondicionado** *(ehl 'ah-ee-reh ah-kohn-dee-see-oh-'nah-doh)*

airport **el aeropuerto** *(ehl ah-eh-roh-'pwehr-toh)*

aisle **el pasillo** *(ehl pah-'see-yoh)*

alarm **la alarma** *(lah ah-'lahr-mah)*

alcohol **el alcohol** *(ehl ahl-koh-'ohl)*

all **todo/toda** *('toh-doh/'toh-dah)*

allergy **la alergia** *(lah ah-'lehr-hee-ah)*

almost **casi** *('kah-see)*

alone **solo/sola** *('soh-loh/'soh-lah)*

although **aunque** *(ah-'oon-keh)*

aluminum **el aluminio** *(ehl ah-loo-'mee-nee-oh)*

always	**siempre** *(see-'ehm-preh)*
ambitious	**ambicioso/ambiciosa** *(ahm-bee-see-'oh-soh/ahm-bee-see-'oh-sah)*
ambulance	**la ambulancia** *(lah ahm-boo-'lahn-see-ah)*
amount	**la cantidad** *(lah kahn-tee-'dahd)*
amperage	**el amperaje** *(ehl ahm-peh-'rah-heh)*
analyst	**el analista/la analista** *(ehl ah-nah-'lees-tah/lah ah-nah-'lees-tah)*
and	**y** *(ee)*
angle	**el ángulo** *(ehl 'ahn-goo-loh)*
angry	**enojado/enojada** *(eh-noh-'hah-doh/eh-noh-'hah-dah)*
ankle	**el tobillo** *(ehl toh-'bee-yoh)*
announcement	**el anuncio** *(ehl ah-'noon-see-oh)*
answering machine	**el contestador telefónico**
	(ehl kohn-tehs-tah-'dohr teh-leh-'foh-nee-koh)
anxious	**ansioso/ansiosa** *(ahn-see-'oh-soh/ahn-see-'oh-sah)*
anyone	**cualquier persona** *(kwahl-kee-'ehr pehr-'soh-nah)*
anything	**cualquier cosa** *(kwahl-kee-'ehr 'koh-sah)*
anywhere	**en cualquier sitio** *(ehn kwahl-kee-'ehr 'see-tee-oh)*
apartment building	**el edificio de apartamentos**
	(ehl eh-dee-'fee-see-oh deh ah-pahr-tah-'mehn-tohs)
apathetic	**apático/apática** *(ah-'pah-tee-koh/ah-'pah-tee-kah)*
appliances	**los electrodomésticos** *(lohs eh-lehk-troh-doh-'mehs-tee-kohs)*
application	**la solicitud** *(lah soh-lee-see-'tood)*
appointment	**la cita** *(lah 'see-tah)*
approach	**el enfoque** *(ehl ehn-'foh-keh)*
appropriate	**apropiado/apropiada** *(ah-proh-pee-'ah-doh/ah-proh-pee-'ah-dah)*
April	**abril** *(ah-'breel)*
apron	**el mandil** *(ehl mahn-'deel)*
arbitration	**el arbitraje** *(ehl ahr-bee-'trah-heh)*
architect	**el arquitecto/la arquitecta**
	(ehl ahr-kee-'tehk-toh/lah ahr-kee-'tehk-tah)
area code	**el código telefónico** *(ehl 'koh-dee-goh teh-leh-'foh-nee-koh)*
area	**el área** *(ehl 'ah-reh-ah)*
argument	**la discusión** *(lah dees-koo-see-'ohn)*
arm	**el brazo** *(ehl 'brah-soh)*
armchair	**el sillón** *(ehl see-'yohn)*
article	**el artículo** *(ehl ahr-'tee-koo-loh)*
artist	**el artista** *(ehl ahr-'tees-tah)*
as	**como** *('koh-moh)*
asbestos	**el amianto** *(ehl ah-mee-'ahn-toh)*
as-is	**tal como está** *(tahl 'koh-moh ehs-'tah)*
assembly	**el montaje** *(ehl mohn-'tah-heh)*
assignments	**las tareas** *(lahs tah-'reh-ahs)*
assistant	**el asistente/la asistenta** *(ehl ah-sees-'tehn-teh/lah ah-sees-'tehn-tah)*

at	**en** *(ehn)*
ATM	**el cajero automático** *(eh kah-'heh-roh aw-toh-'mah-tee-koh)*
attachment	**el adjunto** *(ehl ahd-'hoon-toh)*
August	**agosto** *(ah-'gohs-toh)*
aunt	**la tía** *(lah 'tee-ah)*
authorized	**autorizado/autorizada** *(aw-toh-ree-'sah-doh/aw-toh-ree-'sah-dah)*
automatic	**automático/automática** *(aw-toh-'mah-tee-koh/aw-toh-'mah-tee-kah)*
available	**disponible** *(dees-poh-'nee-bleh)*
avenue	**la avenida** *(lah ah-veh-'nee-dah)*
average	**el promedio** *(ehl proh-'meh-dee-oh)*
award	**el galardón** *(ehl gah-lahr-'dohn)*
ax	**el hacha** *(ehl 'ah-chah)*
baby	**el/la bebé** *(ehl/lah beh-'beh)*
back	**la espalda** *(lah ehs-'pahl-dah)*
backache	**el dolor de espalda** *(ehl doh-'lohr deh ehs-'pahl-dah)*
back order	**el pedido atrasado** *(ehl peh-'dee-doh ah-trah-'sah-doh)*
back pay	**el pago atrasado** *(ehl 'pah-goh ah-trah-'sah-doh)*
back support	**la faja** *(lah 'fah-hah)*
backhoe	**la retroexcavadora** *(lah reh-troh-ex-kah-vah-'doh-rah)*
backwards	**al revés** *(ahl reh-'vehs)*
bad	**malo/mala** *('mah-loh/'mah-lah)*
badge	**la placa** *(lah 'plah-kah)*
bag	**la bolsa** *(lah 'bohl-sah)*
balance (econ.)	**el saldo** *(ehl 'sahl-doh)*
balcony	**el balcón** *(ehl bahl-'kohn)*
bandage	**el vendaje** *(ehl vehn-'dah-heh)*
bank	**el banco** *(ehl 'bahn-koh)*
banquet	**el banquete** *(ehl bahn-'keh-teh)*
bar (metal)	**la barra** *(lah 'bahr-rah)*
barbershop	**la peluquería** *(lah peh-loo-keh-'ree-ah)*
bargain	**la ganga** *(lah 'gahn-gah)*
barrel	**el barril** *(ehl bahr-'reel)*
barrier	**la barrera** *(lah bahr-'reh-rah)*
bartender	**el cantinero** *(ehl kahn-tee-'neh-roh)*
basket	**la canasta** *(lah kah-'nahs-tah)*
bathroom	**el baño** *(ehl 'bahn-yoh)*
battery	**el acumulador** *(ehl ah-koo-moo-lah-'dohr)*
batteries (dry cell)	**las pilas** *(lahs 'pee-lahs)*
beach	**la playa** *(lah 'plah-yah)*
bearing	**el cojinete** *(ehl koh-hee-'neh-teh)*
beauty salon	**el salón de belleza** *(ehl sah-'lohn deh beh-'yeh-sah)*
because	**porque** *('pohr-keh)*

before	**antes** *('ahn-tehs)*
behind	**detrás** *(deh-'trahs)*
bell	**la campana** *(lah kahm-'pah-nah)*
bellhop	**el botones** *(ehl boh-'toh-nehs)*
belt	**la correa** *(lah kohr-'reh-ah)*
belt (clothing)	**el cinturón** *(ehl seen-too-'rohn)*
bench	**el banco** *(ehl 'bahn-koh)*
benefits	**los beneficios** *(lohs beh-neh-'fee-see-ohs)*
bent	**doblado/doblada** *(doh-'blah-doh/doh-'blah-dah)*
bereavement	**estar de luto** *(ehs-'tahr deh 'loo-toh)*
besides	**además** *(ah-deh-'mahs)*
better	**mejor** *(meh-'hohr)*
bicycle	**la bicicleta** *(lah bee-see-'kleh-tah)*
big	**grande** *('grahn-deh)*
bill	**la cuenta** *(lah 'kwehn-tah)*
billboard	**la cartelera** *(lah kahr-teh-'leh-rah)*
binder	**la carpeta** *(lah kahr-'peh-tah)*
bit	**la broca** *(lah 'broh-kah)*
black	**negro/negra** *('neh-groh/'neh-grah)*
blast furnace	**el alto horno** *(ehl 'ahl-toh 'ohr-noh)*
bleach	**el cloro** *(ehl 'kloh-roh)*
blister	**la ampolla** *(lah ahm-'poh-yah)*
block	**el bloque** *(ehl 'bloh-keh)*
blocked	**bloqueado/bloqueada** *(bloh-keh-'ah-doh/bloh-keh-'ah-dah)*
blouse	**la blusa** *(lah 'bloo-sah)*
blower	**el soplador** *(ehl soh-plah-'dohr)*
blue	**azul** *(ah-'sool)*
board	**la tabla** *(lah 'tah-blah)*
boarding pass	**el pase de abordar** *(ehl 'pah-seh deh ah-bohr-'dahr)*
boat	**el barco** *(ehl 'bahr-koh)*
boiler	**la caldera** *(lah kahl-'deh-rah)*
bolt	**el perno** *(ehl 'pehr-noh)*
book	**el libro** *(ehl 'lee-broh)*
booklet	**el librito** *(ehl lee-'bree-toh)*
bookshelf	**el librero** *(ehl lee-'breh-roh)*
bookstore	**la librería** *(lah lee-breh-'ree-ah)*
booth	**el puesto** *(ehl 'pwehs-toh)*
boots	**las botas** *(lahs 'boh-tahs)*
bored	**aburrido/aburrida** *(ah-boor-'ree-doh/ah-boor-'ree-dah)*
boss	**el jefe/la jefa** *(ehl 'heh-feh/lah 'heh-fah)*
bothered	**molesto/molesta** *(moh-'lehs-toh/moh-'lehs-tah)*
bottle	**la botella** *(lah boh-'teh-yah)*
bottom	**el fondo** *(ehl 'fohn-doh)*

box	**la caja** *(lah 'kah-hah)*
boy	**el niño** *(ehl 'neen-yoh)*
brace	**el soporte** *(ehl soh-'pohr-teh)*
bracelet	**el brazalete** *(ehl brah-sah-'leh-teh)*
bracket	**la ménsula** *(lah 'mehn-soo-lah)*
branch	**la sucursal** *(lah soo-koor-'sahl)*
brand	**la marca** *(lah 'mahr-kah)*
brass	**el latón** *(ehl lah-'tohn)*
brave	**valiente** *(vah-lee-'ehn-teh)*
break	**la rotura** *(lah roh-'too-rah)*
breaker	**el cortacircuitos** *(ehl kohr-tah-seer-koo-'ee-tohs)*
breaks (rest)	**las pausas para descansar** *(lahs 'pah-oo-sahs 'pah-rah dehs-kahn-'sahr)*
brick	**el ladrillo** *(ehl lah-'dree-yoh)*
bridge	**el puente** *(ehl 'pwehn-teh)*
briefcase	**el maletín** *(ehl mah-leh-'teen)*
bright	**brillante** *(bree-'yahn-teh)*
brochure	**el folleto** *(ehl foh-'yeh-toh)*
broken	**roto/rota** *('roh-toh/'roh-tah)*
bronze	**el bronce** *(ehl 'brohn-seh)*
broom	**la escoba** *(lah ehs-'koh-bah)*
brother	**el hermano** *(ehl ehr-'mah-noh)*
brother-in-law	**el cuñado** *(ehl koon-'yah-doh)*
brown	**café** *(kah-'feh)*
browser	**el navegador** *(ehl nah-veh-gah-'dohr)*
bruise	**la contusión** *(lah kohn-too-see-'ohn)*
brush	**el cepillo** *(ehl seh-'pee-yoh)*
bucket	**el balde** *(ehl 'bahl-deh)*
building	**el edificio** *(ehl eh-dee-'fee-see-oh)*
bulb	**el foco, la bombilla** *(ehl 'foh-koh, lah bohm-'bee-yah)*
bulldozer	**el tractor oruga** *(ehl trahk-'tohr oh-'roo-gah)*
bulletin board	**el tablón de anuncios** *(ehl tah-'blohn deh ah-'noon-see-ohs)*
bump	**el bulto** *(ehl 'bool-toh)*
bunch	**el ramo** *(ehl 'rah-moh)*
burn	**la quemadura** *(lah keh-mah-'doo-rah)*
burned	**quemado/quemada** *(keh-'mah-doh/keh-'mah-dah)*
burner	**la quemadora** *(lah keh-mah-'doh-rah)*
bus	**el autobús** *(ehl aw-toh-'boos)*
bus stop	**la parada de autobús** *(lah pah-'rah-dah deh aw-toh-'boos)*
busboy	**el ayudante de camarero** *(ehl ah-yoo-'dahn-teh deh kah-mah-'reh-roh)*
business	**el negocio** *(ehl neh-'goh-see-oh)*
busy	**ocupado/ocupada** *(oh-koo-'pah-doh/oh-koo-'pah/dah)*

but	**pero, sino** *('peh-roh, 'see-noh)*
button	**el botón** *(ehl boh-'tohn)*
buyer	**el comprador/la compradora**
	(ehl kohm-prah-'dohr/lah kohm-prah-'doh-rah)
buzzer	**el timbre** *(ehl 'teem-breh)*
by	**por** *(pohr)*
cabinet	**el gabinete** *(ehl gah-bee-'neh-teh)*
cable	**el cable** *(ehl 'kah-bleh)*
cafeteria	**la cafetería** *(lah kah-feh-teh-'ree-ah)*
cage	**la jaula** *(lah 'hah-oo-lah)*
calculator	**la calculadora** *(lah kahl-koo-lah-'doh-rah)*
calendar	**el calendario** *(ehl kah-lehn-'dah-ree-oh)*
camcorder	**la filmadora** *(lah feel-mah-'doh-rah)*
camera	**la cámara** *(lah 'kah-mah-rah)*
campaign	**la campaña** *(lah kahm-'pahn-yah)*
can	**la lata** *(lah 'lah-tah)*
canister	**el bote** *(ehl 'boh-teh)*
canvas	**la lona** *(lah 'loh-nah)*
cap	**la gorra** *(lah 'gohr-rah)*
capable	**capaz** *(kah 'pahs)*
car	**el carro** *(ehl 'kahr-roh)*
car lot	**el lote de carros** *(ehl 'loh-teh deh 'kahr-rohs)*
card	**la tarjeta** *(lah tahr-'heh-tah)*
cardboard	**el cartón** *(ehl kahr-'tohn)*
career	**la carrera** *(lah kahr-'reh-rah)*
careless	**descuidado/descuidada** *(dehs-kwee-'dah-doh/dehs-kwee-'dah-dah)*
cargo	**la carga** *(lah 'kahr-gah)*
carpenter	**el carpintero** *(ehl kahr-peen-'teh-roh)*
carpet	**la alfombra** *(lah ahl-'fohm-brah)*
cart	**el carrito** *(ehl kahr-'ree-toh)*
cartridge	**el cartucho** *(ehl kahr-'too-choh)*
case	**la caja** *(lah 'kah-hah)*
cash	**el efectivo** *(ehl eh-fehk-'tee-voh)*
cash flow	**el flujo de caja** *(ehl 'floo-hoh deh 'kah-hah)*
cash register	**la registradora** *(lah reh-hees-trah-'doh-rah)*
cashier	**el cajero/la cajera** *(ehl kah-'heh-roh/lah kah-'heh-rah)*
cashier's check	**el cheque de caja** *(ehl 'cheh-keh deh 'kah-hah)*
casing	**la cubierta** *(lah koo-bee-'ehr-tah)*
catalogue	**el catálogo** *(ehl kah-'tah-loh-goh)*
ceiling	**el techo** *(ehl 'teh-choh)*
celebration	**la celebración** *(lah seh-leh-brah-see-'ohn)*
cell	**la célula** *(lah 'seh-loo-lah)*

cell phone	el **celular** *(ehl seh-loo-'lahr)*
cement	el **cemento** *(ehl seh-'mehn-toh)*
cement truck	el **camión hormigonero** *(ehl kah-mee-'ohn ohr-mee-goh-'neh-roh)*
center	el **centro** *(ehl 'sehn-troh)*
centimeter	el **centímetro** *(ehl sehn-'tee-meh-troh)*
ceremony	la **ceremonia** *(lah seh-reh-'moh-nee-ah)*
certificate	el **certificado** *(ehl sehr-tee-fee-'kah-doh)*
chain	la **cadena** *(lah kah-'deh-nah)*
chainsaw	la **motosierra** *(lah moh-toh-see-'ehr-rah)*
chair	la **silla** *(lah 'see-yah)*
change	el **cambio** *(ehl 'kahm-bee-oh)*
channel	el **canal** *(ehl kah-'nahl)*
chapter	el **capítulo** *(ehl kah-'pee-too-loh)*
charge	la **carga** *(lah 'kahr-gah)*
charger	la **cargadora** *(lah kahr-gah-'doh-rah)*
chart	el **diagrama** *(ehl dee-ah-'grah-mah)*
check	el **cheque** *(ehl 'cheh-keh)*
chemicals	los **productos químicos** *(lohs proh-'dook-tohs 'kee-mee-kohs)*
chest	el **baúl** *(ehl bah-'ool)*
chest (body)	el **pecho** *(ehl 'peh-choh)*
child care	el **cuidado del niño** *(ehl kwee-'dah-doh dehl 'neen-yoh)*
children	los **niños** *(lohs 'neen-yohs)*
chill	el **escalofrío** *(ehl ehs-kah-loh-'free-oh)*
chipped	**astillado/astillada** *(ahs-tee-'yah-doh/ahs-tee-'yah-dah)*
chisel	el **cincel** *(ehl seen-'sehl)*
chores	las **labores domésticas** *(lahs lah-'boh-rehs doh-'mehs-tee-kahs)*
church	la **iglesia** *(lah eeg-'leh-see-ah)*
circle	el **círculo** *(ehl 'seer-koo-loh)*
circuit	el **circuito** *(ehl seer-'kwee-toh)*
citizen	el **ciudadano/la ciudadana** *(ehl see-oo-dah-'dah-noh/lah see-oo-dah-'dah-nah)*
city	la **ciudad** *(lah see-oo-'dahd)*
city hall	el **municipio** *(ehl moo-nee-'see-pee-oh)*
claim	la **reclamación** *(lah reh-klah-mah-see-'ohn)*
clamp	la **abrazadera** *(lah ah-brah-sah-'deh-rah)*
clasp	el **broche** *(ehl 'broh-cheh)*
class	la **clase** *(lah 'klah-seh)*
clean	**limpio/limpia** *('leem-pee-oh/'leem-pee-ah)*
cleanser	el **limpiador** *(ehl leem-pee-ah-'dohr)*
clerk	el/la **dependiente** *(ehl/lah deh-pehn-dee-'ehn-teh)*
clinic	la **clínica** *(lah 'klee-nee-kah)*
clip	la **sujetadora** *(lah soo-heh-tah-'doh-rah)*
clock	el **reloj** *(ehl reh-'loh)*

closeout	**la liquidación** *(lah lee-kee-dah-see-'ohn)*
clothing	**la ropa** *(lah 'roh-pah)*
cloudy	**nublado/nublada** *(noo-'blah-doh/noo-'blah-dah)*
coal	**el carbón** *(ehl kahr-'bohn)*
code	**el código** *(ehl 'koh-dee-goh)*
coffee shop	**la cafetería** *(lah kah-feh-teh-'ree-ah)*
coil	**el rollo, la bobina** *(ehl 'roh-yoh, lah boh-'bee-nah)*
cold	**frío/fría** *('free-oh/'free-ah)*
cold (illness)	**el resfriado** *(ehl rehs-free-'ah-doh)*
color	**el color** *(ehl koh-'lohr)*
comb	**el peine** *(ehl 'peh-ee-neh)*
comment	**el comentario** *(ehl koh-mehn-'tah-ree-oh)*
commercial	**el comercial** *(ehl koh-mehr-see-'ahl)*
commissions	**las comisiones** *(lahs koh-mee-see-'oh-nehs)*
commitment	**el compromiso** *(ehl kohm-proh-'mee-soh)*
committee	**el comité** *(ehl koh-mee-'teh)*
communications	**las comunicaciones** *(lahs koh-moo-nee-kah-see-'oh-nehs)*
company	**la compañía** *(lah kohm-pah-'nee-ah)*
compartment	**el compartimiento** *(ehl kohm-pahr-tee-mee-'ehn-toh)*
competent	**competente** *(kohm-peh-'tehn-teh)*
competitor	**el competidor/la competidora** *(ehl kohm-peh-tee-'dohr/lah kohm-peh-tee-'doh-rah)*
complaint	**la queja** *(lah 'keh-hah)*
compound	**el compuesto** *(ehl kohm-'pwehs-toh)*
compressor	**el compresor** *(ehl kohm-preh-'sohr)*
computer	**la computadora** *(lah kohm-poo-tah-'doh-rah)*
computer file	**el fichero** *(ehl fee-'cheh-roh)*
concept	**el concepto** *(ehl kohn-'sehp-toh)*
condensers	**los condensadores** *(lohs kohn-dehn-sah-'doh-rehs)*
conditions	**las condiciones** *(lahs kohn-dee-see-'oh-nehs)*
conference	**la conferencia** *(lah kohn-feh-'rehn-see-ah)*
conference call	**la conferencia por teléfono** *(lah kohn-feh-'rehn-see-ah pohr teh-'leh-foh-noh)*
conference room	**la sala de conferencias** *(lah 'sah-lah deh kohn-feh-'rehn-see-ahs)*
confidence	**la confianza** *(lah kohn-fee-'ahn-sah)*
confirmation	**la confirmación** *(lah kohn-feer-mah-see-'ohn)*
conflict	**el conflicto** *(ehl kohn-'fleek-toh)*
confused	**confundido/confundida** *(kohn-foon-'dee-doh/kohn-foon-'dee-dah)*
connection	**la conexión** *(lah kohn-ehk-see-'ohn)*
consultant	**el consultor/la consultora** *(ehl kohn-sool-'tohr/lah kohn-sool-'toh-rah)*
consumer	**el consumidor/la consumidora** *(ehl kohn-soo-mee-'dohr/lah kohn-soo-mee-'doh-rah)*

container	**el contenedor** *(ehl kohn-teh-neh-'dohr)*
contaminated	**contaminado/contaminada** *(kohn-tah-mee-'nah-doh/kohn-tah-mee-'nah-dah)*
content	**el contenido** *(ehl kohn-teh-'nee-doh)*
contract	**el contrato** *(ehl kohn-'trah-toh)*
contractor	**el contratista/la contratista** *(ehl kohn-trah-'tees-tah/lah kohn-trah-'tees-tah)*
control	**el control** *(ehl kohn-'trohl)*
control panel	**el tablero de control** *(ehl tah-'bleh-roh deh kohn-'trohl)*
conveyor belt	**la correa transportadora** *(lah kohr-'reh-ah trahns-pohr-tah-'doh-rah)*
cook	**el cocinero/la cocinera** *(ehl koh-see-'neh-roh/lah koh-see-'neh-rah)*
cool	**fresco/fresca** *('frehs-koh/'frehs-kah)*
coordinator	**el coordinador/la coordinadora** *(ehl koh-ohr-dee-nah-'dohr/lah koh-ohr-dee-nah-'doh-rah)*
copier	**la copiadora** *(lah koh-pee-ah-'doh-rah)*
copper	**el cobre** *(ehl 'koh-breh)*
cord	**el cordón** *(ehl kohr-'dohn)*
cordless	**inalámbrico/inalámbrica** *(een-ah-'lahm-bre-koh/een-ah-'lahm-bree-kah)*
cordless drill	**el taladro portátil** *(ehl tah-'lah-droh pohr-'tah-teel)*
cordless phone	**el teléfono inalámbrico** *(ehl teh-'leh-foh-noh een-ah-'lahm-bree-koh)*
corner	**la esquina** *(lah ehs-'kee-nah)*
corporation	**la corporación** *(lah kohr-poh-rah-see-'ohn)*
correct	**correcto/correcta** *(kohr-'rehk-toh/kohr-'rehk-tah)*
corrosive	**corrosivo/corrosiva** *(kohr-roh-'see-voh/kohr-roh-'see-vah)*
cost	**el costo** *(ehl 'kohs-toh)*
cotton	**el algodón** *(ehl ahl-goh-'dohn)*
cough	**la tos** *(lah tohs)*
counter	**el mostrador** *(ehl mohs-trah-'dohr)*
country	**el país** *(ehl pah-'ees)*
county	**el condado** *(ehl kohn-'dah-doh)*
coupon	**el cupón** *(ehl koo-'pohn)*
courier	**el mensajero/la mensajera** *(ehl mehn-sah-'heh-roh/lah mehn-sah-'heh-rah)*
cousin (female)	**la prima** *(lah 'pree-mah)*
cousin (male)	**el primo** *(ehl 'pree-moh)*
CPR	**la respiración artificial** *(lah rehs-pee-rah-see-'ohn ahr-tee-fee-see-'ahl)*
crane	**la grúa** *(lah 'groo-ah)*
crank	**la manivela** *(lah mah-nee-'veh-lah)*
crate	**la caja de transporte** *(lah 'kah-hah deh trahns-'pohr-teh)*
creativity	**la creatividad** *(lah kreh-ah-tee-vee-'dahd)*

credit	**el crédito** *(ehl 'kreh-dee-toh)*
credit card	**la tarjeta de crédito** *(lah tahr-'heh-tah deh 'kreh-dee-toh)*
criteria	**el criterio** *(ehl kree-'teh-ree-oh)*
crosswalk	**el cruce de peatones** *(ehl 'kroo-seh deh peh-ah-'toh-nehs)*
crowbar	**la palanca** *(lah pah-'lahn-kah)*
crushed	**aplastado/aplastada** *(ah-plahs-'tah-doh/ah-plahs-'tah-dah)*
crutches	**las muletas** *(lahs moo-'leh-tahs)*
cube	**el cubo** *(ehl 'koo-boh)*
cubicle	**la cabina** *(lah kah-'bee-nah)*
cultural differences	**las diferencias culturales** *(lahs dee-feh-'rehn-see-ahs kool-too-'rah-lehs)*
cup	**la taza** *(lah 'tah-sah)*
cupboard	**el armario** *(ehl ahr-'mah-ree-oh)*
current	**la corriente** *(lah kohr-ree-'ehn-teh)*
curve	**la curva** *(lah 'koor-vah)*
cushion	**la almohadilla** *(lah ahl-moh-ah-'dee-yah)*
customer	**el cliente/la clienta** *(ehl klee-'ehn-teh/lah klee-ehn-tah)*
customer service	**el servicio para clientes** *(ehl sehr-'vee-see-oh 'pah-rah klee-'ehn-tehs)*
customs	**la aduana** *(lah ah-'dwah-nah)*
cut	**la cortada** *(lah kohr-'tah-dah)*
cutter	**la cortadora** *(lah kohr-tah-'doh-rah)*
cycle	**el ciclo** *(ehl 'seek-loh)*
cylinder	**el cilindro** *(ehl see-'leen-droh)*
dairy	**la lechería** *(lah leh-cheh-'ree-ah)*
damage	**el daño** *(ehl 'dahn-yoh)*
damaged	**dañado/dañada** *(dahn-'yah-doh/dahn-'yah-dah)*
danger	**el peligro** *(ehl peh-'lee-groh)*
dangerous	**peligroso/peligrosa** *(peh-lee-'groh-soh/peh-lee-'groh-sah)*
data	**los datos** *(lohs 'dah-tohs)*
database	**la base de datos** *(lah 'bah-seh deh 'dah-tohs)*
date	**la fecha** *(lah 'feh-chah)*
date of birth	**fecha de nacimiento** *(lah 'feh-chah deh nah-see-mee-'ehn-toh)*
daughter	**la hija** *(lah 'ee-hah)*
daughter-in-law	**la nuera** *(lah 'nweh-rah)*
day	**el día** *(ehl 'dee-ah)*
DC	**la corriente directa** *(lah kohr-ree-'ehn-teh dee-'rehk-tah)*
deadbolt	**el pestillo** *(ehl pehs-'tee-yoh)*
dealer	**el concesionario/la concesionaria** *(ehl kohn-seh-see-oh-'nah-ree-oh/lah kohn-seh-see-oh-'nah-ree-ah)*
death	**la muerte** *(lah 'mwehr-teh)*
December	**diciembre** *(dee-see-'ehm-breh)*

defective	**defectuoso/defectuosa** *(deh-fehk-too-'oh-soh/deh-fehk-too-'oh-sah)*
degree	**el grado** *(el 'grah-doh)*
delayed	**retrasado/retrasada** *(reh-trah-'sah-doh/reh-trah-'sah-dah)*
delivery	**la entrega** *(lah ehn-'treh-gah)*
delivery truck	**el camión de reparto** *(ehl kah-mee-'ohn deh reh-'pahr-toh)*
demands	**las reclamaciones** *(lahs reh-klah-mah-see-'oh-nehs)*
dentist	**el/la dentista** *(ehl/lah dehn-'tees-tah)*
department	**el departamento** *(ehl deh-pahr-tah-'mehn-toh)*
department store	**la tienda de departamentos**
	(lah tee-'ehn-dah deh deh-pahr-tah-'mehn-tohs)
depth	**la profundidad** *(lah proh-foon-dee-'dahd)*
desert	**el desierto** *(ehl deh-see-'ehr-toh)*
design	**el diseño** *(ehl dee-'sehn-yoh)*
desk	**el escritorio** *(ehl ehs-kree-'toh-ree-oh)*
destroyed	**destruido/destruida** *(dehs-troo-'ee-doh/dehs-troo-'ee-dah)*
detergent	**el detergente** *(ehl deh-tehr-'hehn-teh)*
device	**el aparato** *(ehl ah-pah-'rah-toh)*
diagonal	**diagonal** *(dee-ah-goh-'nahl)*
dial	**el dial** *(ehl dee-'ahl)*
difficult	**difícil** *(dee-'fee-seel)*
digital	**digital** *(dee-hee-'tahl)*
dinner	**la cena** *(lah 'seh-nah)*
diploma	**el diploma** *(ehl dee-'ploh-mah)*
directions	**las instrucciones** *(lahs eens-trook-see-'oh-nehs)*
director	**el director/la directora** *(ehl dee-rehk-'tohr/lah dee-rehk-'toh-rah)*
dirt	**la tierra** *(lah tee-'ehr-rah)*
dirty	**sucio/sucia** *('soo-see-oh/'soo-see-ah)*
disability insurance	**el seguro de incapacidad**
	(ehl seh-'goo-roh deh een-kah-pah-see-'dahd)
disconnected	**desconectado/desconectada**
	(dehs-koh-nehk-'tah-doh/dehs-koh-nehk-'tah-dah)
discount	**el descuento** *(ehl dehs-'kwehn-toh)*
dishonest	**deshonesto/deshonesta** *(dehs-oh-'nehs-toh/dehs-oh-'nehs-tah)*
dishwasher	**el/la lavaplatos** *(ehl/lah lah-vah 'plah-tohs)*
disk	**el disco** *(ehl 'dees-koh)*
dispute	**la disputa** *(lah dees-'poo-tah)*
disrespectful	**irrespetuoso/irrespetuosa**
	(eer-rehs-peh-'twoh-soh/eer-rehs-peh-'twoh-sah)
distance	**la distancia** *(lah dees-'tahn-see-ah)*
distracted	**distraído/distraída** *(dees-trah-'ee-doh/dees-trah-'ee-dah)*
district	**el distrito** *(ehl dees-'tree-toh)*
disturbance	**el disturbio** *(ehl dees-'toor-bee-oh)*
division	**la división** *(lah dee-vee-see-'ohn)*

divorce	**el divorcio** *(ehl dee-'vohr-see-oh)*
dizzy	**mareado/mareada** *(mah-reh-'ah-doh/mah-reh-'ah-dah)*
dock	**el muelle** *(ehl 'mweh-yeh)*
dock charge	**el cargo de muelle** *(ehl 'kahr-goh deh 'mweh-yeh)*
doctor	**el médico/la médica** *(ehl 'meh-dee-koh/lah 'meh-dee-kah)*
document	**el documento** *(ehl doh-koo-'mehn-toh)*
dolley	**el travelín** *(ehl trah-veh-'leen)*
domestic	**doméstico/doméstica** *(doh-'mehs-tee-koh/doh-'mehs-tee-kah)*
door	**la puerta** *(lah 'pwehr-tah)*
door-to-door	**de puerta en puerta** *(deh 'pwehr-tah ehn 'pwehr-tah)*
double	**el doble** *(ehl 'doh-bleh)*
down	**abajo** *(ah-'bah-hoh)*
down payment	**el pago inicial** *(ehl 'pah-goh ee-nee-see-'ahl)*
downtown	**el centro** *(ehl 'sehn-troh)*
dozen	**la docena** *(lah doh-'seh-nah)*
drain	**el drenaje** *(ehl dreh-'nah-heh)*
drawer	**el cajón** *(ehl kah-'hohn)*
drawing	**el dibujo** *(ehl dee-'boo-hoh)*
dress	**el vestido** *(ehl vehs-'tee-doh)*
drill	**el taladro** *(ehl tah-'lah-droh)*
drizzle	**la llovizna** *(lah yoh-'vees-nah)*
drugs	**las drogas** *(lahs 'droh-gahs)*
drum	**el barril** *(ehl bahr-'reel)*
dry cleaners	**la tintorería** *(lah teen-toh-reh-'ree-ah)*
duct	**el conducto** *(ehl kohn-'dook-toh)*
dump truck	**el camión volquete** *(ehl kah-mee-'ohn vohl-'keh-teh)*
dumpster	**el basurero de hierro** *(ehl bah-soo-'reh-roh deh ee-'ehr-roh)*
during	**durante** *(doo-'rahn-teh)*
dust pan	**la recogebasura** *(lah reh-koh-heh-bah-'soo-rah)*
dust	**el polvo** *(ehl 'pohl-voh)*
duties	**los deberes** *(lohs deh-'beh-rehs)*
duty free	**exento de impuestos** *(ex-'ehn-toh deh eem-'pwehs-tohs)*
ear	**el oído** *(ehl oh-'ee-doh)*
earplugs	**los tapones de oídos** *(lohs tah-'poh-nehs deh oh-'ee-dohs)*
early	**temprano/temprana** *(tehm-'prah-noh/tehm-'prah-nah)*
earnings	**las ganancias** *(lahs gah-'nahn-see-ahs)*
earring	**el arete** *(ehl ah-'reh-teh)*
earthquake	**el terremoto** *(ehl tehr-reh-'moh-toh)*
easy	**fácil** *('fah-seel)*
edge	**el borde** *(ehl 'bohr-deh)*
education	**la educación** *(lah eh-doo-kah-see-'ohn)*
efficient	**eficiente** *(eh-fee-see-'ehn-teh)*

eighth	**octavo/octava** *(ohk-'tah-voh/ohk-'tah-vah)*
elbow	**el codo** *(ehl 'koh-doh)*
electrical cable	**el cable eléctrico** *(ehl 'kah-bleh eh-'lehk-tree-koh)*
electrical outlet	**el tomacorriente** *(ehl toh-mah-kor-ree-'ehn-teh)*
electricity	**la electricidad** *(lah eh-lehk-tree-see-'dahd)*
electronic	**electrónico/electrónica** *(eh-lehk-'troh-nee-koh/eh-lehk-'troh-nee-kah)*
elevator	**el ascensor** *(ehl ahs-sehn-'sohr)*
e-mail	**el correo electrónico** *(ehl kohr-'reh-oh eh-lehk-'troh-nee-koh)*
embarrassed	**avergonzado/avergonzada** *(ah-vehr-gohn-'sah-doh/ah-vehr-gohn-'sah-dah)*
employed	**empleado/empleada** *(ehm-pleh-'ah-doh/ehm-pleh-'ah-dah)*
employee	**el empleado/la empleada** *(ehl ehm-pleh-'ah-doh/lah ehm-pleh-'ah-dah)*
employer	**el empresario/la empresaria** *(ehl ehm-preh-'sah-ree-oh/lah ehm-preh-'sah-ree-ah)*
engine	**el motor** *(ehl moh-'tohr)*
engineer	**el ingeniero/la ingeniera** *(ehl een-heh-nee-'eh-roh/lah een-heh-nee-'eh-rah)*
enough	**bastante** *(bahs-'tahn-teh)*
enthusiasm	**el entusiasmo** *(ehl ehn-too-see-'ahs-moh)*
entrance	**la entrada** *(lah ehn-'trah-dah)*
envelope	**el sobre** *(ehl 'soh-breh)*
environmental	**ambiental** *(ahm-bee-'ehn-tahl)*
equals	**es igual a** *(ehs ee-'gwahl ah)*
equipment	**el equipo** *(ehl eh-'kee-poh)*
eraser	**el borrador** *(ehl bohr-rah-'dohr)*
error	**el error** *(ehl ehr-'rohr)*
escalator	**la escalera mecánica** *(lah ehs-kah-'leh-rah meh-'kah-nee-kah)*
even	**llano** *('yah-noh)*
everyone	**todos** *('toh-dohs)*
everything	**todo** *('toh-doh)*
everywhere	**por todas partes** *(pohr 'toh-dahs 'pahr-tehs)*
example	**el ejemplo** *(ehl eh-'hehm-ploh)*
excellent	**excelente** *(ex-seh-'lehn-teh)*
exceptional	**excepcional** *(ex-sehp-see-oh-'nahl)*
exhaust	**el escape** *(ehl ehs-'kah-peh)*
exhausted	**agotado/agotada** *(ah-goh-'tah-doh/ah-goh-'tah-dah)*
exit	**la salida** *(lah sah-'lee-dah)*
expenses	**los gastos** *(lohs 'gahs-tohs)*
expensive	**caro/cara** *('kah-roh/'kah-rah)*
expertise	**la competencia** *(lah kohm-peh-'tehn-see-ah)*
explosion	**la explosión** *(lah ex-ploh-see-'ohn)*
explosive	**el explosivo** *(ehl ex-ploh-'see-voh)*

express mail	**el correo expreso** *(ehl kohr-'reh-oh ex-'preh-soh)*
extension cord	**el cable de extensión** *(ehl 'kah-bleh deh ex-tehn-see-'ohn)*
extension	**la extensión** *(lah ex-tehn-see-'ohn)*
eye	**el ojo** *(ehl 'oh-hoh)*
fabric	**la tela** *(lah 'teh-lah)*
fabulous	**fabuloso/fabulosa** *(fah-boo-'loh-soh/fah-boo-'loh-sah)*
face	**la cara** *(lah 'kah-rah)*
facility	**la instalación** *(lah eens-tah-lah-see-'ohn)*
factory	**la fábrica** *(lah 'fah-bree-kah)*
facts	**los hechos** *(lohs 'eh-chohs)*
faint	**desmayado/desmayada** *(dehs-mah-'yah-doh/dehs-mah-'yah-dah)*
fall (noun)	**la caída** *(lah kah-'ee-dah)*
fall (season)	**el otoño** *(ehl oh-'tohn-yoh)*
fall equipment	**la protección contra caídas** *(lah proh-tehk-see-'ohn 'kohn-trah kah-'ee-dahs)*
family	**la familia** *(lah fah-'mee-lee-ah)*
family business	**la empresa familiar** *(lah ehm-'preh-sah fah-mee-lee-'ahr)*
fan	**el ventilador** *(ehl vehn-tee-lah-'dohr)*
fantastic	**fantástico/fantástica** *(fahn-'tahs-tee-koh/fahn-'tahs-tee-kah)*
far	**lejos** *('leh-hohs)*
farm	**la finca** *(lah 'feen-kah)*
farmer	**el granjero/la granjera** *(ehl grahn-'heh-roh/lah grahn-'heh-rah)*
fast	**rápido/rápida** *('rah-pee-doh/'rah-pee-dah)*
fastener	**el cierre** *(ehl see-'ehr-reh)*
faster	**más rápido** *(mahs 'rah-pee-doh)*
fat	**gordo/gorda** *('gohr-doh/'gohr-dah)*
father	**el padre** *(ehl 'pah-dreh)*
father-in-law	**el suegro** *(ehl 'sweh-groh)*
faucet	**el grifo** *(ehl 'gree-foh)*
fax machine	**el fax** *(ehl fahks)*
February	**febrero** *(feh-'breh-roh)*
feeder	**la alimentadora** *(lah ah-lee-mehn-tah-'doh-rah)*
felony	**el delito mayor** *(ehl deh-'lee-toh mah-'yohr)*
fence	**la cerca** *(lah 'sehr-kah)*
festival	**el festival** *(ehl fehs-tee-'vahl)*
fever	**la fiebre** *(lah fee-'eh-breh)*
fiberglass	**la fibra de vidrio** *(lah 'fee-brah deh 'veed-ree-oh)*
field	**el campo** *(ehl 'kahm-poh)*
fifth	**quinto/quinta** *('keen-toh/'keen-tah)*
fight	**la pelea** *(lah peh-'leh-hah)*
file	**el archivo** *(ehl ahr-'chee-voh)*
file (tool)	**la lima** *(lah 'lee-mah)*

film	**la película** *(lah peh-'lee-koo-lah)*
filter	**el filtro** *(ehl 'feel-troh)*
finance	**las finanzas** *(lahs fee-'nahn-sahs)*
finger	**el dedo** *(ehl 'deh-doh)*
fire	**el fuego** *(ehl 'fweh-goh)*
fire department	**el departamento de bomberos** *(ehl deh-pahr-tah-'mehn-toh deh bohm-'beh-rohs)*
fire drill	**el simulacro de incendio** *(ehl see-moo-'lahk-roh deh een-'sehn-dee-oh)*
firearm	**el arma de fuego** *(ehl 'ahr-mah deh 'fweh-goh)*
fired	**despedido/depedida** *(dehs-peh-'dee-doh/dehs-peh-'dee-dah)*
firefighter	**el bombero/la bombera** *(ehl bohm-'beh-roh/lah bohm-'beh-rah)*
firm	**la empresa** *(lah ehm-'preh-sah)*
first	**primero/primera** *(pree-'meh-roh/pree-'meh-rah)*
first aid	**los primeros auxilios** *(lohs pree-'meh-rohs ah-ook-'see-lee-ohs)*
first name	**el primer nombre** *(ehl pree-'mehr 'nohm-breh)*
flames	**las llamas** *(lahs 'yah-mahs)*
flammable	**inflamable** *(een-flah-'mah-bleh)*
flatbed truck	**el camión de plataforma** *(ehl kah-mee-'ohn deh plah-tah-'fohr-mah)*
flight	**el vuelo** *(ehl voo-'eh-loh)*
flight number	**el número del vuelo** *(ehl 'noo-meh-roh deh voo-'eh-loh)*
flood	**la inundación** *(lah ee-noon-dah-see-'ohn)*
floor	**el piso** *(ehl 'pee-soh)*
floor tile	**la baldosa** *(lah bahl-'doh-sah)*
flow	**el flujo** *(ehl 'floo-hoh)*
flower shop	**la floristería** *(lah floh-rees-teh-'ree-ah)*
flu	**la influenza** *(lah een-floo-'ehn-sah)*
fluid ounce	**la onza fluida** *(lah 'ohn-sah floo-'ee-dah)*
foam	**la espuma** *(lah ehs-'poo-mah)*
folder	**la carpeta** *(lah kahr-'peh-tah)*
food	**la comida** *(lah koh-'mee-dah)*
foot	**el pie** *(ehl pee-'eh)*
for	**para, por** *('pah-rah, pohr)*
for example	**por ejemplo** *(pohr eh-'hehm-ploh)*
force	**la fuerza** *(lah 'fwehr-sah)*
forecast	**el pronóstico** *(ehl proh-'nohs-tee-koh)*
foreign	**extranjero/extranjera** *(ex-trahn-'heh-roh/ex-trahn-'heh-rah)*
forest	**el bosque** *(ehl 'bohs-keh)*
forge	**la fragua** *(lah 'frah-gwah)*
forklift	**la carretilla elevadora** *(lah kahr-reh-'tee-yah eh-leh-vah-'doh-rah)*
form	**el formulario** *(ehl fohr-moo-'lah-ree-oh)*
foul language	**el lenguaje sucio** *(ehl lehn-'gwah-heh 'soo-see-oh)*
fountain	**la fuente** *(lah 'fwehn-teh)*

fourth	**cuarto/cuarta** *('kwahr-toh/'kwahr-tah)*
fraction	**la fracción** *(lah frahk-see-'ohn)*
franchise	**la concesión** *(lah kohn-seh-see-'ohn)*
fraud	**el fraude** *(ehl 'frah-oo-deh)*
free	**gratuito/gratuita** *(grah-too-'ee-toh/grah-too-'ee-tah)*
freight	**el flete** *(ehl 'fleh-teh)*
Friday	**el viernes** *(ehl vee-'ehr-nehs)*
friend	**el amigo/la amiga** *(ehl ah-'mee-goh/lah ah-'mee-gah)*
friendly	**amistoso/amistosa** *(ah-mees-'toh-soh/ah-mees-'toh-sah)*
from	**de** *(deh)*
frost	**la escarcha** *(lah ehs-'kahr-chah)*
frustrated	**frustrado/frustrada** *(froos-'trah-doh/froos-'trah-dah)*
fuel	**el combustible** *(ehl kohm-boos-'tee-bleh)*
full name	**el nombre completo** *(ehl 'nohm-breh kohm-'pleh-toh)*
full-time	**el tiempo completo** *(ehl tee-'ehm-poh kohm-'pleh-toh)*
fumes	**las emanaciones** *(lahs eh-mah-nah-see-'oh-nehs)*
funny	**chistoso/chistosa** *(chees-'toh-soh/chees-'toh-sah)*
furniture	**los muebles** *(lohs 'mweh-blehs)*
fuse	**el fusible** *(ehl foo-'see-bleh)*
gallon	**el galón** *(ehl gah-'lohn)*
games	**los juegos** *(lohs 'hweh-gohs)*
gap	**el hueco** *(ehl 'hweh-koh)*
garden	**el jardín** *(ehl hahr-'deen)*
gardener	**el jardinero** *(ehl hahr-dee-'neh-roh)*
gas	**el gas** *(ehl gahs)*
gas meter	**el medidor de gas** *(ehl meh-dee-'dohr deh gahs)*
gas station	**la gasolinera** *(lah gah-soh-lee-'neh-rah)*
gasoline	**la gasolina** *(lah gah-soh-'lee-nah)*
gate	**el portón** *(ehl pohr-'tohn)*
gauge	**el indicador** *(ehl een-dee-kah-'dohr)*
gear	**el engranaje** *(ehl ehn-grah-'nah-heh)*
generator	**el generador** *(ehl heh-neh-rah-'dohr)*
gift	**el regalo** *(ehl reh-'gah-loh)*
girl	**la niña** *(lah 'neen-yah)*
glass	**el vidrio** *(ehl 'vee-dree-oh)*
glass (drinking)	**el vaso** *(ehl 'vah-soh)*
global	**mundial** *(moon-dee-'ahl)*
gloves	**los guantes** *(lohs 'gwahn-tehs)*
glue	**el pegamento** *(ehl peh-gah-'mehn-toh)*
goal	**la meta** *(lah 'meh-tah)*
goggles	**las gafas** *(lahs 'gah-fahs)*
good	**bueno/buena** *('bweh-noh/'bweh-nah)*

goods	**los bienes** *(lohs bee-'eh-nehs)*
GPS	**el sistema de posicionamiento global**
	(ehl sees-'teh-mah deh poh-see-see-oh-nah-'mee-'ehn-toh gloh-'bahl)
gram	**el gramo** *(ehl 'grah-moh)*
granddaughter	**la nieta** *(lah nee-'eh-tah)*
grandfather	**el abuelo** *(ehl ah-'bweh-loh)*
grandmother	**la abuela** *(lah ah-'bweh-lah)*
grandson	**el nieto** *(ehl nee-'eh-toh)*
graph	**el gráfico** *(ehl 'grah-fee-koh)*
gravel	**la grava** *(lah 'grah-vah)*
gray	**gris** *(grees)*
grease	**la grasa** *(lah 'grah-sah)*
green	**verde** *('vehr-deh)*
green card	**la tarjeta verde** *(lah tahr-'heh-tah 'vehr-deh)*
grievances	**las quejas** *(lahs 'keh-hahs)*
grinder	**el molinero** *(ehl moh-lee-'neh-roh)*
groove	**la muesca** *(lah 'mwehs-kah)*
group	**el grupo** *(ehl 'groo-poh)*
guarantee	**la garantía** *(lah gah-rahn-'tee-ah)*
guide	**el/la guía** *(ehl/lah 'gee-ah)*
guidelines	**las pautas** *(lahs 'pah-oo-tahs)*
hacksaw	**la sierra de metales** *(lah see-'ehr-rah deh meh-'tah-lehs)*
hail	**el granizo** *(ehl grah-'nee-soh)*
hair	**el pelo** *(ehl 'peh-loh)*
hair net	**la redecilla del pelo** *(lah reh-deh-'see-yah dehl 'peh-loh)*
hairbrush	**el cepillo** *(ehl seh-'pee-yoh)*
hairspray	**la laca** *(lah 'lah-kah)*
half	**la mitad** *(lah mee-'tahd)*
hallway	**el corredor** *(ehl kohr-reh-'dohr)*
hammer	**el martillo** *(ehl mahr-'tee-yoh)*
hand	**la mano** *(lah 'mah-noh)*
handful	**el puñado** *(ehl poon-'yah-doh)*
handle	**la perilla** *(lah peh-'ree-yah)*
handling	**los gastos de tramitación**
	(lohs 'gahs-tohs deh trah-mee-tah-see-'ohn)
handsaw	**el serrucho, la sierra** *(ehl sehr-'roo-choh, lah see-'ehr-rah)*
handsome	**guapo/guapa** *('gwah-poh/'gwah-pah)*
hard	**duro/dura** *('doo-roh/'doo-rah)*
hard drive	**el disco duro** *(ehl 'dees-koh 'doo-roh)*
hard hat	**el casco** *(ehl 'kahs-koh)*
harness	**el correaje** *(ehl kohr-reh-'ah-heh)*
hat	**el sombrero** *(ehl sohm-'breh-roh)*

hatch	**la escotilla** *(lah ehs-koh-'tee-yah)*
hazard	**el peligro** *(ehl peh-'lee-groh)*
he	**él** *(ehl)*
head	**la cabeza** *(lah kah-'beh-sah)*
headache	**el dolor de cabeza** *(ehl doh-'lohr deh kah-'beh-sah)*
headphones	**los auriculares** *(lohs aw-ree-koo-'lah-rehs)*
headquarters	**la oficina principal** *(lah oh-fee-'see-nah preen-see-'pahl)*
headset	**los auriculares con micrófono** *(lohs aw-ree-koo-'lah-rehs kohn mee-'kroh-foh-noh)*
healthy	**saludable** *(sah-loo-'dah-bleh)*
heart	**el corazón** *(ehl koh-rah-'sohn)*
heart attack	**el infarto** *(ehl een-'fahr-toh)*
heat	**el calor** *(ehl kah-'lohr)*
heater	**el calentador** *(ehl kah-lehn-tah-'dohr)*
heating	**la calefacción** *(lah kah-leh-fahk-see-'ohn)*
heatstroke	**la insolación** *(lah een-soh-lah-see-'ohn)*
heavy	**pesado/pesada** *(peh-'sah-doh/peh-'sah-dah)*
height	**la altura** *(lah ahl-'too-rah)*
helicopter	**el helicóptero** *(ehl eh-lee-'kohp-teh-roh)*
helmet	**el casco** *(ehl 'kahs-koh)*
helper	**el ayudante/la ayudanta** *(ehl ah-yoo-'dahn-teh/lah ah-yoo-'dahn-tah)*
her	**su, sus** *(soo, soos)*
here	**aquí** *(ah-'kee)*
hers	**suya, suyas** *('soo-yah, 'soo-yahs)*
high	**alto/alta** *('ahl-toh/'ahl-tah)*
highway	**la carretera** *(lah kahr-reh-'teh-rah)*
hinge	**la bisagra** *(lah bee-'sah-grah)*
hip	**la cadera** *(lah kah-'deh-rah)*
his	**su, sus** *(soo, soos)*
hole	**el hoyo** *(ehl 'oh-yoh)*
home office	**la oficina matriz** *(lah oh-fee-'see-nah mah-'trees)*
honesty	**la honradez** *(lah ohn-rah-'dehs)*
hook	**el gancho** *(ehl 'gahn-choh)*
horn	**la bocina** *(lah boh-'see-nah)*
horsepower	**el caballo de fuerza** *(ehl kah-'bah-yoh deh 'fwehr-sah)*
hose	**la manguera** *(lah mahn-'geh-rah)*
hospital	**el hospital** *(ehl ohs-pee-'tahl)*
hot	**caliente** *(kah-lee-'ehn-teh)*
hotel	**el hotel** *(ehl oh-'tehl)*
house	**la casa** *(lah 'kah-sah)*
How?	**¿Cómo?** *('koh-moh)*
How many?	**¿Cuántos?/¿Cuántas?** *('kwahn-tohs/'kwahn-tahs)*

How much?	**¿Cuánto?** *('kwahn-toh)*
however	**sin embargo** *(seen ehm-'bahr-goh)*
human resources	**los recursos humanos** *(lohs reh-'koor-sohs oo-'mah-nohs)*
hurricane	**el huracán** *(ehl oo-rah-'kahn)*
husband	**el esposo, el marido** *(ehl ehs-'poh-soh, ehl mah-'ree-doh)*
hydraulic	**hidráulico/hidráulica** *(ee-'drah-oo-lee-koh/ee-'drah-oo-lee-kah)*
I	**yo** *(yoh)*
ice	**el hielo** *(ehl ee-'eh-loh)*
icon	**el ícono** *(ehl 'ee-koh-noh)*
idea	**la idea** *(lah ee-'deh-ah)*
identification	**la identificación** *(lah ee-dehn-tee-fee-kah-see-'ohn)*
ill	**enfermo/enferma** *(ehn-'fehr-moh/ehn-'fehr-mah)*
illegal	**ilegal** *(ee-leh-'gahl)*
illness	**la enfermedad** *(lah ehn-fehr-meh-'dahd)*
imported	**importado/importada** *(eem-pohr-'tah-doh/eem-pohr-'tah-dah)*
in front	**enfrente** *(ehn-'frehn-teh)*
in	**en** *(ehn)*
inch	**la pulgada** *(lah pool-'gah-dah)*
included	**incluido/incluida** *(een-kloo-'ee-doh/een-kloo-'ee-dah)*
incompetent	**incompetente** *(een-kohm-peh-tehn-teh)*
incomplete	**incompleto/incompleta** *(een-kohm-'pleh-toh/een-kohm-'pleh-tah)*
incorrect	**incorrecto/incorrecta** *(een-kohr-'rehk-toh/een-kohr-'rehk-tah)*
incredible	**increíble** *(een-kreh-'ee-bleh)*
independent	**independiente** *(een-deh-pehn-dee-'ehn-teh)*
index	**el índice** *(ehl 'een-dee-seh)*
industrial complex	**el complejo industrial** *(ehl kohm-'pleh-hoh een-doos-tree-'ahl)*
industrious	**trabajador/trabajadora** *(trah-bah-hah-'dohr/trah-bah-hah-'doh-rah)*
inexpensive	**barato/barata** *(bah-'rah-toh/bah-'rah-tah)*
information	**la información** *(lah een-fohr-mah-see-'ohn)*
initiative	**la iniciativa** *(lah ee-nee-see-ah-'tee-vah)*
injury	**la herida** *(lah eh-'ree-dah)*
ink	**la tinta** *(lah 'teen-tah)*
inoperative	**inoperante** *(ee-noh-peh-'rahn-teh)*
input	**la aportación** *(lah ah-pohr-tah-see-'ohn)*
inside	**adentro** *(ah-'dehn-troh)*
installment	**el plazo** *(ehl 'plah-soh)*
institution	**la institución** *(lah eens-tee-too-see-'ohn)*
instructions	**las instrucciones** *(lahs eens-trook-see-'oh-nehs)*
instrument	**el instrumento** *(el eens-troo-'mehn-toh)*
insurance	**el seguro** *(ehl seh-'goo-roh)*
intelligent	**inteligente** *(een-teh-lee-'hehn-teh)*

intercom	**el intercomunicador** *(ehl een-tehr-koh-moo-nee-kah-'dohr)*
interested	**interesado/interesada** *(een-teh-reh-'sah-doh/een-teh-reh-'sah-dah)*
interim	**provisional** *(proh-vee-see-oh-nahl)*
international	**internacional** *(een-tehr-nah-see-oh-'nahl)*
Internet	**el internet** *(ehl een-tehr-'neht)*
interpretation	**la interpretación** *(lah een-tehr-preh-tah-see-'ohn)*
interstate	**interestatal** *(een-tehr-ehs-tah-'tahl)*
interview	**la entrevista** *(lah ehn-treh-'vees-tah)*
in-the-red	**endeudado/endeudada** *(ehn-deh-oo-'dah-doh/ehn-deh-oo-'dah-dah)*
inventory	**las existencias** *(lahs ex-ees-'tehn-see-ahs)*
invoice	**la factura** *(lah fahk-'too-rah)*
iron	**el hierro** *(ehl ee-'ehr-roh)*
irresponsible	**irresponsable** *(eer-rehs-pohn-'sah-bleh)*
issue (subject)	**el asunto** *(ehl ah-'soon-toh)*
jacket	**la chaqueta** *(lah chah-'keh-tah)*
jackhammer	**el martillo neumático** *(ehl mahr-'tee-yoh neh-oo-'mah-tee-koh)*
janitor	**el conserje** *(ehl kohn-'sehr-heh)*
January	**enero** *(eh-'neh-roh)*
jar	**la jarra** *(lah 'hahr-rah)*
jaw	**la mandíbula** *(lah mahn 'doo boo lah)*
jealous	**celoso/celosa** *(seh-'loh-soh/seh-'loh-sah)*
job	**el trabajo** *(ehl trah-'bah-hoh)*
job application	**la solicitud de trabajo** *(lah soh-lee-see-'tood deh trah-'bah-hoh)*
joist	**la vigueta** *(lah vee-'geh-tah)*
July	**julio** *('hoo-lee-oh)*
June	**junio** *('hoo-nee-'oh)*
key	**la tecla** *(lah 'teh-klah)*
key (lock)	**la llave** *(lah 'yah-veh)*
keyboard	**el teclado** *(ehl teh-'klah-doh)*
kidneys	**los riñones** *(lohs reen-'yoh-nehs)*
kilogram	**el kilogramo** *(ehl kee-loh-'grah-moh)*
kilometer	**el kilómetro** *(ehl kee-'loh-meh-troh)*
kind	**amable** *(ah-'mah-bleh)*
kit	**el estuche** *(eh ehs-'too-cheh)*
knee	**la rodilla** *(lah roh-'dee-yah)*
kneepads	**las rodilleras** *(lahs roh-dee-'yeh-rahs)*
knob	**el tirador** *(ehl tee-rah-'dohr)*
label	**la etiqueta** *(lah eh-tee-'keh-tah)*
laboratory	**el laboratorio** *(ehl lah-boh-rah-'toh-ree-oh)*
laborer	**el obrero/la obrera** *(ehl oh-'breh-roh/lah oh-'breh-rah)*

ladder	**la escalera** *(lah ehs-kah-'leh-rah)*
ladle	**el cucharón** *(ehl koo-chah-'rohn)*
lake	**el lago** *(ehl 'lah-goh)*
lamp	**la lámpara** *(lah 'lahm-pah-rah)*
language	**el lenguaje** *(ehl lehn-'gwah-heh)*
laptop	**la computadora portátil** *(lah kohm-poo-tah-'doh-rah pohr-'tah-teel)*
large	**grande** *('grahn-deh)*
laser	**el láser** *(ehl 'lah-sehr)*
last	**último/última** *('ool-tee-moh/'ool-tee-mah)*
last name	**el apellido** *(ehl ah-peh-'yee-doh)*
last night	**anoche** *(ah-'noh-cheh)*
latch	**el cerrojo** *(ehl sehr-'roh-hoh)*
late	**tarde** *('tahr-deh)*
later	**luego** *('lweh-goh)*
lathe	**el torno** *(ehl 'tohr-noh)*
laundromat	**la lavandería** *(lah lah-vahn-deh-'ree-ah)*
laws	**las leyes** *(lahs 'leh-yehs)*
lawsuit	**el pleito** *(ehl 'pleh-ee-toh)*
lawyer	**el abogado/la abogada** *(ehl ah-boh-'gah-doh/lah ah-boh-'gah-dah)*
leather	**el cuero** *(ehl 'kweh-roh)*
left	**la izquierda** *(lah ees-kee-'ehr-dah)*
length	**el largo** *(ehl 'lahr-goh)*
lesson	**la lección** *(lah lehk-see-'ohn)*
letter	**la letra** *(lah 'leh-trah)*
letter (mail)	**la carta** *(lah 'kahr-tah)*
level	**el nivel** *(ehl nee-'vehl)*
lever	**la palanca** *(lah pah-'lahn-kah)*
librarian	**el bibliotecario/la bibliotecaria** *(ehl bee-blee-oh-teh-'kah-ree-oh/ lah bee-blee-oh-teh-'kah-ree-ah)*
library	**la biblioteca** *(lah bee-blee-oh-'teh-kah)*
license	**la licencia** *(lah lee-sehn-see-ah)*
light	**la luz** *(lah loos)*
light (weight)	**ligero/ligera** *(lee-heh-roh/lee-heh-rah)*
lightbulb	**el foco** *(ehl 'foh-koh)*
lighting	**la iluminación** *(lah ee-loo-mee-nah-see-'ohn)*
lightning	**el relámpago** *(ehl reh-'lahm-pah-goh)*
line	**la línea** *(lah 'lee-neh-ah)*
lining	**el forro** *(ehl 'fohr-roh)*
liquid	**el líquido** *(ehl 'lee-kee-doh)*
list	**la lista** *(lah 'lees-tah)*
liter	**el litro** *(ehl 'lee-troh)*
little	**chico/chica** *('chee-koh/'chee-kah)*
load	**la carga** *(lah 'kahr-gah)*

loader	**la cargadora** *(lah kahr-'gah-'doh-rah)*
lobby	**el vestíbulo** *(ehl vehs-'tee-boo-loh)*
local	**local** *(loh-'kahl)*
lock	**la cerradura** *(lah sehr-rah-'doo-rah)*
logo	**el logotipo** *(ehl loh-goh-'tee-poh)*
long	**largo/larga** *('lahr-goh/'lahr-gah)*
loose	**suelto/suelta** *('swehl-toh/'swehl-tah)*
loss	**la pérdida** *(lah 'pehr-dee-dah)*
lost	**perdido/perdida** *(pehr-'dee-doh/pehr-'dee-dah)*
lost and found	**la oficina de objetos perdidos** *(lah oh-fee-'see-nah deh ohb-'heh-tohs pehr-'dee-dohs)*
luggage	**el equipaje** *(ehl eh-kee-'pah-heh)*
lumber (piece)	**el madero** *(ehl mah-'deh-roh)*
lungs	**los pulmones** *(lohs pool-'moh-nehs)*
machine	**la máquina** *(lah 'mah-kee-nah)*
machinist	**el operario de máquina** *(ehl oh-peh-'rah-ree-oh deh 'mah-kee-nah)*
magazine	**la revista** *(lah reh-'vees-tah)*
magnet	**el imán** *(ehl ee-'mahn)*
maiden name	**el nombre de soltera** *(ehl 'nohm-breh deh sohl-'teh-rah)*
mail	**el correo** *('ehl kohr-'reh-oh)*
mail carrier	**el/la cartero** *(ehl/lah kahr-'teh-roh)*
mail order	**el pedido por correo** *(ehl peh-'dee-doh pohr kohr-'reh-oh)*
mailbox	**el buzón** *(ehl boo-'sohn)*
mailing list	**la planilla de direcciones** *(lah plah-'nee-yah deh dee-rehk-see-'oh-nehs)*
mailroom	**la oficina de correspondencia** *(lah oh-fee-'see-nah deh kohr-rehs-pohn-'dehn-see-ah)*
maintenance	**el mantenimiento** *(ehl mahn-teh-nee-mee-'ehn-toh)*
makeup	**el maquillaje** *(ehl mah-kee-'yah-heh)*
malfunction	**la disfunción** *(lah dees-foon-see-'ohn)*
mallet	**el mazo** *(ehl 'mah-soh)*
man	**el hombre** *(ehl 'ohm-breh)*
manager	**el gerente/la gerenta** *(ehl heh-'rehn-teh/lah heh-'rehn-tah)*
manner	**la manera** *(lah mah-'neh-rah)*
manpower	**la mano de obra** *(lah 'mah-noh deh 'oh-brah)*
manufacturer	**el/la fabricante** *(ehl/la fah-bree-'kahn-teh)*
manufacturing	**la fabricación** *(lah fah-bree-kah-see-'ohn)*
map	**el mapa** *(ehl 'mah-pah)*
march (strike)	**la manifestación** *(lah mah-nee-fehs-tah-see-'ohn)*
March	**marzo** *('mahr-soh)*
margin	**el margen** *(ehl 'mahr-hehn)*
marital status	**el estado civil** *(ehl ehs-'tah-doh see-'veel)*

mark	**la marca** *(lah 'mahr-kah)*
markdown	**la reducción de precio** *(lah reh-dook-see-'ohn deh 'preh-see-oh)*
marker	**el marcador** *(ehl mahr-kah-'dohr)*
marketing	**el mercadeo** *(ehl mehr-kah-'deh-oh)*
markup	**el aumento de precio** *(ehl aw-'mehn-toh deh 'preh-see-oh)*
married	**casado/casada** *(kah-'sah-doh/kah-'sah-dah)*
marvelous	**maravilloso/maravillosa** *(mah-rah-vee-'yoh-soh/mah-rah-vee-'yoh-sah)*
mask	**la máscara** *(lah 'mahs-kah-rah)*
materials	**los materiales** *(lohs mah-teh-ree-'ah-lehs)*
mathematics	**las matemáticas** *(lahs mah-teh-'mah-tee-kahs)*
mature	**maduro/madura** *(mah-'doo-roh/mah-'doo-rah)*
maximum	**el máximo** *(ehl 'mahk-see-moh)*
May	**mayo** *('mah-yoh)*
mean	**cruel** *(kroo-'ehl)*
measles	**el sarampión** *(ehl sah-rahm-pee-'ohn)*
measurement	**la medida** *(lah meh-'dee-dah)*
measures	**las medidas** *(lahs meh-'dee-dahs)*
measuring tape	**la cinta de medir** *(lah 'seen-tah deh meh-'deer)*
mechanic	**el mecánico/la mecánica** *(ehl meh-'kah-nee-koh/lah meh-'kah-nee-kah)*
medical insurance	**el seguro médico** *(ehl seh-'goo-roh 'meh-dee-koh)*
medication	**el medicamento** *(ehl meh-dee-kah-'mehn-toh)*
medicine	**la medicina** *(lah meh-dee-'see-nah)*
meeting	**la reunión** *(lah reh-oo-nee-'ohn)*
membership	**la afiliación** *(lah ah-fee-lee-ah-see-'ohn)*
memo	**el memorandum** *(ehl meh-moh-'rahn-doom)*
memory	**la memoria** *(lah meh-'moh-ree-ah)*
menu	**el menú** *(ehl meh-'noo)*
merchandise	**las mercancías** *(lahs mehr-kahn-'see-ahs)*
mesh	**la malla** *(lah 'mah-yah)*
message	**el mensaje** *(ehl mehn-'sah-heh)*
metal	**el metal** *(ehl meh-'tahl)*
meter (device)	**el medidor** *(ehl meh-dee-'dohr)*
meter (measurement)	**el metro** *(ehl 'meh-troh)*
method	**el método** *(ehl 'meh-toh-doh)*
microphone	**el micrófono** *(ehl mee-'kroh-foh-noh)*
midnight	**la medianoche** *(lah meh-dee-ah-'noh-cheh)*
mile	**la milla** *(lah 'mee-yah)*
mill	**el molino** *(ehl moh-'lee-noh)*
mine	**mío/mía** *('mee-oh/'mee-ah)*
minimum	**el mínimo** *(ehl 'mee-nee-moh)*
minus	**menos** *('meh-nohs)*

Miss	**señorita** *(sehn-yoh-'ree-tah)*
missing	**perdido/perdida** *(pehr-'dee-doh/pehr-'dee-dah)*
model	**el modelo** *(ehl moh-'deh-loh)*
Monday	**el lunes** *(ehl 'loo-nehs)*
money order	**el giro postal** *(ehl 'hee-roh pohs-'tahl)*
money	**el dinero** *(ehl dee-'neh-roh)*
monitor	**el monitor** *(ehl moh-nee-'tohr)*
month	**el mes** *(ehl mehs)*
mop	**el trapeador** *(ehl trah-peh-ah-'dohr)*
morale	**la moral** *(lah moh-'rahl)*
most	**la mayoría** *(lah mah-yoh-'ree-ah)*
mother	**la madre** *(lah 'mah-dreh)*
mother-in-law	**la suegra** *(lah 'sweh-grah)*
motherboard	**la placa madre** *(lah 'plah-'kah 'mah-dreh)*
motorcycle	**la motocicleta** *(lah moh-toh-see-'kleh-tah)*
motto	**el lema** *(ehl 'leh-mah)*
mountain	**la montaña** *(lah mohn-'tahn-yah)*
mouse	**el ratón** *(ehl rah-'tohn)*
mouth	**la boca** *(lah 'boh-kah)*
movie theater	**el cine** *(ehl 'see-neh)*
Mr., man	**señor** *(sehn-'yohr)*
Mrs., lady	**señora** *(sehn-'yoh-rah)*
mumps	**las paperas** *(lahs pah-'peh-rahs)*
museum	**el museo** *(ehl moo-'seh-oh)*
musician	**el/la músico** *(ehl/lah 'moo-see-koh)*
my	**mi, mis** *(mee, mees)*
nail	**el clavo** *(ehl 'klah-voh)*
name	**el nombre** *(ehl 'nohm-breh)*
nationality	**la nacionalidad** *(lah nah-see-oh-nah-lee-'dahd)*
near	**cerca** *('sehr-kah)*
neat	**limpio/limpia** *('leem-pee-oh/'leem-pee-ah)*
neck	**el cuello** *(ehl 'kweh-yoh)*
necklace	**el collar** *(ehl koh-'yahr)*
negligent	**negligente** *(neh-glee-'hehn-teh)*
negotiation	**la negociación** *(lah neh-goh-see-ah-see-'ohn)*
neighbor	**el vecino/la vecina** *(ehl veh-'see-noh/lah veh-'see-nah)*
neighborhood	**el vecindario** *(ehl veh-seen-'dah-ree-oh)*
nephew	**el sobrino** *(ehl soh-'bree-noh)*
nervous	**nervioso/nerviosa** *(nehr-vee-'oh-soh/nehr-vee-'oh-sah)*
net, network	**la red** *(lah rehd)*
net sales	**las ventas netas** *(lahs 'vehn-tahs 'neh-tahs)*
never	**nunca** *('noon-kah)*

new	**nuevo/nueva** *('nweh-voh/'nweh-vah)*
newspaper	**el periódico** *(ehl peh-ree-'oh-dee-koh)*
next	**siguiente, próximo** *(see-gee-'ehn-teh, 'prohk-see-moh)*
next to	**al lado** *(ahl 'lah-doh)*
nice	**simpático/simpática** *(seem-'pah-tee-koh/seem-'pah-tee-kah)*
niece	**la sobrina** *(lah soh-'bree-nah)*
ninth	**noveno/novena** *(noh-'veh-noh/noh-'veh-nah)*
no one	**nadie** *('nah-dee-eh)*
noise	**el ruido** *(ehl roo-'ee-doh)*
none	**ninguno/ninguna** *(neen-'goo-noh/neen-'goo-nah)*
nonprofit	**sin fines lucrativos** *(seen 'fee-nehs loo-krah-'tee-vohs)*
noon	**el mediodía** *(ehl meh-dee-oh-'dee-ah)*
nose	**la nariz** *(lah nah-'rees)*
not yet	**todavía no** *(toh-dah-'vee-ah noh)*
nothing	**nada** *('nah-dah)*
notice	**el anuncio** *(ehl ah-'noon-see-oh)*
November	**noviembre** *(noh-vee-'ehm-breh)*
nowhere	**en ningún sitio** *(ehn neen-'goon 'see-tee-oh)*
nozzle	**el pitón** *(ehl pee-'tohn)*
number	**el número** *(ehl 'noo-meh-roh)*
nurse	**el enfermero/la enfermera**
	(ehl ehn-fehr-'meh-roh/lah ehn-fehr-'meh-rah)
nut	**la tuerca** *(lah 'twehr-kah)*
objective	**el objetivo** *(ehl ohb-heh-'tee-voh)*
occupation	**la ocupación** *(lah oh-koo-pah-see-'ohn)*
October	**octubre** *(ohk-'too-breh)*
of	**de** *(deh)*
of, from the	**del** *(dehl)*
offer	**la oferta** *(lah oh-'fehr-tah)*
office	**la oficina** *(lah oh-fee-'see-nah)*
office building	**el edificio de oficinas** *(ehl eh-dee-'fee-see-oh deh oh-fee-'see-nahs)*
office clerk	**el/la oficinista** *(ehl/lah oh-fee-see-'nees-tah)*
oil	**el aceite** *(ehl ah-'seh-ee-teh)*
old	**viejo/vieja** *(vee-'eh-hoh/vee-'eh-hah)*
older	**mayor** *(mah-'yohr)*
on	**en** *(ehn)*
online	**en línea** *(ehn 'lee-neh-ah)*
only	**solamente** *(soh-lah-'mehn-teh)*
operation	**la operación** *(lah oh-peh-rah-see-'ohn)*
opinion	**la opinión** *(lah oh-pee-nee-'ohn)*
opportunity	**la oportunidad** *(lah oh-pohr-too-nee-'dahd)*
or	**o** *(oh)*

orange	**anaranjado/anaranjada** *(ah-nah-rahn-'hah-doh/ah-nah-rahn-'hah-dah)*
order	**el pedido** *(ehl peh-'dee-doh)*
organization	**la organización** *(lah ohr-gah-nee-sah-see-'ohn)*
organized	**organizado/organizada** *(ohr-gah-nee-'sah-doh/ohr-gah-nee-'sah-dah)*
organizer	**el organizador/la organizadora** *(ehl ohr-gah-nee-sah-'dohr/lah ohr-gah-nee-sah-'doh-rah)*
ounce	**la onza** *(lah 'ohn-sah)*
our	**nuestro/nuestra** *('nwehs-troh/'nwehs-trah)*
out of service	**fuera de servicio** *('fweh-rah deh sehr-'vee-see-oh)*
outfit	**el conjunto** *(ehl kohn-'hoon-toh)*
outlet	**la salida** *(lah sah-'lee-dah)*
outside	**afuera** *(ah-foo-'eh-rah)*
outskirts	**las afueras** *(lahs ah-foo-'eh-rahs)*
outstanding	**sobresaliente** *(soh-breh-sah-lee-'ehn-teh)*
over	**sobre** *('soh-breh)*
over there	**allá** *(ah-'yah)*
overalls	**los pantalones de peto** *(lohs pahn-tah-'loh-nehs deh 'peh-toh)*
overcoat	**el abrigo** *(ehl ah-'bree-goh)*
overdue	**vencido/vencida** *(vehn-'see-doh/vehn-'see-dah)*
overhead costs	**los costos generales** *(lohs 'kohs-tohs heh-neh-'rah-lehs)*
overloaded	**sobrecargado/sobrecargada** *(soh-breh-kahr-'gah-doh/soh-breh-kahr-'gah-dah)*
overnight	**de un día para otro** *(deh oon 'dee-ah 'pah-rah 'oh-troh)*
owner	**el dueño/la dueña** *(ehl 'dwehn-yoh/lah 'dwehn-yah)*
oxygen	**el oxígeno** *(ehl ohk-'see-heh-noh)*
P.M.	**de la tarde** *(deh lah 'tahr-deh)*
package	**el paquete** *(ehl pah-'keh-teh)*
padlock	**el candado** *(ehl kahn-'dah-doh)*
page	**la página** *(lah 'pah-hee-nah)*
paid	**pagado/pagada** *(pah-'gah-doh/pah-'gah-dah)*
paid-in-full	**pagado en su totalidad** *(pah-'gah-doh ehn soo toh-tah-lee-'dahd)*
pain	**el dolor** *(ehl doh-'lohr)*
paint	**la pintura** *(lah peen-'too-rah)*
paintbrush	**la brocha para pintar** *(lah 'broh-chah 'pah-rah peen-'tahr)*
painter	**el pintor/la pintora** *(ehl peen-'tohr/lah peen-'toh-rah)*
pair	**el par** *(ehl pahr)*
pallet	**la plataforma** *(lah plah-tah-'fohr-mah)*
pamphlet	**el folleto** *(ehl foh-'yeh-toh)*
panel	**el panel** *(ehl pah-'nehl)*
pants	**los pantalones** *(lohs pahn-tah-'loh-nehs)*
paper clips	**los sujetapapeles** *(lohs soo-heh-tah-pah-'peh-lehs)*

paper cutter	**la cortapapeles** *(lah kohr-tah-pah-'peh-lehs)*
paper shredder	**la trituradora** *(lah tree-too-rah-'doh-rah)*
paper	**el papel** *(ehl pah-'pehl)*
parallel	**paralelo/paralela** *(pah-rah-'leh-loh/pah-rah-'leh-lah)*
paramedic	**el paramédico/la paramédica**
	(ehl pah-rah-'meh-dee-koh/lah pah-rah-'meh-dee-kah)
parents	**los padres** *(lohs 'pah-drehs)*
park	**el parque** *(ehl 'pahr-keh)*
parking lot	**el estacionamiento** *(ehl ehs-tah-see-oh-nah-mee-'ehn-toh)*
part	**la parte** *(lah 'pahr-teh)*
partition	**el divisor** *(ehl dee-vee-'sohr)*
partner	**el socio/la socia** *(ehl 'soh-see-oh/lah 'soh-see-ah)*
part-time	**el medio tiempo** *(ehl 'meh-dee-oh tee-'ehm-poh)*
party	**la fiesta** *(lah fee-'ehs-tah)*
passport	**el pasaporte** *(ehl pah-sah-'pohr-teh)*
password	**la contraseña** *(lah kohn-trah-'sehn-yah)*
paste	**la pasta** *(lah 'pahs-tah)*
patent	**la patente** *(lah pah-'tehn-teh)*
patience	**la paciencia** *(lah pah-see-'ehn-see-ah)*
pattern	**el patrón** *(ehl pah-'trohn)*
pay	**el pago** *(ehl 'pah-goh)*
paycheck	**la paga** *(lah 'pah-gah)*
payload	**la carga útil** *(lah 'kahr-gah 'oo-teel)*
payment	**el pago** *(ehl 'pah-goh)*
PDA	**la computadora de bolsillo**
	(lah kohm-poo-tah-'doh-rah deh bohl-'see-yoh)
pen	**el lapicero** *(ehl lah-pee-'seh-roh)*
pencil	**el lápiz** *(ehl 'lah-pees)*
pencil sharpener	**el sacapuntas** *(ehl sah-kah-'poon-tahs)*
people	**la gente** *(lah 'hehn-teh)*
percentage	**el porcentaje** *(ehl pohr-sehn-'tah-heh)*
perfume	**el perfume** *(ehl pehr-'foo-meh)*
periodically	**periódicamente** *(peh-ree-oh-dee-kah-'mehn-teh)*
person	**la persona** *(lah pehr-'soh-nah)*
personal hygiene	**la higiene personal** *(lah ee-hee-'eh-neh pehr-soh-'nahl)*
pharmacy	**la farmacia** *(lah fahr-'mah-see-ah)*
Phillips head	**el destornillador de cruz** *(ehl dehs-tohr-nee-yah-'dohr deh kroos)*
phone service	**el servicio telefónico** *(ehl sehr-'vee-see-oh teh-leh-'foh-nee-koh)*
photo	**la foto** *(lah 'foh-toh)*
physical abuse	**el abuso físico** *(ehl ah-'boo-soh 'fee-see-koh)*
physical disabilities	**las incapacidades físicas**
	(lahs een-kah-pah-see-'dah-dehs 'fee-see-kahs)
physical exam	**el examen físico** *(ehl ex-'ah-mehn 'fee-see-koh)*

pick	el **pico** *(ehl 'pee-koh)*
pickup truck	la **camioneta** *(lah kah-mee-oh-'neh-tah)*
picnic	el **picnic** *(ehl 'peek-neek)*
picture	la **pintura** *(lah peen-'too-rah)*
piece	el **pedazo** *(ehl peh-'dah-soh)*
pilot	el/la **piloto** *(ehl/lah pee-'loh-toh)*
pipe	la **tubería** *(lah too-beh-'ree-ah)*
place	el **lugar** *(ehl loo-'gahr)*
place of birth	el **lugar de nacimiento** *(ehl loo-gahr deh nah-see-mee-'ehn-toh)*
place of employment	el **lugar de empleo** *(ehl loo-'gahr deh ehm-'pleh-oh)*
plan	el **plan** *(ehl plahn)*
plane	el **avión** *(ehl ah-vee-'ohn)*
planner	el **planificador/la planificadora** *(ehl plah-nee-fee-kah-'dohr/lah plah-nee-fee-kah-'doh-rah)*
plant	la **planta** *(lah 'plahn-tah)*
plaster	el **yeso** *(ehl 'yeh-soh)*
plastic	el **plástico** *(ehl 'plahs-tee-koh)*
platform	la **plataforma** *(lah plah-tah-'fohr-mah)*
player	el **tocador** *(ehl toh-kah-'dohr)*
pliers	las **pinzas** *(lahs 'peen-sahs)*
plug	el **enchufe** *(ehl ehn-'choo-feh)*
plumber	el **plomero** *(ehl ploh-'meh-roh)*
plumbing	la **plomería** *(lah ploh-meh-'ree-ah)*
plus	**más** *(mahs)*
plywood	la **madera terciada** *(lah mah-'deh-rah tehr-see-'ah-dah)*
point	el **punto** *(ehl 'poon-toh)*
pointer	el **señalador** *(ehl sehn-yah-lah-'dohr)*
poisonous	**venenoso/venenosa** *(veh-neh-'noh-soh/veh-neh-'noh-sah)*
police	la **policía** *(lah poh-lee-'see-ah)*
policy	la **política** *(lah poh-'lee-tee-kah)*
polite	**cortés** *(kohr-'tehs)*
poll	la **encuesta** *(lah ehn-'kwehs-tah)*
poor	**pobre** *('poh-breh)*
poorly	**mal** *(mahl)*
portable	**portátil** *(pohr-'tah-teel)*
portfolio	el **portafolio** *(ehl pohr-tah-'foh-lee-oh)*
portion	la **porción** *(lah pohr-see-'ohn)*
position (job)	el **puesto** *(ehl 'pwehs-toh)*
position	la **posición** *(lah poh-see-see-'ohn)*
post	el **poste** *(ehl 'pohs-teh)*
post office	la **oficina de correo** *(lah oh-fee-'see-nah deh kohr-'reh-oh)*
postage stamp	la **estampilla** *(lah ehs-tahm-'pee-yah)*
poster	el **cartel** *(ehl kahr-'tehl)*

pound	**la libra** *(lah 'lee-brah)*
powder	**el polvo** *(ehl 'pohl-voh)*
power	**la potencia** *(lah poh-'tehn-see-ah)*
power line	**la línea de transmisión** *(lah 'lee-neh-ah deh trahns-mee-see-'ohn)*
pregnant	**embarazada** *(ehm-bah-rah-'sah-dah)*
president	**el presidente/la presidenta** *(ehl preh-see-'dehn-teh/lah preh-see-'dehn-tah)*
pressure	**la presión** *(lah preh-see-'ohn)*
pretty	**bonito/bonita** *(boh-'nee-toh/boh-nee-tah)*
previous employer	**el empresario previo/la empresaria previa** *(ehl ehm-preh-'sah-ree-oh 'preh-vee-oh/lah ehm-preh-'sah-ree-ah 'preh-vee-ah)*
price	**el precio** *(ehl 'preh-see-oh)*
principle	**el principio** *(ehl preen-'see-pee-oh)*
printer	**la impresora** *(lah eem-preh-'soh-rah)*
private	**privado/privada** *(pree-'vah-doh/pree-'vah-dah)*
prize	**el premio** *(ehl 'preh-mee-oh)*
procedure	**el procedimiento** *(ehl proh-seh-dee-mee-'ehn-toh)*
production	**la producción** *(lah proh-dook-see-'ohn)*
products	**los productos** *(lohs proh-'dook-tohs)*
profession	**la profesión** *(lah proh-feh-see-'ohn)*
profit	**la ganancia** *(lah gah-'nahn-see-ah)*
program	**el programa** *(ehl proh-'grah-mah)*
prohibited	**prohibido/prohibida** *(proh-ee-'bee-doh/proh-ee-'bee-dah)*
project	**el proyecto** *(ehl proh-'yehk-toh)*
projector	**el proyector** *(ehl proh-yehk-'tohr)*
property	**la propiedad** *(lah proh-pee-eh-'dahd)*
proposal	**la propuesta** *(lah proh-'pwehs-tah)*
public	**el público** *(ehl 'poo-blee-koh)*
public telephone	**el teléfono público** *(ehl teh-'leh-foh-noh 'poo-blee-koh)*
publicity	**la publicidad** *(lah poo-blee-see-'dahd)*
pump	**la bomba** *(lah 'bohm-bah)*
punctual	**puntual** *(poon-'twahl)*
puncture	**la punción** *(lah poon-see-'ohn)*
purple	**morado/morada** *(moh-'rah-doh/moh-'rah-dah)*
purpose	**el propósito** *(ehl proh-'poh-see-toh)*
qualified	**calificado/calificada** *(kah-lee-fee-'kah-doh/kah-lee-fee-'kah-dah)*
quality	**la calidad** *(lah kah-lee-'dahd)*
quality control	**el control de calidad** *(ehl kohn-'trohl deh kah-lee-'dahd)*
quantity	**la cantidad** *(lah kahn-tee-'dahd)*
quart	**el cuarto** *(ehl 'kwahr-toh)*
quarter	**cuarto/cuarta** *('kwahr-toh/'kwahr-tah)*
question	**la pregunta** *(lah preh-'goon-tah)*

quiet	**quieto/quieta** *(kee-'eh-toh/kee-'eh-tah)*
quota	**la cuota** *(lah 'kwoh-tah)*
race	**la raza** *(lah 'rah-sah)*
racial discrimination	**la discriminación racial** *(lah dees-kree-mee-nah-see-'ohn rah-see-'ahl)*
radioactive	**radiactivo/radiactiva** *(rah-dee-ahk-'tee-voh/rah-dee-ahk-'tee-vah)*
railing	**la baranda** *(lah bah-'rahn-dah)*
rain	**la lluvia** *(lah 'yoo-vee-ah)*
raincoat	**el impermeable** *(ehl eem-pehr-meh-'ah-bleh)*
raise	**el aumento de sueldo** *(ehl aw-mehn-toh deh 'swehl-doh)*
ramp	**la rampa** *(lah 'rahm-pah)*
ranch	**el rancho** *(ehl 'rahn-choh)*
rare	**raro/rara** *('rah-roh/'rah-rah)*
rate	**la tasa** *(lah 'tah-sah)*
ratio	**la proporción** *(lah proh-pohr-see-'ohn)*
raw material	**la materia prima** *(lah mah-'teh-ree-ah 'pree-mah)*
reason	**la razón** *(lah rah-'sohn)*
rebate	**la rebaja** *(lah reh-'bah-hah)*
receipt	**el recibo** *(ehl reh-'see-boh)*
receiving	**la admisión** *(lah ahd-mee-see-'ohn)*
reception desk	**la recepción** *(lah reh-sehp-see-'ohn)*
receptionist	**el/la recepcionista** *(ehl/lah reh-sehp-see-oh-'nees-tah)*
recommendation	**la recomendación** *(lah reh-koh-mehn-dah-see-'ohn)*
record	**el récor** *(ehl 'reh-kohr)*
recorder	**la grabadora** *(lah grah-bah-'doh-rah)*
recruiter	**el reclutador/la reclutadora** *(ehl reh-kloo-tah-'dohr/lah reh-kloo-tah-'doh-rah)*
red	**rojo/roja** *('roh-hoh/'roh-hah)*
red tape	**los trámites burocráticos** *(lohs 'trah-mee-tehs boo-roh-'krah-tee-kohs)*
reduction	**la reducción** *(lah reh-dook-see-'ohn)*
references	**las referencias** *(lahs reh-feh-'rehn-see-ahs)*
refund	**el reembolso** *(ehl reh-ehm-'bohl-soh)*
region	**la región** *(lah reh-ee-'ohn)*
regularly	**regularmente** *(reh-goo-lahr-'mehn-teh)*
regulations	**los reglamentos** *(lohs reh-glah-'mehn-tohs)*
relationship	**la relación** *(lah reh-lah-see-'ohn)*
relatives	**los parientes** *(lohs pah-ree-'ehn-tehs)*
remarkable	**notable** *(noh-'tah-bleh)*
remote control	**el control remoto** *(ehl kohn-'trohl reh-'moh-toh)*
rental car	**el carro para alquilar** *(ehl 'kahr-roh 'pah-rah ahl-kee-'lahr)*
report	**el reporte, el informe** *(ehl reh-'pohr-teh, ehl een-'fohr-meh)*

representative	**el/la representante** *(ehl/lah reh-preh-sehn-'tahn-teh)*
research	**la investigación** *(lah een-vehs-tee-gah-see-'ohn)*
respect	**el respeto** *(ehl rehs-'peh-toh)*
response	**la respuesta** *(lah rehs-'pwehs-tah)*
responsibility	**la responsabilidad** *(lah rehs-pohn-sah-bee-lee-'dahd)*
restaurant	**el restaurante** *(ehl rehs-tah-oo-'rahn-teh)*
restricted	**limitado/limitada** *(lee-mee-'tah-doh/lee-mee-'tah-dah)*
restrooms	**los servicios higiénicos** *(lohs sehr-'vee-see-ohs ee-hee-'eh-nee-kohs)*
results	**los resultados** *(lohs reh-sool-'tah-dohs)*
résumé	**el currículum** *(ehl koor-'ree-koo-loom)*
retail price	**el precio al por menor** *(ehl 'preh-see-oh ahl pohr meh-'nohr)*
retirement package	**el paquete de jubilación** *(ehl pah-'keh-teh deh hoo-bee-lah-see-'ohn)*
return	**la devolución** *(lah deh-voh-loo-see-'ohn)*
reward	**la recompensa** *(lah reh-kohm-'pehn-sah)*
ribbon	**la cinta** *(lah 'seen-tah)*
rich	**rico/rica** *('ree-koh/'ree-kah)*
right	**la derecha** *(lah deh-'reh-chah)*
rights	**los derechos** *(lohs deh-'reh-chohs)*
ring	**el anillo** *(ehl ah-'nee-yoh)*
risk	**el riesgo** *(ehl ree-'ehs-goh)*
risky	**arriesgado/arriesgada** *(ahr-ree-ehs-'gah-doh/ahr-ree-ehs-'gah-dah)*
river	**el río** *(ehl 'ree-oh)*
road	**el camino** *(ehl kah-'mee-noh)*
robbery	**el robo** *(ehl 'roh-boh)*
robot	**el robot** *(ehl roh-'boht)*
roof	**el tejado** *(ehl teh-'hah-doh)*
room	**el cuarto** *(ehl 'kwahr-toh)*
room capacity	**la capacidad del recinto** *(lah kah-pah-see-'dahd dehl reh-'seen-toh)*
roommate	**el compañero/la compañera de cuarto** *(ehl kohm-pahn-'yeh-roh/lah kohm-pahn-'yeh-rah deh 'kwahr-toh)*
rope	**la soga** *(lah 'soh-gah)*
route	**la ruta** *(lah 'roo-tah)*
router	**el encaminador** *(ehl ehn-kah-mee-nah-'dohr)*
row	**la fila** *(lah 'fee-lah)*
rubber	**la goma** *(lah 'goh-mah)*
rubber bands	**las ligas** *(lahs 'lee-gahs)*
rude	**grosero/grosera** *(groh-'seh-roh/groh-'seh-rah)*
ruined	**arruinado/arruinada** *(ahr-roo-ee-'nah-doh/ahr-roo-ee-'nah-dah)*
rule	**la regla** *(lah 'reh-glah)*
ruler	**la regla** *(lah 'reh-glah)*
sack	**el saco** *(ehl 'sah-koh)*
sad	**triste** *('trees-teh)*

safe	**la caja fuerte** *(lah 'kah- hah 'fwehr-teh)*
safe (secure)	**seguro/segura** *(seh-'goo-roh/seh-'goo-rah)*
safety	**la seguridad** *(lah seh-goo-ree-'dahd)*
safety glasses	**los lentes de protección** *(lohs 'lehn-tehs deh proh-tehk-see-'ohn)*
safety manual	**el manual de seguridad** *(ehl mahn-wahl deh seh-goo-ree-'dahd)*
safety outfit	**el conjunto de seguridad** *(ehl kohn-'hoon-toh deh seh-goo-ree-'dahd)*
safety standards	**los estándares de seguridad** *(lohs ehs-'tahn-dah-rehs deh seh-goo-ree-'dahd)*
salary	**el salario** *(ehl sah-'lah-ree-oh)*
sale	**la venta** *(lah 'vehn-tah)*
sales budget	**el presupuesto de ventas** *(ehl preh-soo-'pwehs-toh deh 'vehn-tahs)*
sales items	**los artículos de venta** *(lohs ahr-'tee-koo-lohs deh 'vehn-tah)*
sales tax	**el impuesto de ventas** *(ehl eem-'pwehs-toh deh 'vehn-tahs)*
salesperson	**el vendedor/la vendedora** *(ehl vehn-deh-'dohr/lah vehn-deh-'doh-rah)*
sand	**la arena** *(lah ah-'reh-nah)*
Saturday	**el sábado** *(ehl 'sah-bah-doh)*
scaffold	**el andamio** *(ehl ahn-'dah-mee-oh)*
scale	**la báscula** *(lah 'bahs-koo-lah)*
scanner	**el escáner** *(ehl ehs-'kah-nehr)*
schedule	**el horario** *(ehl oh-'rah-ree-oh)*
school	**la escuela** *(lah ehs-'kweh-lah)*
scissors	**las tijeras** *(lahs tee-'heh-rahs)*
Scotch® tape	**la cinta adhesiva** *(lah 'seen-tah ah-deh-'see-vah)*
scrap	**el desecho** *(ehl dehs-'eh-choh)*
screen	**la pantalla** *(lah pahn-'tah-yah)*
screw	**el tornillo** *(ehl tohr-'nee-yoh)*
screwdriver	**el destornillador** *(ehl dehs-tohr-nee-yah-'dohr)*
season	**la estación** *(lah ehs-tah-see-'ohn)*
seat	**el asiento** *(ehl ah-see-'ehn-toh)*
second	**segundo/segunda** *(seh-'goon-doh/seh-'goon-dah)*
secretary	**el secretario/la secretaria** *(ehl seh-kreh-'tah-ree-oh/lah seh-kreh-'tah-ree-ah)*
section	**la sección** *(lah sehk-see-'ohn)*
secure	**seguro/segura** *(seh-'goo-roh/seh-'goo-rah)*
security	**la seguridad** *(lah seh-goo-ree-'dahd)*
security code	**el código de seguridad** *(ehl 'koh-dee-goh deh seh-goo-ree-'dahd)*
security system	**el sistema de seguridad** *(ehl sees-'teh-mah deh seh-goo-ree-'dahd)*
segment	**el segmento** *(ehl sehg-'mehn-toh)*
seizure	**el ataque** *(ehl ah-'tah-keh)*
self-service	**el autoservicio** *(ehl aw-toh-sehr-'vee-see-oh)*
seminar	**el seminario** *(ehl seh-mee-'nah-ree-oh)*
semitrailer	**el semirremolque** *(ehl seh-mee-reh-'mohl-keh)*

seniority	**la precedencia** *(lah preh-seh-'dehn-see-ah)*
September	**septiembre** *(sehp-tee-'ehm-breh)*
series	**la serie** *(lah 'seh-ree-eh)*
service	**el servicio** *(ehl sehr-'vee-see-oh)*
set	**el juego** *(ehl 'hweh-goh)*
seventh	**séptimo/séptima** *('sehp-tee-moh/'sehp-tee-mah)*
severance pay	**la indemnización por despedida**
	(lah een-dehm-nee-sah-see-'ohn pohr dehs-peh-'dee-dah)
sex	**el sexo** *(ehl 'sehk-soh)*
sexual harassment	**el acosamiento sexual** *(ehl ah-koh-sah-mee-'ehn-toh sehk-soo-'ahl)*
shape	**la forma** *(lah 'fohr-mah)*
she	**ella** *('eh-yah)*
shed	**el cobertizo** *(ehl koh-behr-'tee-soh)*
sheet	**la hoja** *(lah 'oh-hah)*
shelf	**la repisa** *(lah reh-'pee-sah)*
shift	**el turno de trabajo** *(ehl 'toor-noh deh trah-'bah-hoh)*
shin guards	**las espinilladeras** *(lahs ehs-pee-nee-yah-'deh-rahs)*
shipment	**el envío** *(ehl ehn-'vee-oh)*
shipper	**el fletador/la fletadora** *(ehl fleh-tah-'dohr/lah fleh-tah-'doh-rah)*
shipping	**el envío, el transporte** *(ehl ehn-'vee-oh, ehl trahns-'pohr-teh)*
shirt	**la camisa** *(lah kah-'mee-sah)*
shop	**el taller** *(ehl tah-'yehr)*
shopper	**el comprador/la compradora**
	(ehl kohm-prah-'dohr/lah kohm-prah-'doh-rah)
shopping center	**el centro comercial** *(ehl 'sehn-troh koh-mehr-see-'ahl)*
short (in height)	**bajo/baja** *('bah-hoh/'bah-hah)*
short (in length)	**corto/corta** *('kohr-toh/'kohr-tah)*
shorts	**los calzoncillos** *(lohs kahl-sohn-'see-yohs)*
shoulder	**el hombro** *(ehl 'ohm-broh)*
shovel	**la pala** *(lah 'pah-lah)*
show	**el espectáculo** *(ehl ehs-pehk-'tah-koo-loh)*
showcase	**la vitrina** *(lah vee-'tree-nah)*
showroom	**la sala de exhibición** *(lah 'sah-lah deh ex-ee-bee-see-'ohn)*
sick	**enfermo/enferma** *(ehn-'fehr-moh/ehn-'fehr-mah)*
sick leave	**los días pagados por enfermedad**
	(lohs 'dee-ahs pah-'gah-dohs pohr ehn-fehr-meh-'dahd)
sign	**el letrero** *(ehl leh-'treh-roh)*
signature	**la firma** *(lah 'feer-mah)*
sign-in sheet	**la lista de registración** *(lah 'lees-tah deh reh-hees-trah-see-'ohn)*
simulator	**la simuladora** *(lah see-moo-lah-'doh-rah)*
since	**desde** *('dehs-deh)*
sincerity	**la sinceridad** *(lah seen-seh-ree-'dahd)*
single	**soltero/soltera** *(sohl-'teh-roh/sohl-'teh-rah)*

sister	**la hija** *(lah 'ee-hah)*
sister-in-law	**la cuñada** *(lah koo-'nyah-dah)*
site	**el sitio** *(ehl 'see-tee-oh)*
sixth	**sexto/sexta** *('sex-toh/'sex-tah)*
size	**el tamaño** *(ehl tah-'mahn-yoh)*
skill	**la aptitud** *(lah ahp-tee-'tood)*
skilled	**experto/experta** *(ex-'pehr-toh/ex-'pehr-tah)*
skin	**la piel** *(lah pee-'ehl)*
skirt	**la falda** *(lah 'fahl-dah)*
sleepy	**soñoliento/soñolienta** *(sohn-yoh-lee-'ehn-toh/sohn-yoh-lee-'ehn-tah)*
slip	**el papelito** *(ehl pah-peh-'lee-toh)*
slogan	**el eslogan** *(ehl ehs-'loh-gahn)*
sloppy	**desaliñado/desaliñada** *(deh-sah-leen-'yah-doh/deh-sah-leen-'yah-dah)*
slow	**lento/lenta** *('lehn-toh/lehn-tah)*
slower	**más despacio** *(mahs dehs-'pah-see-oh)*
small bottle	**el frasco** *(ehl 'frahs-koh)*
small business	**la pequeña empresa** *(lah peh-'kehn-yah ehm-'preh-sah)*
small	**chico/chica** *('chee-koh/'chee-kah)*
smell	**el olor** *(ehl oh-'lohr)*
smoke	**el humo** *(ehl 'oo-moh)*
snow	**la nieve** *(lah nee-'eh-veh)*
so	**así que** *(ah-'see keh)*
soap	**el jabón** *(ehl hah-'bohn)*
social security number	**el número de seguro social** *(ehl 'noo-meh-roh deh seh-'goo-roh soh-see-'ahl)*
socks	**los calcetines** *(lohs kahl-seh-'tee-nehs)*
sofa	**el sofá** *(ehl soh-'fah)*
some	**unos/unas, algunos/algunas** *('oo-nohs/'oo-nahs, ahl-'goo-nohs/ahl-'goo-nahs)*
someone	**alguien** *('ahl-gee-ehn)*
something	**algo** *('ahl-goh)*
sometimes	**a veces** *(ah 'veh-sehs)*
somewhere	**en algún sitio** *(ehn ahl-'goon 'see-tee-oh)*
son	**el hijo** *(ehl 'ee-hoh)*
son-in-law	**el yerno** *(ehl 'yehr-noh)*
soon	**pronto** *('prohn-toh)*
sore	**dolorido/dolorida** *(doh-loh-'ree-doh/doh-loh-'ree-dah)*
sound	**el sonido** *(ehl soh-'nee-doh)*
space	**el espacio** *(ehl ehs-'pah-see-oh)*
spark	**la chispa** *(lah 'chees-pah)*
speaker (device)	**el altavoz** *(ehl ahl-tah-'vohs)*
specialty	**la especialidad** *(lah ehs-peh-see-ah-lee-'dahd)*

speed	**la velocidad** *(lah veh-loh-see-'dahd)*
sponge	**la esponja** *(lah ehs-'pohn-hah)*
sportcoat	**el saco** *(ehl 'sah-koh)*
spring (coil)	**el resorte** *(ehl reh-'sohr-teh)*
spring (season)	**la primavera** *(lah pree-mah-'veh-rah)*
sprinkler system	**el sistema de regadío** *(ehl sees-'teh-mah deh reh-gah-'dee-oh)*
square	**el cuadrado** *(ehl kwah-'drah-doh)*
SSI	**el seguro de seguridad social** *(ehl seh-'goo-roh deh seh-goo-ree-'dahd soh-see-'ahl)*
stacker	**la apiladora** *(lah ah-pee-lah-'doh-rah)*
stadium	**el estadio** *(ehl ehs-'tah-dee-oh)*
stain	**la mancha** *(lah 'mahn-chah)*
stairs	**las escaleras** *(lahs ehs-kah-'leh-rahs)*
stamp	**el sello** *(ehl 'seh-yoh)*
staple	**la grapa** *(lah 'grah-pah)*
stapler	**la engrapadora** *(lah ehn-grah-pah-'doh-rah)*
station	**la estación** *(lah ehs-tah-see-'ohn)*
stationery	**los objetos de escritorio** *(lohs ohb-'heh-tohs deh ehs-kree-'toh-ree-oh)*
steam	**el vapor** *(ehl vah-'pohr)*
steel	**el acero** *(ehl ah-'seh-roh)*
steps	**los escalones** *(lohs ehs-kah-'loh-nehs)*
stick	**el palo** *(ehl 'pah-loh)*
still	**aún, todavía** *(ah-'oon, toh-dah-'vee-ah)*
stock	**la reserva** *(lah reh-'sehr-vah)*
stomach	**el estómago** *(ehl ehs-'toh-mah-goh)*
stomachache	**el dolor de estómago** *(ehl doh-'lohr deh ehs-'toh-mah-goh)*
stone	**la piedra** *(lah pee-'eh-drah)*
stool	**el banquillo** *(ehl bahn-'kee-yoh)*
stop sign	**la señal de parada** *(lah sehn-'yahl deh pah-'rah-dah)*
store	**la tienda** *(lah tee-'ehn-dah)*
storeroom	**el depósito** *(ehl deh-'poh-see-toh)*
storm	**la tormenta** *(lah tohr-'mehn-tah)*
straight	**recto/recta** *('rehk-toh/'rehk-tah)*
straight ahead	**adelante** *(ah-deh-'lahn-teh)*
strap	**la correa** *(lah kohr-'reh-ah)*
strategy	**la estrategia** *(lah ehs-trah-'teh-ee-ah)*
street	**la calle** *(lah 'kah-yeh)*
strike	**la huelga** *(lah 'hwehl-gah)*
string	**la cuerda** *(lah 'kwehr-dah)*
stripe	**la franja** *(lah 'frahn-hah)*
strong	**fuerte** *('fwehr-teh)*
stuck	**pegado/pegada** *(peh-'gah-doh/peh-'gah-dah)*
style	**el estilo** *(ehl ehs-'tee-loh)*

subdivision	**la subdivisión** *(lah soob-dee-vee-see-'ohn)*
subject	**el tema** *(ehl 'teh-mah)*
subway	**el metro** *(ehl 'meh-troh)*
successful	**exitoso/exitosa** *(ex-ee-'toh-soh/ex-ee-'toh-sah)*
suggestion	**la sugerencia** *(lah soo-heh-'rehn-see-ah)*
suit	**el traje** *(ehl 'trah-heh)*
suitcase	**la maleta** *(lah mah-'leh-tah)*
sum	**la suma** *(lah 'soo-mah)*
summer	**el verano** *(ehl veh-'rah-noh)*
sun	**el sol** *(ehl sohl)*
Sunday	**el domingo** *(ehl doh-'meen-goh)*
sunglasses	**los lentes de sol** *(lohs 'lehn-tehs deh sohl)*
sunstroke	**la insolación** *(lah een-soh-lah-see-'ohn)*
supermarket	**el supermercado** *(ehl soo-pehr-mehr-'kah-doh)*
supervisor	**el supervisor/la supervisora** *(ehl soo-pehr-vee-'sohr/lah soo-pehr-vee-'soh-'rah)*
supplier	**el abastecedor/la abastecedora** *(ehl ah-bahs-teh-seh-'dohr/lah ah-bahs-teh-seh-'doh-rah)*
supplies	**los suministros** *(lohs soo-mee-'nees-trohs)*
surplus	**el exceso** *(ehl ex-'seh-soh)*
SUV	**el vehículo deportivo utilitario** *(ehl veh-'ee-koo-loh deh-pohr-'tee-voh oo-tee-lee-'tah-ree-oh)*
switch	**el interruptor** *(ehl een-tehr-roop-'tohr)*
switchboard	**el tablero de distribución** *(ehl tah-'bleh-roh deh dees-tree-boo-see-'ohn)*
symbol	**el símbolo** *(ehl 'seem-boh-loh)*
system	**el sistema** *(ehl sees-'teh-mah)*
table	**la mesa** *(lah 'meh-sah)*
tablespoon	**la cucharada** *(lah koo-chah-'rah-dah)*
tacks	**las tachuelas** *(lahs tach-'weh-lahs)*
tailor	**el/la sastre** *(ehl/lah 'sahs-treh)*
tall	**alto/alta** *('ahl-toh/'ahl-tah)*
tank	**el tanque** *(ehl 'tahn-keh)*
tanker truck	**el camión cisterna** *(ehl kah-mee-'ohn sees-'tehr-nah)*
tape	**la cinta** *(lah 'seen-tah)*
tape measure	**la cinta de medir** *(lah 'seen-tah deh meh-'deer)*
tardiness	**las tardanzas** *(lahs tahr-'dahn-sahs)*
tasks	**las faenas** *(lahs fah-'eh-nahs)*
tax	**el impuesto** *(ehl eem-'pwehs-toh)*
taxi	**el taxi** *(ehl 'tahk-see)*
teacher	**el maestro/la maestra** *(ehl mah-'ehs-troh/lah mah-'ehs-trah)*
tear	**el rasgón** *(ehl rahs-'gohn)*

teaspoon	**la cucharadita** *(lah koo-chah-rah-'dee-tah)*
technician	**el/la técnico** *(ehl/lah 'tehk-nee-koh)*
technique	**la técnica** *(lah 'tehk-nee-kah)*
teenager	**el muchacho/la muchacha** *(ehl moo-'chah-choh/ lah moo-'chah-chah)*
teeth	**los dientes** *(lohs dee-'ehn-tehs)*
telephone	**el teléfono** *(ehl teh-'leh-foh-noh)*
telephone number	**el número de teléfono** *(ehl 'noo-meh-roh deh teh-'leh-foh-noh)*
temperature	**la temperatura** *(lah tehm-peh-rah-'too-rah)*
tennis shoes	**las zapatillas** *(lahs sah-pah-'tee-yahs)*
tenth	**décimo/décima** *('deh-see-moh/'deh-see-mah)*
terrible	**terrible** *(tehr-'ree-bleh)*
territory	**el territorio** *(ehl tehr-ree-'toh-ree-oh)*
text	**el texto** *(ehl 'tehks-toh)*
the (pl.)	**los, las** *(lohs, lahs)*
the (sing.)	**el, la** *(ehl, lah)*
theater	**el teatro** *(ehl teh-'ah-troh)*
their	**su, sus** *(soo, soos)*
theirs	**suyo, suyos/suya, suyas** *('soo-yoh, 'soo-yohs/'soo-yah, 'soo-yahs)*
theme	**el tema** *(ehl 'teh-mah)*
then	**entonces** *(ehn-'tohn-sehs)*
there are	**hay** *('ah-ee)*
there is	**hay** *('ah-ee)*
there	**allí** *(ah-'yee)*
thermometer	**el termómetro** *(ehl tehr-'moh-meh-troh)*
thermos	**el termo** *(ehl 'tehr-moh)*
thermostat	**el termostato** *(ehl tehr-mohs-'tah-toh)*
they	**ellos/ellas** *('eh-yohs/'eh-yahs)*
thin	**delgado/delgada** *(dehl-'gah-doh/dehl-'gah-dah)*
thing	**la cosa** *(lah 'koh-sah)*
third	**tercero/tercera** *(tehr-'seh-roh/tehr-'seh-rah)*
thought	**el pensamiento** *(ehl pehn-sah-mee-'ehn-toh)*
thread	**el hilo** *(ehl 'ee-loh)*
threat	**la amenaza** *(lah ah-meh-'nah-sah)*
through	**por** *(pohr)*
thunder	**el trueno** *(ehl troo-'eh-noh)*
Thursday	**el jueves** *(ehl 'hweh-vehs)*
tie	**la corbata** *(lah kohr-'bah-tah)*
tight	**apretado/apretada** *(ah-preh-'tah-doh/ah-preh-'tah-dah)*
time	**la hora** *(lah 'oh-rah)*
timecard	**el horario** *(ehl oh-'rah-ree-oh)*
time clock	**el registrador de tiempo** *(ehl reh-hees-trah-'dohr deh tee-'ehm-poh)*
time frame	**el lapso de tiempo** *(ehl 'lahp-soh deh tee-'ehm-poh)*
timer	**el contador** *(ehl kohn-tah-'dohr)*

times	**veces** *('veh-sehs)*
tip	**la propina** *(lah proh-'pee-nah)*
tire	**el neumático** *(ehl neh-oo-'mah-tee-koh)*
tired	**cansado/cansada** *(kahn-'sah-doh/kahn-'sah-dah)*
title	**el título** *(ehl 'tee-too-loh)*
to	**a** *(ah)*
today	**hoy** *('oh-ee)*
toll booth	**la cabina de peaje** *(lah kah-'bee-nah deh peh-'ah-heh)*
tomorrow	**mañana** *(mahn-'yah-nah)*
ton	**la tonelada** *(lah toh-neh-'lah-dah)*
tongs	**las tenazas** *(lahs teh-'nah-sahs)*
tongue	**la lengua** *(lah 'lehn-gwah)*
too much	**demasiado** *(deh-mah-see-'ah-doh)*
tools	**las herramientas** *(lahs ehr-rah-mee-'ehn-tahs)*
toothache	**el dolor de muela** *(ehl doh-'lohr deh 'mweh-lah)*
topic	**la cuestión** *(lah kwehs-tee-'ohn)*
torch	**la antorcha** *(lah ahn-'tohr-chah)*
torn	**rasgado/rasgada** *(rahs-'gah-doh/rahs-'gah-dah)*
tornado	**el tornado** *(ehl tohr-'nah-doh)*
tow truck	**la grúa** *(lah 'groo-ah)*
towel	**la toalla** *(lah toh-'ah-yah)*
tower	**la torre** *(lah 'tohr-reh)*
town	**el pueblo** *(ehl 'pweh-bloh)*
toxic	**tóxico/tóxica** *('tohk-see-koh/'tohk-see-kah)*
track	**el carril** *(ehl kahr-'reel)*
tractor trailer	**el camión tractor** *(ehl kah-mee-'ohn trahk-'tohr)*
trademark	**la marca registrada** *(lah 'mahr-kah reh-hees-'trah-dah)*
traffic signal	**el semáforo** *(ehl seh-'mah-foh-roh)*
train	**el tren** *(ehl trehn)*
train station	**la estación de tren** *(lah ehs-tah-see-'ohn deh trehn)*
trained	**entrenado/entrenada** *(ehn-treh-'nah-doh/ehn-treh-'nah-dah)*
training	**el entrenamiento** *(ehl ehn-treh-nah-mee-'ehn-toh)*
training manual	**el manual de instrucciones** *(ehl mah-'nwahl deh eens-trook-see-'oh-nehs)*
training room	**la sala de entrenamiento** *(lah 'sah-lah deh ehn-treh-nah-mee-'ehn-toh)*
transcript	**la transcripción** *(lah trahns-kreep-see-'ohn)*
transformer	**el transformador** *(ehl trahns-fohr-mah-'dohr)*
translator	**el traductor/la traductora** *(ehl trah-dook-'tohr/lah trah-dook-'toh-rah)*
transportation	**el transporte** *(ehl trahns-'pohr-teh)*
trash	**la basura** *(lah bah-'soo-rah)*
trash basket	**el cesto de basura** *(ehl 'sehs-toh deh bah-'soo-rah)*

trashbag	**la bolsa de basura** *(lah 'bohl-sah deh bah-'soo-rah)*
trashcan	**el bote de basura** *(ehl 'boh-teh deh bah-'soo-rah)*
traveler's check	**el cheque de viajero** *(ehl 'cheh-keh deh vee-ah-'heh-roh)*
tray	**la bandeja** *(lah bahn-'deh-hah)*
trend	**la tendencia** *(lah tehn-'dehn-see-ah)*
triangle	**el triángulo** *(ehl tree-'ahn-goo-loh)*
tripod	**el trípode** *(ehl 'tree-poh-deh)*
trowel	**la paleta** *(lah pah-'leh-tah)*
truck	**el camión** *(ehl kah-mee-'ohn)*
truck driver	**el camionero/la camionera** *(ehl kah-mee-oh-'neh-roh/lah kah-mee-oh-'neh-rah)*
truckload	**la camionada** *(lah kah-mee-oh-'nah-dah)*
T-shirt	**la camiseta** *(lah kah-mee-'seh-tah)*
tub	**la tina** *(lah 'tee-nah)*
tube	**el tubo** *(ehl 'too-boh)*
Tuesday	**el martes** *(ehl 'mahr-tehs)*
tunnel	**el túnel** *(ehl 'too-nehl)*
turbine	**la turbina** *(lah toor-'bee-nah)*
TV	**el televisor** *(ehl teh-leh-vee-'sohr)*
twice	**dos veces** *(dohs 'veh-sehs)*
twisted	**torcido/torcida** *(tohr-'see-doh/tohr-'see-dah)*
two-way radio	**el radioteléfono portátil** *(ehl rah-dee-oh-teh-'leh-foh-noh pohr-'tah-teel)*
typical	**típico/típica** *('tee-pee-koh/'tee-pee-kah)*
ugly	**feo/fea** *('feh-oh/'feh-ah)*
umbrella	**el paraguas** *(ehl pah-'rah-gwahs)*
unacceptable	**inaceptable** *(een-ah-sehp-'tah-bleh)*
uncle	**el tío** *(ehl 'tee-oh)*
uncomfortable	**incómodo/incómoda** *(een-'koh-moh-doh/een-'koh-moh-dah)*
under	**debajo** *(deh-'bah-hoh)*
unemployment	**el desempleo** *(ehl deh-sehm-'pleh-oh)*
uneven	**desigual** *(deh-see-'gwahl)*
unhappy	**descontento/descontenta** *(dehs-kohn-'tehn-toh/dehs-kohn-'tehn-tah)*
uniform	**el uniforme** *(ehl oo-nee-'fohr-meh)*
union	**el sindicato** *(ehl seen-dee-'kah-toh)*
unit	**la unidad** *(lah oo-nee-'dahd)*
United States	**los Estados Unidos** *(lohs ehs-'tah-dohs oo-'nee-dohs)*
university	**la universidad** *(lah oo-nee-vehr-see-'dahd)*
until	**hasta** *('ahs-tah)*
up	**arriba** *(ahr-'ree-bah)*
upset	**amargado/amargada** *(ah-mahr-'gah-doh/ah-mahr-'gah-dah)*
upside down	**boca abajo** *('boh-kah ah-'bah-hoh)*

urgency	**la urgencia** *(lah oor-'hehn-see-ah)*
used	**usado/usada** *(oo-'sah-doh/oo-'sah-dah)*
vacation days	**los días de vacaciones** *(lohs 'dee-ahs deh vah-kah-see-'oh-nehs)*
valley	**el valle** *(ehl 'vah-yeh)*
valuable	**valioso/valiosa** *(vah-lee-'oh-soh/vah-lee-'oh-sah)*
value	**el valor** *(ehl vah-lohr)*
valve	**la válvula** *(lah 'vahl-voo-lah)*
van	**la furgoneta** *(lah foor-goh-'neh-tah)*
vandalism	**el vandalismo** *(ehl vahn-dah-'lees-moh)*
vending machine	**la máquina vendedora** *(lah 'mah-kee-nah vehn-deh-'doh-rah)*
vest	**el chaleco** *(ehl chah-'leh-koh)*
vice	**la prensa sujetadora** *(lah 'prehn-sah soo-heh-tah-'doh-rah)*
vice-president	**el vicepresidente/la vicepresidenta**
	(ehl vee-seh-preh-see-'dehn-teh/lah vee-seh-preh-see-'dehn-tah)
video conferencing	**la conferencia por video**
	(lah kohn-feh-'rehn-see-ah pohr vee-'deh-oh)
visitor	**el/la visitante** *(ehl/lah vee-see-'tahn-teh)*
voice mail	**el telemensaje** *(ehl teh-leh-mehn-'sah-heh)*
voided	**cancelado/cancelada** *(kahn-seh-'lah-doh/kahn-seh-'lah-dah)*
voltage	**el voltaje** *(ehl vohl-'tah-heh)*
wage	**el sueldo** *(ehl 'swehl-doh)*
waiter	**el mesero/la mesera** *(ehl meh-'seh-roh/lah meh-'seh-rah)*
waiting room	**la sala de espera** *(lah 'sah-lah deh ehs-'peh-rah)*
walkway	**el pasillo** *(ehl pah-'see-yoh)*
wall	**la pared** *(lah pah-'rehd)*
warehouse	**el almacén** *(ehl ahl-mah-'sehn)*
warm	**caluroso/calurosa** *(kah-loo-'roh-soh/kah-loo-'roh-sah)*
warning	**el aviso, la advertencia** *(ehl ah-'vee-soh, lah ahd-vehr-'tehn-see-ah)*
warrant	**la orden de la corte** *(lah 'ohr-dehn deh lah 'kohr-teh)*
washer	**la arandela** *(lah ah-rahn-'deh-lah)*
waste	**los residuos** *(lohs reh-'see-dwohs)*
watch	**el reloj de pulsera** *(ehl reh-'loh deh pool-'seh-rah)*
water	**el agua** *(ehl 'ah-gwah)*
water fountain	**la fuente de agua** *(lah 'fwehn-teh deh 'ah-gwah)*
water valve	**la válvula de agua** *(lah 'vahl-voo-lah deh 'ah-gwah)*
watt	**el vatio** *(ehl 'vah-tee-oh)*
way	**el modo** *(ehl 'moh-doh)*
we	**nosotros/nosotras** *(noh-'soh-trohs/noh-'soh-trahs)*
weak	**débil** *('deh-beel)*
weather	**el tiempo** *(ehl tee-'ehm-poh)*
web site	**el sitio web** *(ehl 'see-tee-oh oo-'ehb)*

Wednesday	el **miércoles** *(ehl mee-'ehr-koh-lehs)*
week	la **semana** *(lah seh-'mah-nah)*
weekend	el **fin de la semana** *(ehl feen deh lah seh-'mah-nah)*
weight	el **peso** *(ehl 'peh-soh)*
What?	¿**Qué?** *(keh)*
wheel	la **rueda** *(lah 'rweh-dah)*
wheelbarrow	la **carretilla** *(lah kahr-reh-'tee-yah)*
wheelchair	la **silla de ruedas** *(lah 'see-yah deh roo-'eh-dahs)*
When?	¿**Cuándo?** *('kwahn-doh)*
Where?	¿**Dónde?** *('dohn-deh)*
Which?	¿**Cuál?** *(kwahl)*
while	**mientras** *(mee-'ehn-trahs)*
whistle	el **silbato** *(ehl seel-'bah-toh)*
white	**blanco/blanca** *('blahn-koh/'blahn-kah)*
whiteboard	la **pizarra blanca** *(lah pee-'sahr-rah 'blahn-kah)*
Who?	¿**Quién?** *(kee-'ehn)*
wholesale price	el **precio al por mayor** *(ehl 'preh-see-oh ahl pohr mah-'yohr)*
Whose?	¿**De quién?** *(deh kee-'ehn)*
Why?	¿**Por qué?** *(pohr keh)*
widow	la **viuda** *(lah vee-'oo-dah)*
width	la **anchura** *(lah ahn-'choo-rah)*
wife	la **esposa** *(lah ehs-'poh-sah)*
wind	el **viento** *(ehl vee-'ehn-toh)*
window	la **ventana** *(lah vehn-'tah-nah)*
winter	el **invierno** *(ehl een-vee-'ehr-noh)*
wire	el **alambre** *(ehl ah-'lahm-breh)*
with	**con** *(kohn)*
without	**sin** *(seen)*
woman	la **mujer** *(lah moo-'hehr)*
wood	la **madera** *(lah mah-'deh-rah)*
wool	la **lana** *(lah 'lah-nah)*
work	el **trabajo** *(ehl trah-'bah-hoh)*
work center	el **centro de trabajo** *(ehl 'sehn-troh deh trah-'bah-hoh)*
work permit	el **permiso de trabajo** *(ehl pehr-'mee-soh deh trah-'bah-hoh)*
worker	el **trabajador/la trabajadora**
	(ehl trah-bah-hah-'dohr/lah trah-bah-hah-'doh-rah)
Workman's Comp	la **compensación laboral**
	(lah kohm-pehn-sah-see-'ohn lah-boh-'rahl)
worktable	la **mesa de trabajo** *(lah 'meh-sah deh trah-'bah-hoh)*
worried	**preocupado/preocupada**
	(preh-oh-koo-'pah-doh/preh-oh-koo-'pah-dah)
worse	**peor** *(peh-'ohr)*
worthless	**sin valor** *(seen vah-'lohr)*

wrench	**la llave inglesa** *(lah 'yah-veh een-'gleh-sah)*
wrist	**la muñeca** *(lah moon-'yeh-kah)*
yard	**la yarda** *(lah 'yahr-dah)*
year	**el año** *(ehl 'ahn-yoh)*
yellow	**amarillo** *(ah-mah-'ree-yoh)*
yellow pages	**las páginas amarillas** *(lahs 'pah-ee-'nahs ah-mah-'ree-yahs)*
yesterday	**ayer** *(ah-'yehr)*
you (formal, sing.)	**usted** *(oos-'tehd)*
you (formal, pl.)	**ustedes** *(oos-'teh-dehs)*
young	**joven** *('hoh-vehn)*
your (inf.)	**tu, tus** *(too, toos)*
your (formal)	**su, sus** *(soo, soos)*
yours (inf.)	**tuyo, tuyos/ tuya, tuyas** *('too-yoh, 'too-yohs/too-yah, 'too-yahs)*
yours (formal)	**suyo, suyos/ suya, suyas** *('soo-yoh, 'soo-yohs/soo-yah, 'soo-yahs)*
zip code	**la zona postal** *(la 'soh-nah pohs-'tahl)*
zone	**la zona** *(lah 'soh-nah)*

English-Spanish Glossary (Verbs)

to absorb	**absorber** *(ahb-sohr-'behr)*
to accept	**aceptar** *(ah-sehp-'tahr)*
to add	**agregar** *(ah-'greh-'gahr)*
to add (math)	**sumar** *(soo-'mahr)*
to adjust	**ajustar** *(ah-hoos-'tahr)*
to admit	**admitir** *(ahd-mee-'teer)*
to advertise	**anunciar** *(ah-noon-see-'ahr)*
to advise	**aconsejar** *(ah-'kohn-seh-hahr)*
to align	**alinear** *(ah-lee-neh-'ahr)*
to allow	**permitir** *(pehr-mee-'teer)*
to alter	**alterar** *(ahl-teh-'rahr)*
to analyze	**analizar** *(ah-nah-lee-'sahr)*
to answer	**contestar** *(kohn-tehs-'tahr)*
to antagonize	**antagonizar** *(ahn-tah-goh-nee-'sahr)*
to apply	**solicitar** *(soh-lee-see-'tahr)*
to approve	**aprobar** *(ah-proh-'bahr)*
to argue	**argumentar** *(ahr-goo-mehn-'tahr)*
to arrive	**llegar** *(yeh-'gahr)*
to ask	**preguntar** *(preh-goon-'tahr)*
to ask for	**pedir** *(peh-'deer)*
to assemble	**armar** *(ahr-'mahr)*
to assure	**asegurar** *(ah-seh-goo-'rahr)*
to attach	**unir** *(oo-'neer)*
to attend	**asistir** *(ah-sees-'teer)*
to avoid	**evitar** *(eh-vee-'tahr)*
to be	**estar, ser** *(ehs-'tahr, sehr)*
to be able to	**poder** *(poh-'dehr)*
to begin	**empezar** *(ehm-peh-'sahr)*
to bend	**doblar** *(doh-'blahr)*
to bother	**molestar** *(moh-lehs-'tahr)*
to break	**romper** *(rohm-'pehr)*
to breathe	**respirar** *(rehs-pee-'rahr)*
to bring	**traer** *(trah-'ehr)*
to build	**construir** *(kohns-troo-'eer)*
to burn	**quemar** *(keh-'mahr)*
to bury	**enterrar** *(ehn-tehr-'rahr)*
to buy	**comprar** *(kohm-'prahr)*

to calculate	**calcular** *(kahl-koo-'lahr)*
to call	**llamar** *(yah-'mahr)*
to calm down	**calmar** *(kahl-'mahr)*
to cancel	**cancelar** *(kahn-seh-'lahr)*
to carry	**llevar** *(yeh-'vahr)*
to center	**centrar** *(sehn-'trahr)*
to change	**cambiar** *(kahm-bee-'ahr)*
to charge	**cobrar** *(koh-'brahr)*
to check	**revisar** *(reh-vee-'sahr)*
to clarify	**aclarar** *(ah-klah-'rahr)*
to clean	**limpiar** *(leem-pee-'ahr)*
to click	**hacer "clic"** *(ah-'sehr kleek)*
to climb	**subir** *(soo-'beer)*
to close	**cerrar** *(sehr-'rahr)*
to collect	**coleccionar** *(koh-lehk-see-oh-'nahr)*
to combine	**combinar** *(kohm-bee-'nahr)*
to come	**venir** *(veh-'neer)*
to commit	**comprometerse** *(kohm-proh-meh-'tehr-seh)*
to confirm	**confirmar** *(kohn-feer-'mahr)*
to connect	**conectar** *(koh-nehk-'tahr)*
to consult	**consultar** *(kohn-sool-'tahr)*
to continue	**continuar** *(kohn-tee-'nwahr)*
to control	**controlar** *(kohn-troh-'lahr)*
to converse	**conversar** *(kohn-vehr-'sahr)*
to cooperate	**cooperar** *(koh-oh-peh-'rahr)*
to coordinate	**coordinar** *(koh-ohr-dee-'nahr)*
to correct	**corregir** *(kohr-reh-'heer)*
to counsel	**aconsejar** *(ah-kohn-seh-'hahr)*
to cover	**tapar** *(tah-'pahr)*
to cross	**cruzar** *(kroo-'sahr)*
to cut	**cortar** *(kohr-'tahr)*
to deactivate	**desactivar** *(dehs-ahk-tee-'vahr)*
to defend	**defender** *(deh-fehn-'dehr)*
to delete	**eliminar** *(eh-lee-mee-'nahr)*
to deliver	**repartir** *(reh-pahr-'teer)*
to demand	**exigir** *(ex-ee-'heer)*
to demonstrate	**demostrar** *(deh-mohs-'trahr)*
to deny	**negar** *(neh-'gahr)*
to deposit	**depositar** *(deh-poh-see-'tahr)*
to describe	**describir** *(dehs-kree-'beer)*
to design	**diseñar** *(dee-sehn-'yahr)*
to develop	**desarollar** *(deh-sahr-roh-'yahr)*

to disassemble	**desarmar** *(dehs-ahr-'mahr)*
to disconnect	**desconectar** *(dehs-koh-nehk-'tahr)*
to discuss	**discutir** *(dees-koo-'teer)*
to distribute	**distribuir** *(dees-tree-boo-'eer)*
to divide	**dividir** *(dee-vee-'deer)*
to do	**hacer** *(ah-'sehr)*
to download	**bajar** *(bah-'hahr)*
to draw	**dibujar** *(dee-boo-'hahr)*
to drill	**taladrar** *(tah-lah-'drahr)*
to drink	**beber** *(beh-'behr)*
to drive	**manejar** *(mah-neh-'hahr)*
to dry	**secar** *(seh-'kahr)*
to dump	**botar** *(boh-'tahr)*
to eat	**comer** *(koh-'mehr)*
to empty	**vaciar** *(vah-see-'ahr)*
to enclose	**encerrar** *(ehn-sehr-'rahr)*
to encourage	**animar** *(ah-nee-'mahr)*
to end	**terminar** *(tehr-mee-'nahr)*
to enforce	**hacer cumplir** *(ah-'sehr koom-'pleer)*
to enter	**entrar** *(ehn-'trahr)*
to establish	**establecer** *(ehs-tah-bleh-'sehr)*
to evaluate	**evaluar** *(eh-vah-loo-'ahr)*
to examine	**examinar** *(ex-ah-mee-nahr)*
to exceed	**sobrepasar** *(soh-breh-pah-'sahr)*
to exhibit	**exhibir** *(ex-ee-'beer)*
to explain	**explicar** *(ex-plee-'kahr)*
to export	**exportar** *(ex-pohr-'tahr)*
to faint	**desmayarse** *(dehs-mah-'yahr-seh)*
to fall	**caerse** *(kah-'ehr-seh)*
to fasten	**fijar** *(fee-'hahr)*
to feel	**sentir** *(sehn-'teer)*
to fight	**pelear** *(peh-leh-'ahr)*
to file	**archivar** *(ahr-chee-'vahr)*
to fill	**llenar** *(yeh-'nahr)*
to find	**encontrar** *(ehn-kohn-'trahr)*
to finish	**terminar** *(tehr-mee-'nahr)*
to fire (someone)	**despedir** *(dehs-peh-'deer)*
to flip	**voltear** *(vohl-teh-'ahr)*
to follow	**seguir** *(seh-'geer)*
to forget	**olvidar** *(ohl-vee-'dahr)*
to form	**formar** *(fohr-'mahr)*

to forward	**reenviar** *(reh-ehn-vee-'ahr)*
to function	**funcionar** *(foon-see-oh-'nahr)*
to give	**dar** *(dahr)*
to glue	**pegar** *(peh-'gahr)*
to go	**ir** *(eer)*
to gossip	**chismear** *(chees-meh-'ahr)*
to grab	**agarrar** *(ah-gahr-'rahr)*
to guarantee	**garantizar** *(gah-rahn-tee-'sahr)*
to guess	**adivinar** *(ah-dee-vee-'nahr)*
to hang	**colgar** *(kohl-'gahr)*
to haul	**transportar** *(trahns-pohr-'tahr)*
to have	**tener** *(teh-'nehr)*
to heat	**calentar** *(kah-lehn-'tahr)*
to help	**ayudar** *(ah-yoo-'dahr)*
to hide	**esconder** *(ehs-kohn-'dehr)*
to hire	**contratar** *(kohn-trah-'tahr)*
to hold	**sostener** *(sohs-teh-'nehr)*
to identify	**identificar** *(ee-dehn-tee-fee-'kahr)*
to implement	**poner en práctica** *(poh-'nehr ehn 'prahk-tee-kah)*
to import	**importar** *(eem-pohr-'tahr)*
to improve	**mejorar** *(meh-hoh-'rahr)*
to include	**incluir** *(een-kloo-'eer)*
to indicate	**indicar** *(een-dee-'kahr)*
to insert	**meter** *(meh-'tehr)*
to insist	**insistir** *(een-sees-'teer)*
to inspect	**inspeccionar** *(eens-pehk-see-oh-'nahr)*
to install	**instalar** *(eens-tah-'lahr)*
to invest	**invertir** *(een-vehr-'teer)*
to investigate	**investigar** *(een-vehs-tee-'gahr)*
to join	**unir** *(oo-'neer)*
to join (sign up)	**afiliarse** *(ah-fee-lee-'ahr-seh)*
to last	**durar** *(doo-'rahr)*
to lead	**dirigir** *(dee-ree-'heer)*
to learn	**aprender** *(ah-prehn-'dehr)*
to leave	**salir** *(sah-'leer)*
to lie	**mentir** *(mehn-'teer)*
to lift	**levantar** *(leh-vahn-'tahr)*
to line up	**alinear** *(ah-lee-neh-'ahr)*

to listen	**escuchar** *(ehs-koo-'chahr)*
to live	**vivir** *(vee-'veer)*
to load	**cargar** *(kahr-'gahr)*
to lock	**cerrar con llave** *(sehr-'rahr kohn 'yah-veh)*
to look	**mirar** *(mee-'rahr)*
to look for	**buscar** *(boos-'kahr)*
to loosen	**soltar** *(sohl-'tahr)*
to lose	**perder** *(pehr-'dehr)*
to lower	**bajar** *(bah-'hahr)*
to maintain	**mantener** *(mahn-teh-'nehr)*
to make	**hacer** *(ah-'sehr)*
to manage	**manejar** *(mah-neh-'hahr)*
to mark	**marcar** *(mahr-'kahr)*
to measure	**medir** *(meh-'deer)*
to meet	**reunirse** *(reh-oo-'neer-seh)*
to mix	**mezclar** *(mehs-'klahr)*
to modify	**modificar** *(moh-dee-fee-'kahr)*
to monitor	**vigilar** *(vee-hee-'lahr)*
to motivate	**motivar** *(moh-tee-'vahr)*
to mount	**montar** *(mohn-'tahr)*
to move	**mover** *(moh-'vehr)*
to move (residence)	**mudarse** *(moo-'dahr-seh)*
to multiply	**multiplicar** *(mool-tee-plee-'kahr)*
to negotiate	**negociar** *(neh-goh-see-'ahr)*
to notice	**notar** *(noh-'tahr)*
to obey	**obedecer** *(oh-beh-deh-'sehr)*
to observe	**observar** *(ohb-sehr-'vahr)*
to offer	**ofrecer** *(oh-freh-'sehr)*
to open	**abrir** *(ah-'breer)*
to operate	**operar** *(oh-peh-'rahr)*
to order	**pedir** *(peh-'deer)*
to organize	**organizar** *(ohr-gah-nee-'sahr)*
to overcharge	**cobrar en exceso** *(koh-'brahr ehn ex-'seh-soh)*
to overload	**sobrecargar** *(soh-breh-kahr-'gahr)*
to overspend	**gastar más de la cuenta** *(gahs-'tahr mahs deh lah 'kwehn-tah)*
to owe	**deber** *(deh-'behr)*
to package	**empaquetar** *(ehm-pah-keh-'tahr)*
to paint	**pintar** *(peen-tahr)*
to park	**estacionar** *(ehs-tah-see-oh-'nahr)*

to participate	**participar** *(pahr-tee-see-'pahr)*
to patch	**remendar** *(reh-mehn-'dahr)*
to pause	**pausar** *(pah-oo-'sahr)*
to pay	**pagar** *(pah-'gahr)*
to permit	**permitir** *(pehr-mee-'teer)*
to persuade	**persuadir** *(pehr-soo-ah-'deer)*
to pick up	**recoger** *(reh-koh-'hehr)*
to pile	**amontonar** *(ah-mohn-toh-'nahr)*
to place	**colocar** *(koh-loh-'kahr)*
to plan	**planear** *(plah-neh-'ahr)*
to plug in	**enchufar** *(ehn-choo-'fahr)*
to postpone	**posponer** *(pohs-poh-'nehr)*
to pour	**verter** *(vehr-'tehr)*
to practice	**practicar** *(prahk-tee-'kahr)*
to prep	**dejar listo** *(deh-'hahr 'lees-toh)*
to prepare	**preparar** *(preh-pah-'rahr)*
to press	**oprimir** *(oh-pree-'meer)*
to print	**imprimir** *(eem-pree-'meer)*
to process	**tramitar** *(trah-mee-'tahr)*
to produce	**producir** *(proh-doo-'seer)*
to program	**programar** *(proh-grah-'mahr)*
to prohibit	**prohibir** *(proh-ee-'beer)*
to promise	**prometer** *(proh-meh-'tehr)*
to protect	**proteger** *(proh-teh-'hehr)*
to prove	**probar** *(proh-'bahr)*
to provide	**proveer** *(proh-veh-'ehr)*
to pull	**jalar** *(hah-'lahr)*
to push	**empujar** *(ehm-poo-'hahr)*
to put	**poner** *(poh-'nehr)*
to put away	**guardar** *(gwahr-'dahr)*
to put inside	**meter** *(meh-'tehr)*
to quit	**renunciar** *(reh-noon-see-'ahr)*
to raise	**levantar** *(leh-vahn-'tahr)*
to reach	**alcanzar** *(ahl-kahn-'sahr)*
to read	**leer** *(leh-'ehr)*
to receive	**recibir** *(reh-see-'beer)*
to recognize	**reconocer** *(reh-koh-noh-'sehr)*
to recommend	**recomendar** *(reh-koh-mehn-'dahr)*
to record	**documentar** *(doh-koo-mehn-'tahr)*
to redo	**rehacer** *(reh-ah-'sehr)*
to reduce	**reducir** *(reh-doo-'seer)*

to refer	**referir** *(reh-feh-'reer)*
to refill	**rellenar** *(reh-yeh-'nahr)*
to refuse	**negarse** *(neh-'gahr-seh)*
to reject	**rechazar** *(reh-chah-'sahr)*
to relax	**relajarse** *(reh-lah-'hahr-seh)*
to remember	**recordar** *(reh-kohr-'dahr)*
to remove	**sacar** *(sah-'kahr)*
to repair	**reparar** *(reh-pah-'rahr)*
to repeat	**repetir** *(reh-peh-'teer)*
to replace	**reemplazar** *(reh-ehm-plah-'sahr)*
to reply	**responder** *(rehs-pohn-'dehr)*
to represent	**representar** *(reh-preh-sehn-'tahr)*
to rest	**descansar** *(dehs-kahn-'sahr)*
to retire	**jubilar** *(hoo-bee-'lahr)*
to return	**volver** *(vohl-'vehr)*
to review	**repasar** *(reh-pah-'sahr)*
to ruin	**arruinar** *(ahr-roo-ee-'nahr)*
to run	**correr** *(kohr-'rehr)*
to save	**ahorrar** *(ah-ohr-'rahr)*
to say	**decir** *(deh-'seer)*
to scrub	**fregar** *(freh-'gahr)*
to search	**buscar** *(boos-'kahr)*
to see	**ver** *(vehr)*
to select	**escoger** *(ehs-koh-'hehr)*
to sell	**vender** *(vehn-'dehr)*
to send	**enviar** *(ehn-vee-'ahr)*
to separate	**separar** *(seh-pah-'rahr)*
to serve	**servir** *(sehr-'veer)*
to set up	**erigir** *(eh-ree-'heer)*
to settle	**arreglar** *(ahr-reh-'glahr)*
to shape	**formar** *(fohr-'mahr)*
to share	**compartir** *(kohm-pahr-teer)*
to shift	**cambiar** *(kahm-bee-'ahr)*
to ship	**enviar** *(ehn-vee-'ahr)*
to sign	**firmar** *(feer-'mahr)*
to sit down	**sentarse** *(sehn-'tahr-seh)*
to sleep	**dormir** *(dohr-'meer)*
to sort	**clasificar** *(klah-see-fee-'kahr)*
to speak	**hablar** *(ah-'blahr)*
to spend	**gastar** *(gahs-'tahr)*
to spill	**derramar** *(dehr-rah-'mahr)*

to spin	**girar** *(hee-'rahr)*
to spray	**rociar** *(roh-see-'ahr)*
to spread	**repartir** *(reh-pahr-'teer)*
to stabilize	**estabilizar** *(ehs-tah-bee-lee-'sahr)*
to stack	**apilar** *(ah-pee-'lahr)*
to stain	**manchar** *(mahn-'chahr)*
to stamp	**estampar** *(ehs-tahm-'pahr)*
to start up	**arrancar** *(ahr-rahn-'kahr)*
to step	**pisar** *(pee-'sahr)*
to stop	**parar** *(pah-'rahr)*
to straighten	**enderezar** *(ehn-deh-reh-'sahr)*
to stretch	**estirar** *(ehs-tee-'rahr)*
to study	**estudiar** *(ehs-too-dee-'ahr)*
to suggest	**sugerir** *(soo-heh-'reer)*
to support	**sostener** *(sohs-teh-'nehr)*
to surround	**rodear** *(roh-deh-'ahr)*
to suspend	**suspender** *(soos-pehn-'dehr)*
to sweep	**barrer** *(bahr-'rehr)*
to take	**tomar** *(toh-'mahr)*
to teach	**enseñar** *(ehn-sehn-'yahr)*
to tell	**decir** *(deh-'seer)*
to tell time	**decir la hora** *(deh-'seer lah 'oh-rah)*
to test	**probar** *(proh-'bahr)*
to thank	**agradecer** *(ah-grah-deh-'sehr)*
to think	**pensar** *(pehn-'sahr)*
to throw	**tirar** *(tee-'rahr)*
to throw away	**botar** *(boh-'tahr)*
to tie	**amarrar** *(ah-mahr-'rahr)*
to tighten	**apretar** *(ah-preh-'tahr)*
to touch	**tocar** *(toh-'kahr)*
to train	**entrenar** *(ehn-treh-'nahr)*
to transfer	**transferir** *(trahns-feh-'reer)*
to transmit	**transmitir** *(trahns-mee-'teer)*
to transport	**transportar** *(trahns-pohr-'tahr)*
to travel	**viajar** *(vee-ah-'hahr)*
to try	**tratar** *(trah-'tahr)*
to turn	**voltear** *(vohl-teh-'ahr)*
to turn off	**apagar** *(ah-pah-'gahr)*
to turn on	**encender** *(ehn-sehn-'dehr)*
to twist	**torcer** *(tohr-'sehr)*

to understand	**entender** *(ehn-tehn-'dehr)*
to unload	**descargar** *(dehs-kahr-'gahr)*
to unplug	**desenchufar** *(dehs-ehn-choo-'fahr)*
to unroll	**desenrollar** *(dehs-ehn-roh-'yahr)*
to upgrade	**mejorar** *(meh-hoh-'rahr)*
to use	**usar** *(oo-'sahr)*
to verify	**verificar** *(veh-ree-fee-'kahr)*
to visit	**visitar** *(vee-see-'tahr)*
to wait	**esperar** *(ehs-peh-'rahr)*
to walk	**caminar** *(kah-mee-'nahr)*
to want	**querer** *(keh-'rehr)*
to wash	**lavar** *(lah-'vahr)*
to watch	**vigilar** *(vee-hee-'lahr)*
to water	**regar** *(reh-'gahr)*
to weld	**soldar** *(sohl-'dahr)*
to wet	**mojar** *(moh-'hahr)*
to wipe	**quitar frotando** *(kee-'tahr froh-'tahn-doh)*
to withstand	**aguantar** *(ah-gwahn-'tahr)*
to work	**trabajar** *(trah-bah-'hahr)*
to write	**escribir** *(ehs-kree-'beer)*
to yell	**gritar** *(gree-'tahr)*

Numbers Chart

0	**cero** *('seh-roh)*
1	**uno** *('oo-noh)*
2	**dos** *(dohs)*
3	**tres** *(trehs)*
4	**cuatro** *('kwah-troh)*
5	**cinco** *('seehn-koh)*
6	**seis** *('seh-ees)*
7	**siete** *(see-'eh-teh)*
8	**ocho** *('oh-choh)*
9	**nueve** *(noo-'eh-veh)*
10	**diez** *(dee-'ehs)*
11	**once** *('ohn-seh)*
12	**doce** *('doh-seh)*
13	**trece** *('treh-seh)*
14	**catorce** *(kah-'tohr-seh)*
15	**quince** *('keen-seh)*
16	**dieciséis** *(dee-ehs-ee-'seh-ees)*
17	**diecisiete** *(dee-ehs-ee-see-'eh-teh)*
18	**dieciocho** *(dee-ehs-ee-'oh-choh)*
19	**diecinueve** *(dee-ehs-ee-noo-'eh-veh)*
20	**veinte** *('veh-een-teh)*
30	**treinta** *('treh-een-tah)*
40	**cuarenta** *(kwah-'rehn-tah)*
50	**cincuenta** *(seen-'kwehn-tah)*
60	**sesenta** *(seh-'sehn-tah)*
70	**setenta** *(seh-'tehn-tah)*
80	**ochenta** *(oh-'chehn-tah)*
90	**noventa** *(noh-'vehn-tah)*
100	**cien** *(see-'ehn)*
200	**doscientos** *(dohs-see-'ehn-tohs)*
300	**trescientos** *(trehs-see-'ehn-tohs)*
400	**cuatrocientos** *(kwah-troh-see-'ehn-tohs)*
500	**quinientos** *(keen-ee-'ehn-tohs)*
600	**seiscientos** *(seh-ee-see-'ehn-tohs)*
700	**setecientos** *(seh-teh-see-'ehn-tohs)*
800	**ochocientos** *(oh-choh-see-'ehn-tohs)*
900	**novecientos** *(noh-veh-see-'ehn-tohs)*
1000	**mil** *(meel)*

Metric Conversion Table

Length—Longitud *(lohn-hee-'tood)*

1 centimeter = 0.3937 inches
1 inch = 2.54 centimeters
1 foot = 30.48 centimeters
1 foot = 0.3048 meters
1 yard = 0.9144 meters
1 meter = 1.093613 yards
1 kilometer = 0.621 miles
1 mile = 1.609344 kilometers

Weight—Peso *('peh-soh)*

1 gram = 0.353 ounces
1 ounce = 28.35 grams
1 pound = 453.6 grams
1 pound = 0.4563 kilograms
1 kilogram = 2.2046 pounds
1 American ton = 0.907 metric tons
1 metric ton = 1.1 American tons

Volume and Capacity—Volumen y capacidad *(voh-'loo-mehn ee kah-pah-see-'dahd)*

1 milliliter = 0.034 fluid ounces
1 milliliter = 0.2 teaspoons
1 fluid ounce = 29.6 milliliters
1 teaspoon ≐ 5 milliliters
1 cup = 0.24 liters
1 pint = 0.473 liters
1 quart = 0.95 liters
1 liter = 4.227 cups
1 liter = 0.264 gallons
1 gallon = 3.785 liters

Area—Area *('ah-reh-ah)*

1 square centimeter = 0.155 square inches
1 square inch = 6.4516 square centimeters
1 square foot = 929 square centimeters
1 acre = 0.405 hectares
1 hectare = 2.471 acres
1 square kilometer = 0.386 square miles
1 square mile = 2.59 square kilometers

Specialized Vocabulary for Employers

CHILDCARE, CONSTRUCTION, FOOD SERVICES, HOUSECLEANING, LANDSCAPING, TAILORING AND DRY-CLEANING, VEHICLE REPAIR

In addition to the material presented in Chapters One to Six, employers may also require vocabulary in Spanish that targets their specialized fields of work. The following are some key examples. Be creative with your skills as you practice each new word:

Childcare
El cuidado de niños
(ehl kwee-'dah-doh deh 'neen-yohs)

action figure	**la figura de acción** *(lah fee-'goo-rah deh ahk-see-'ohn)*
aerobics	**el aeróbic** *(ehl ah-eh-'roh-beek)*
art	**el arte** *(ehl 'ahr-teh)*
baby	**el bebé** *(ehl beh-'beh)*
ball	**la pelota** *(lah peh-'loh-tah)*
ballet	**el ballet** *(ehl bah-'leh)*
balloon	**el globo** *(ehl 'gloh-boh)*
baseball	**el béisbol** *(ehl 'beh-ees-bohl)*
basketball	**el básquetbol** *(ehl 'bahs-keht-bohl)*
bassinet	**el bacinete** *(ehl bah-see-'neh-teh)*
bear	**el oso** *(ehl 'oh-soh)*
behavior	**el comportamiento** *(ehl kohm-pohr-tah-mee-'ehn-toh)*
bib	**el babero** *(ehl bah-'beh-roh)*
bike	**la bicicleta** *(lah bee-see-'kleh-tah)*
bird	**el pájaro** *(ehl 'pah-hah-roh)*
blanket	**la cobija** *(lah koh-'bee-hah)*
blocks	**los bloques** *(lohs 'bloh-kehs)*
bowling	**el boliche** *(ehl boh-'lee-cheh)*
cartoons	**los dibujos animados** *(lohs dee-'boo-hohs ah-nee-'mah-dohs)*
cat	**el gato** *(ehl 'gah-toh)*
checkers	**el juego de damas** *(ehl 'hweh-goh deh 'dah-mahs)*
chicken	**el pollo** *(ehl 'poh-yoh)*
circus	**el circo** *(ehl 'seer-koh)*
coloring book	**el libro de pintar** *(ehl 'lee-broh deh peen-'tahr)*
costume	**el disfraz** *(ehl dees-'frahs)*
court	**la cancha** *(lah 'kahn-chah)*
cow	**la vaca** *(lah 'vah-kah)*
crayons	**los gises** *(lohs 'gee-sehs)*
crib	**la cuna** *(lah 'koo-nah)*
dancing	**el baile** *(ehl 'bah-ee-leh)*

diaper	**el pañal** *(ehl pahn-'yahl)*
dinosaur	**el dinosaurio** *(ehl dee-noh-'sah-oo-ree-oh)*
dog	**el perro** *(ehl 'pehr-roh)*
doll	**la muñeca** *(lah moon-'yeh-kah)*
drawing	**el dibujo** *(ehl dee-boo-'hoh)*
duck	**el pato** *(ehl 'pah-toh)*
DVDs	**los vídeos** *(lohs 'vee-deh-ohs)*
elephant	**el elefante** *(ehl eh-leh-'fahn-teh)*
exercise	**el ejercicio** *(ehl eh-hehr-'see-see-'oh)*
fish	**el pez** *(ehl pehs)*
fishing	**la pesca** *(lah pehs-'kah)*
football	**el fútbol americano** *(ehl 'foot-bohl ah-meh-ree-'kah-noh)*
game	**el juego** *(ehl 'hweh-goh)*
giraffe	**la jirafa** *(lah hee-'rah-fah)*
gymnastics	**la gimnasia** *(lah heem-'nah-see-ah)*
hiking	**la caminata** *(lah kah-mee-'nah-tah)*
horse	**el caballo** *(ehl kah-'bah-yoh)*
horseback riding	**la equitación** *(lah eh-kee-tah-see-'ohn)*
infant car seat	**el asiento infantil para carro**
	(ehl ah-see-'ehn-toh een-fahn-'teel 'pah-rah 'kahr-roh)
jogging	**el trote** *(ehl 'troh-teh)*
joke	**el chiste** *(ehl 'chees-teh)*
kite	**la cometa** *(lah koh-'meh-tah)*
laughter	**la risa** *(lah 'ree-sah)*
lion	**el león** *(eh leh-'ohn)*
magic	**la magia** *(lah 'mah-hee-ah)*
match	**el partido** *(ehl pahr-'tee-doh)*
meal	**la comida** *(lah koh-'mee-dah)*
modeling clay	**la plastilina** *(lah plahs-tee-'lee-nah)*
monkey	**el mono** *(ehl 'moh-noh)*
mouse	**el ratón** *(ehl rah-'tohn)*
movies	**las películas** *(lahs peh-'lee-koo-lahs)*
music	**la música** *(lah 'moo-see-kah)*
nanny	**la niñera** *(lah neen-'yeh-rah)*
nap	**la siesta** *(lah see-'ehs-tah)*
nurse	**la enfermera** *(lah ehn-fehr-'meh-rah)*
nursing bottle	**el biberón** *(ehl bee-beh-'rohn)*
pacifier	**el chupete** *(ehl choo-'peh-teh)*
painting	**la pintura** *(lah peen-'too-rah)*
parade	**el desfile** *(ehl dehs-'fee-leh)*
pig	**el cerdo** *(ehl 'sehr-doh)*
playground	**el campo de recreo** *(ehl 'kahm-poh deh reh-'kreh-oh)*
playing cards	**los naipes** *(lohs 'nah-ee-pehs)*

pony	el **caballito** *(ehl kah-bah-'yee-toh)*
pool	la **piscina** *(lah pee-'see-nah)*
practice	la **práctica** *(lah 'prahk-tee-kah)*
puppet	el **títere** *(ehl 'tee-teh-reh)*
puzzle	el **rompecabezas** *(ehl rohm-peh-kah-'beh-sahs)*
rabbit	el **conejo** *(ehl koh-'neh-hoh)*
reading	la **lectura** *(lah lehk-'too-rah)*
rollerblades	los **patines** *(lohs pah-'tee-nehs)*
running	la **carrera** *(lah kahr-'reh-rah)*
scooter	el **escúter** *(ehl ehs-'koo-tehr)*
sheep	la **oveja** *(lah oh-'veh-hah)*
skateboard	la **patineta** *(lah pah-tee-'neh-tah)*
sled	el **trineo** *(ehl tree-'neh-oh)*
slide	el **resbalador** *(ehl rehs-bah-lah-'dohr)*
smile	la **sonrisa** *(lah sohn-'ree-sah)*
soccer	el **fútbol** *(ehl 'foot-bohl)*
song	la **canción** *(lah kahn-see-'ohn)*
sports	los **deportes** *(lohs deh-'pohr-tehs)*
story	el **cuento** *(ehl 'kwehn-'toh)*
stroller	el **cochecillo** *(ehl koh-cheh-'see-yoh)*
stuffed animals	los **animales de peluche** *(lohs ah-nee-'mah-lehs deh peh-'loo-cheh)*
swimming	la **natación** *(lah nah-tah-see-'ohn)*
swing	el **columpio** *(ehl koh-'loom-pee-oh)*
tears	las **lágrimas** *(lah 'lah-gree-mahs)*
tennis	el **tenis** *(ehl 'teh-nees)*
tiger	el **tigre** *(ehl 'tee-greh)*
toy car	el **carrito** *(ehl kahr-'ree-toh)*
toy train	el **tren de juguete** *(ehl trehn deh hoo-'geh-teh)*
toy	el **juguete** *(ehl hoo-'geh-teh)*
trick	el **truco** *(ehl 'troo-koh)*
tricycle	el **triciclo** *(ehl tree-'see-kloh)*
video game	el **videojuego** *(ehl vee-deh-oh 'hweh-goh)*
volleyball	el **vólibol** *(ehl 'voh-lee-bohl)*
wagon	el **carrito** *(ehl kahr-'ree-'toh)*
zebra	la **cebra** *(lah 'seh-brah)*
zoo	el **zoológico** *(ehl soh-oh-'loh-hee-koh)*

Construction
La construcción
(lah kohns-trook-see-'ohn)

aluminum	el **aluminio** *(ehl ah-loo-'mee-nee-oh)*
apprentice	el **aprendiz** *(ehl ah-prehn-'dees)*

architect	el **arquitecto** *(ehl ahr-kee-'tehk-toh)*
bit	la **broca** *(lah 'broh-kah)*
blade	la **cuchilla** *(lah koo-'chee-yah)*
bolt	el **perno** *(ehl 'pehr-noh)*
brick	el **ladrillo** *(ehl lah-'dree-yoh)*
builder	el **constructor** *(ehl kohns-trook-'tohr)*
bulldozer	el **tractor oruga** *(ehl trahk-'tohr oh-'roo-gah)*
carpenter	el **carpintero** *(ehl kahr-peen-'teh-roh)*
cement truck	la **mezcladora de cemento** *(lah mehs-klah-'doh-rah deh seh-'mehn-toh)*
chain	la **cadena** *(lah kah-'deh-nah)*
chainsaw	la **motosierra** *(lah moh-toh-see-'ehr-rah)*
chisel	el **cincel** *(ehl seen-'sehl)*
clamp	la **prensa de sujetar** *(lah 'prehn-sah deh soo-heh-'tahr)*
compressor	el **compresor de aire** *(ehl kohm-preh-'sohr deh 'ah-ee-reh)*
contractor	el **contratista** *(ehl kohn-trah-'tees-tah)*
copper	el **cobre** *(ehl 'koh-breh)*
drill	el **taladro** *(ehl tah-'lah-droh)*
driller	la **perforadora** *(lah pehr-foh-rah-'doh-rah)*
dry waller	el **yesero** *(ehl yeh-'seh-roh)*
dump truck	el **camión volquete** *(ehl kah-mee-'ohn vohl-'keh-teh)*
dumpster	el **basurero de hierro** *(ehl bah-soo-'reh-roh deh ee-'ehr-roh)*
electric cord	el **cordón eléctrico** *(ehl kohr-'dohn eh-'lehk-tree-koh)*
electrician	el **electricista** *(ehl eh-lehk-tree-'sees-tah)*
engineer	el **ingeniero** *(ehl een-heh-nee-'eh-roh)*
equipment	el **equipo** *(ehl eh-'kee-poh)*
file	la **lima** *(lah 'lee-mah)*
floor tile	la **loseta** *(lah loh-'seh-tah)*
foreman	el **capataz** *(ehl kah-pah-'tahs)*
generator	el **generador** *(ehl heh-neh-rah-'dohr)*
glass	el **vidrio** *(ehl 'veed-ree-oh)*
glue	el **pegamento** *(ehl peh-gah-'mehn-toh)*
hacksaw	la **sierra para metales** *(lah see-'ehr-rah 'pah-rah meh-'tah-lehs)*
hammer	el **martillo** *(ehl mahr-'tee-yoh)*
helper	el **ayudante** *(ehl ah-yoo-'dahn-teh)*
inspector	el **inspector** *(ehl eens-pehk-'tohr)*
installer	el **instalador** *(ehl eens-tah-lah-'dohr)*
iron	el **hierro** *(ehl ee-'ehr-roh)*
laborer	el **obrero** *(ehl oh-'breh-roh)*
ladder	la **escalera** *(lah ehs-kah-'leh-rah)*
level	el **nivel** *(ehl nee-'vehl)*
loader	la **cargadora** *(lah kahr-gah-'doh-rah)*
lumber	las **tablas** *(lahs 'tah-blahs)*

mallet	**el mazo** *(ehl 'mah-soh)*
materials	**los materiales** *(lohs mah-teh-ree-'ah-lehs)*
measuring tape	**la cinta de medir** *(lah 'seen-tah deh meh-'deer)*
metal	**el metal** *(ehl meh-'tahl)*
nails	**los clavos** *(lohs 'klah-vohs)*
nut	**la tuerca** *(lah 'twehr-kah)*
paint brush	**la brocha de pintar** *(lah 'broh-chah deh peen-'tahr)*
paint	**la pintura** *(lah peen-'too-rah)*
painter	**el pintor** *(ehl peen-'tohr)*
Phillips screwdriver	**el destornillador en cruz** *(ehl dehs-tohr-nee-yah-'dohr ehn kroos)*
plaster	**el yeso** *(ehl 'yeh-soh)*
plastic	**el plástico** *(ehl 'plahs-tee-koh)*
pliers	**los alicates** *(lohs ah-lee-'kah-tehs)*
plumber	**el plomero** *(ehl ploh-'meh-roh)*
plumbing	**la plomería** *(lah ploh-meh-'ree-ah)*
plywood	**la madera contrachapada** *(lah mah-'deh-rah kohn-trah-chah-'pah-dah)*
prybar	**la palanca** *(lah pah-'lahn-kah)*
pump	**la bomba** *(lah 'bohm-bah)*
rope	**la soga** *(lah 'soh-gah)*
rubber	**la goma** *(lah 'goh-mah)*
sandpaper	**el papel de lija** *(ehl pah-'pehl deh 'lee-hah)*
saw	**la sierra** *(lah see-'ehr-rah)*
sawhorse	**el caballete** *(ehl kah-bah-'yeh-teh)*
scaffold	**el andamio** *(ehl ahn-'dah-mee-oh)*
scraper	**el raspador** *(ehl rahs-pah-'dohr)*
screwdriver	**el destornillador** *(ehl dehs-tohr-nee-yah-'dohr)*
screws	**los tornillos** *(lohs tohr-'nee-yos)*
sledge	**la almádena** *(lah ahl-'mah-deh-nah)*
socket wrench	**la llave de cubo** *(lah 'yah-veh deh 'koo-boh)*
steel	**el acero** *(ehl ah-'seh-roh)*
stonemason	**el albañil** *(ehl ahl-bahn-'eel)*
sub-contractor	**el subcontratista** *(ehl soob-kohn-trah-'tees-tah)*
tank truck	**el camión cisterna** *(ehl kah-mee-'ohn sees-'tehr-nah)*
tape	**la cinta** *(lah 'seen-tah)*
toolbox	**la caja de herramientas** *(lah 'kah-hah deh ehr-rah-mee-'ehn-tahs)*
tools	**las herramientas** *(lahs ehr-rah-mee-'ehn-tahs)*
trailer	**el remolque** *(ehl reh-'mohl-keh)*
trash bag	**la bolsa de basura** *(lah 'bohl-sah deh bah-'soo-rah)*
trashcan	**el cesto de basura** *(ehl 'sehs-toh deh bah-'soo-rah)*
trowel	**la llana** *(lah 'yah-nah)*
truck	**el camión** *(ehl kah-mee-'ohn)*
truck driver	**el camionero** *(ehl kah-mee-oh-'neh-roh)*

wall tile	**el azulejo** *(ehl ah-soo-'leh-hoh)*
wheelbarrow	**la carretilla** *(lah kahr-reh-'tee-yah)*
wire brush	**el cepillo de alambre** *(ehl seh-'pee-yoh deh ah-'lahm-breh)*
wire	**el alambre** *(ehl ah-'lahm-breh)*
wirecutters	**los cortaalambres** *(lohs kohr-tah-ah-'lahm-brehs)*
wood	**la madera** *(lah mah-'deh-rah)*
worksite	**la zona de trabajo** *(lah 'soh-nah deh trah-'bah-hoh)*
wrecking ball	**la bola de demolición** *(lah 'boh-lah deh deh-moh-lee-see-'ohn)*
wrench	**la llave inglesa** *(lah 'yah-veh een-'gleh-sah)*

Food Services
El servicio de alimentos
(ehl sehr-'vee-see-oh deh ah-lee-'mehn-tohs)

apple	**la manzana** *(lah mahn-'sah-nah)*
apricot	**el durazno** *(ehl doo-'rahs-noh)*
apron	**el delantal** *(ehl deh-lahn-'tahl)*
bacon	**el tocino** *(ehl toh-'see-noh)*
banana	**el plátano** *(ehl 'plah-tah-noh)*
bartender	**el cantinero** *(ehl kahn-tee-'neh-roh)*
beans	**los frijoles** *(lohs free-'hoh-lehs)*
beef	**la carne de res** *(lah 'kahr-neh deh rehs)*
beer	**la cerveza** *(lah sehr-'veh-sah)*
beet	**la remolacha** *(lah reh-moh-'lah-chah)*
blender	**la licuadora** *(lah lee-kwah-'doh-rah)*
bowl	**el plato hondo** *(ehl 'plah-toh 'ohn-doh)*
bread	**el pan** *(ehl pahn)*
breakfast	**el desayuno** *(ehl dehs-ah-'yoo-noh)*
broccoli	**el brócoli** *(ehl 'broh-koh-lee)*
busboy	**el ayudante de camarero**
	(ehl ah-yoo-'dahn-teh deh kah-mah-'reh-roh)
butter	**la mantequilla** *(lah mahn-teh-'kee-yah)*
cabbage	**el repollo** *(ehl reh-'poh-yoh)*
cake	**la torta** *(lah 'tohr-tah)*
can opener	**el abrelatas** *(ehl ah-breh-'lah-tahs)*
candy	**los dulces** *(lohs 'dool-sehs)*
cantaloupe	**el melón** *(ehl meh-'lohn)*
carrot	**la zanahoria** *(lah sah-nah-'oh-ree-ah)*
celery	**el apio** *(ehl 'ah-pee-oh)*
cereal	**el cereal** *(ehl seh-reh-'ahl)*
cheese	**el queso** *(ehl 'keh-soh)*
cherry	**la cereza** *(lah seh-'reh-sah)*

chicken	**el pollo** *(ehl 'poh-yoh)*
coconut	**el coco** *(ehl 'koh-koh)*
coffee	**el café** *(ehl kah-'feh)*
coffeepot	**la cafetera** *(lah kah-feh-'teh-rah)*
cook	**el cocinero** *(ehl koh-see-'neh-roh)*
cookie	**la galleta** *(lah gah-'yeh-tah)*
corn	**el maíz** *(ehl mah-'ees)*
cream	**la crema** *(lah 'kreh-mah)*
cucumber	**el pepino** *(ehl peh-'pee-noh)*
cup	**la taza** *(lah 'tah-sah)*
decaffeinated coffee	**el café descafeinado** *(ehl kah-'feh dehs-kah-feh-ee-'nah-doh)*
dessert	**el postre** *(ehl 'pohs-treh)*
diet soda	**la soda dietética** *(lah 'soh-dah dee-eh-'teh-tee-kah)*
dinner	**la cena** *(lah 'seh-nah)*
dishwasher	**el lavaplatos** *(ehl lah-vah-'plah-tohs)*
drink	**la bebida** *(lah beh-'bee-dah)*
eggs	**los huevos** *(los 'hweh-vohs)*
fat	**la grasa** *(lah 'grah-sah)*
fish	**el pescado** *(ehl pehs-'kah-doh)*
fork	**el tenedor** *(ehl teh-neh-'dohr)*
freezer	**el congelador** *(ehl kohn-heh-lah-'dohr)*
fruit	**la fruta** *(lah 'froo-tah)*
garbage disposal	**el desechador** *(ehl dehs-eh-chah-'dohr)*
glass	**el vaso** *(ehl 'vah-soh)*
grape	**la uva** *(lah 'oo-vah)*
grapefruit	**la toronja** *(lah toh-'rohn-hah)*
grill	**la parrilla** *(lah pahr-'ree-yah)*
gum	**el chicle** *(ehl 'cheek-leh)*
hairnet	**la redecilla** *(lah reh-deh-'see-yah)*
ham	**el jamón** *(ehl hah-'mohn)*
hamburger	**la hamburguesa** *(lah ahm-boor-'geh-sah)*
honey	**la miel** *(lah mee-'ehl)*
hot chocolate	**el chocolate caliente** *(ehl choh-koh-'lah-teh kah-lee-'ehn-teh)*
hot dog	**el perro caliente** *(ehl 'pehr-roh kah-lee-'ehn-teh)*
hot pepper	**el chile** *(ehl 'chee-leh)*
ice cream	**el helado** *(ehl eh-'lah-doh)*
iced tea	**el té helado** *(ehl teh eh-'lah-doh)*
jello	**la gelatina** *(lah heh-'lah-'tee-nah)*
juice	**el jugo** *(ehl 'hoo-goh)*
knife	**el cuchillo** *(ehl koo-'chee-yoh)*
lemon	**el limón** *(ehl lee-'mohn)*
lemonade	**la limonada** *(lah lee-moh-'nah-dah)*
lettuce	**la lechuga** *(lah leh-'choo-gah)*

liquor	el **licor** *(ehl lee-'kohr)*
lunch	el **almuerzo** *(ehl ahl-'mwehr-soh)*
margarine	la **margarina** *(lah mahr-gah-'ree-nah)*
marmalade	la **mermelada** *(lah mehr-meh-'lah-dah)*
mayonnaise	la **mayonesa** *(lah mah-yoh-'neh-sah)*
meat	la **carne** *(lah 'kahr-neh)*
microwave	la **microonda** *(lah mee-kroh-'ohn-dah)*
milk	la **leche** *(lah 'leh-cheh)*
mixer	la **batidora** *(lah bah-tee-'doh-rah)*
mushrooms	los **champiñones** *(lohs chahm-peen-'yoh-nehs)*
mustard	la **mostaza** *(lah mohs-tah-sah)*
napkin	la **servilleta** *(lah sehr-vee-'yeh-tah)*
natural food	la **comida natural** *(lah koh-'mee-dah nah-too-'rahl)*
noodles	los **fideos** *(lohs fee-'deh-ohs)*
onion	la **cebolla** *(lah seh-'boh-yah)*
orange	la **naranja** *(lah nah-'rahn-hah)*
organic food	la **comida orgánica** *(lah koh-'mee-dah ohr-'gah-nee-kah)*
oven	el **horno** *(ehl 'ohr-noh)*
pan	el **sartén** *(ehl sahr-'tehn)*
pancake	el **panqueque** *(ehl pahn-'keh-keh)*
peach	el **melocotón** *(ehl meh-loh-koh-'tohn)*
pear	la **pera** *(lah 'peh-rah)*
peas	las **arvejitas** *(lahs ahr-veh-'hee-tahs)*
pepper	la **pimienta** *(lah pee-mee-'ehn-tah)*
pepper shaker	el **pimentero** *(ehl pee-mehn-'teh-roh)*
pickle	el **encurtido** *(ehl ehn-koor-'tee-doh)*
pie	el **pastel** *(ehl pahs-'tehl)*
pitcher	el **cántaro** *(ehl 'kahn-tah-roh)*
pizza	la **pizza** *(lah 'pee-tzah)*
plate	el **plato** *(ehl 'plah-toh)*
platter	la **fuente** *(lah 'fwehn-teh)*
pork	el **cerdo** *(ehl 'sehr-doh)*
pot	la **olla** *(lah 'oh-yah)*
potato	la **papa** *(lah 'pah-pah)*
pudding	el **budín** *(ehl boo-'deen)*
radish	el **rábano** *(ehl 'rah-bah-noh)*
refrigerator	el **refrigerador** *(ehl reh-free-heh-rah-'dohr)*
restaurant	el **restaurante** *(ehl rehs-tah-oo-'rahn-teh)*
rice	el **arroz** *(ehl ahr-'rohs)*
roast beef	el **rósbif** *(ehl 'rohs-beef)*
rolls	los **panecillos** *(lohs pah-neh-'see-yohs)*
salad	la **ensalada** *(lah ehn-sah-'lah-dah)*
salad dressing	la **salsa para ensalada** *(lah 'sahl-sah 'pah-rah ehn-sah-'lah-dah)*

salt	**la sal** *(lah sahl)*
salt shaker	**el salero** *(ehl sah-'leh-roh)*
sandwich	**el emparedado** *(ehl ehm-pah-reh-'dah-doh)*
sauce	**la salsa** *(lah 'sahl-sah)*
saucer	**el platillo** *(ehl plah-'tee-yoh)*
sausage	**la salchicha** *(lah sahl-'chee-chah)*
seafood	**el marisco** *(ehl mah-'rees-koh)*
shake	**el batido** *(ehl bah-'tee-doh)*
skim milk	**la leche descremada** *(lah 'leh-cheh dehs-kreh-'mah-dah)*
soft drink	**el refresco** *(ehl reh-'frehs-koh)*
soup	**la sopa** *(lah 'soh-pah)*
spaghetti	**el espagueti** *(ehl ehs-pah-'geh-tee)*
spinach	**la espinaca** *(lah ehs-pee-'nah-kah)*
spoon	**la cuchara** *(lah koo-'chah-rah)*
squash	**el zapallo** *(ehl sah-'pah-yoh)*
steak	**el bistec** *(ehl bees-'tehk)*
stove	**la estufa** *(lah ehs-'too-fah)*
strawberry	**la fresa** *(lah 'freh-sah)*
sugar	**el azúcar** *(ehl ah-'soo-kahr)*
tablecloth	**el mantel** *(ehl mahn-'tehl)*
tea	**el té** *(ehl teh)*
toast	**el pan tostado** *(ehl pahn tohs-'tah-doh)*
toaster	**el tostador** *(ehl tohs-tah-'dohr)*
tomato	**el tomate** *(ehl toh-'mah-teh)*
tuna	**el atún** *(ehl ah-'toon)*
turkey	**el pavo** *(ehl 'pah-voh)*
uniform	**el uniforme** *(ehl oo-nee-'fohr-meh)*
vegetables	**los vegetales** *(lohs veh-heh-'tah-lehs)*
vegetarian food	**la comida vegetariana** *(lah koh-'mee-dah veh-heh-tah-ree-'ah-nah)*
waiter	**el mesero** *(ehl meh-'seh-roh)*
waitress	**la mesera** *(lah meh-'seh-rah)*
wine	**el vino** *(ehl 'vee-noh)*
yogurt	**el yogúr** *(ehl yoh-'goor)*

Housecleaning
La limpieza de la casa
(lah leem-pee-'eh-sah deh lah 'kah-sah)

air conditioner	**el acondicionador de aire** *(ehl ah-kohn-dee-see-oh-nah-'dohr deh 'ah-ee-reh)*
air freshener	**el ambientador** *(ehl ahm-bee-ehn-tah-'dohr)*
alarm	**la alarma** *(lah ah-'lahr-mah)*
answering machine	**la contestadora** *(lah kohn-tehs-tah-'doh-rah)*

apartment	el **apartamento** *(ehl ah-pahr-tah-'mehn-toh)*
appliance	el **electrodoméstico** *(ehl eh-lehk-troh-doh-'mehs-tee-koh)*
armchair	el **sillón** *(ehl see-'yohn)*
attic	el **desván** *(ehl dehs-'vahn)*
audio system	el **sistema de audio** *(ehl sees-'teh-mah deh 'aw-dee-oh)*
awning	el **toldo** *(ehl 'tohl-doh)*
bathroom	el **baño** *(ehl 'bahn-yoh)*
bathtub	la **tina** *(lah 'tee-nah)*
bed	la **cama** *(lah 'kah-mah)*
bedroom	el **dormitorio** *(ehl dohr-mee-'toh-ree-oh)*
bedspread	la **cubrecama** *(lah koo-breh-'kah-mah)*
blanket	la **frazada** *(lah frah-'sah-dah)*
bleach	el **cloro** *(ehl 'kloh-roh)*
blinds	las **persianas** *(lahs pehr-see-'ah-nahs)*
broom	la **escoba** *(lah ehs-'koh-bah)*
brush	el **cepillo** *(ehl seh-'pee-yoh)*
bucket	el **balde** *(ehl 'bahl-deh)*
cable box	la **caja del cable** *(lah 'kah-hah dehl 'kah-bleh)*
carpeting	el **alfombrado** *(ehl ahl-fohm-'brah-doh)*
chair	la **silla** *(lah 'see-yah)*
chest	el **baúl** *(ehl bah-'ool)*
chimney	la **chimenea** *(lah chee-meh-'neh-ah)*
cleanser	el **limpiador** *(ehl leem-pee-ah-'dohr)*
clock	el **reloj** *(ehl reh-'loh)*
closet	el **ropero** *(ehl roh-'peh-roh)*
cobwebs	las **telarañas** *(lahs teh-lah-'rahn-yahs)*
computer	la **computadora** *(lah kohm-poo-tah-'doh-rah)*
condominium	el **condominio** *(ehl kohn-doh-'mee-nee-oh)*
cottage	el **chalet** *(ehl chah-'leh)*
curtain	la **cortina** *(lah kohr-'tee-nah)*
deck	la **terraza** *(lah tehr-'rah-sah)*
dining room	el **comedor** *(ehl koh-meh-'dohr)*
dirt	la **suciedad** *(lah soo-see-eh-'dahd)*
dishwasher	el **lavaplatos** *(ehl lah-vah-'plah-tohs)*
dispenser	el **dispensador** *(ehl dees-pehn-sah-'dohr)*
drain	el **drenaje** *(ehl dreh-'nah-heh)*
dresser	el **tocador** *(ehl toh-kah-'dohr)*
driveway	la **entrada de carros** *(lah ehn-'trah-dah deh 'kahr-rohs)*
dryer	la **secadora** *(lah seh-kah-'doh-rah)*
dust	el **polvo** *(ehl 'pohl-voh)*
dustpan	la **pala de recoger basura** *(lah 'pah-lah deh reh-koh-'hehr bah-'soo-rah)*
fan	el **ventilador** *(ehl vehn-tee-lah-'dohr)*

farmhouse	**la granja** *(lah 'grahn-hah)*
faucet	**el grifo** *(ehl 'gree-foh)*
feather duster	**el plumero** *(ehl ploo-'meh-roh)*
fireplace	**el fogón** *(ehl foh-'gohn)*
flooring	**el piso** *(ehl 'pee-soh)*
fountain	**la fuente** *(lah 'fwehn-teh)*
freezer	**el congelador** *(ehl kohn-heh-lah-'dohr)*
garage	**el garaje** *(ehl gah-'rah-heh)*
garbage disposal	**el desechador** *(ehl dehs-eh-chah-'dohr)*
garden	**el jardín** *(ehl hahr-'deen)*
gardener	**el jardinero/la jardinera** *(ehl hahr-dee-'neh-roh/lah hahr-dee-'neh-rah)*
gardening	**la jardinería** *(lah hahr-dee-neh-'ree-ah)*
grease	**la grasa** *(lah 'grah-sah)*
heater	**el calentador** *(ehl kah-lehn-tah-'dohr)*
home theater	**el cine de hogar** *(ehl 'see-neh deh oh-'gahr)*
hot water heater	**el calentador de agua** *(ehl kah-lehn-tah-'dohr deh 'ah-gwah)*
house	**la casa** *(lah 'kah-sah)*
housekeeper	**el criado** *(ehl kree-'ah-doh)*
key	**la llave** *(lah 'yah-veh)*
kitchen	**la cocina** *(lah koh-'see-nah)*
lamp	**la lámpara** *(lah 'lahm-pah-rah)*
lawn	**el césped** *(ehl 'sehs-pehd)*
lightbulb	**el foco** *(ehl 'foh-koh)*
lighting	**la iluminación** *(lah ee-loo-mee-nah-see-'ohn)*
living room	**la sala** *(lah 'sah-lah)*
magazine	**la revista** *(lah reh-'vees-tah)*
mansion	**la mansión** *(lah mahn-see-'ohn)*
mask	**la máscara** *(lah 'mahs-kah-rah)*
microwave	**el microonda** *(ehl mee-kroh-'ohn-dah)*
mop	**el trapeador** *(ehl trah-peh-ah-'dohr)*
mud	**el lodo** *(ehl 'loh-doh)*
newspaper	**el periódico** *(ehl peh-ree-'oh-dee-koh)*
nightstand	**la mesita de noche** *(lah meh-'see-tah deh 'noh-cheh)*
oven	**el horno** *(ehl 'ohr-noh)*
paper towel	**la toalla de papel** *(lah toh-'ah-yah deh pah-'pehl)*
patio	**el patio** *(ehl 'pah-tee-oh)*
phone	**el teléfono** *(ehl teh-'leh-foh-noh)*
pillow	**la almohada** *(lah ahl-moh-'ah-dah)*
pillowcase	**la funda de almohada** *(lah 'foon-dah deh ahl-moh-'ah-dah)*
planter	**el macetero** *(ehl mah-seh-'teh-roh)*
porch	**el porche** *(ehl 'pohr-cheh)*
radio	**el radio** *(ehl 'rah-dee-oh)*

rag	**el trapo** *(ehl 'trah-poh)*
recorder	**la grabadora** *(lah grah-bah-'doh-rah)*
refrigerator	**el refrigerador** *(ehl reh-free-heh-rah-'dohr)*
scouring pad	**la almohadilla abrasiva** *(lah ahl-moh-ah-'dee-yah ah-brah-'see-vah)*
scrub brush	**el cepillo de fregar** *(ehl seh-'pee-yoh deh freh-'gahr)*
sheet	**la sábana** *(lah 'sah-bah-nah)*
shower	**la ducha** *(lah 'doo-chah)*
shutters	**los postigos** *(lohs pohs-'tee-gohs)*
sink	**el lavabo** *(ehl lah-'vah-boh)*
soap	**el jabón** *(ehl hah-'bohn)*
sofa	**el sofá** *(ehl soh-'fah)*
sponge	**la esponja** *(lah ehs-'pohn-hah)*
stain	**la mancha** *(lah 'mahn-chah)*
stereo	**el estéreo** *(ehl ehs-'teh-reh-oh)*
stove	**la estufa** *(lah ehs-'too-fah)*
table	**la mesa** *(lah 'meh-sah)*
toilet paper	**el papel higiénico** *(ehl pah-'pehl ee-hee-'eh-nee-koh)*
toilet	**el excusado** *(ehl ex-koo-'sah-doh)*
towel	**la toalla** *(lah toh-'ah-yah)*
trash	**la basura** *(lah bah-'soo-rah)*
trash basket	**el cesto de basura** *(ehl 'sehs-toh deh bah-'soo-rah)*
trashcan	**el bote de basura** *(ehl 'boh-teh deh bah-'soo-rah)*
TV	**el televisor** *(ehl teh-leh-vee-'sohr)*
urinal	**el orinal** *(ehl oh-ree-'nahl)*
vacuum cleaner	**la aspiradora** *(lah ahs-pee-rah-'doh-rah)*
washer	**la lavadora** *(lah lah-vah-'doh-rah)*
wax	**la cera** *(lah 'seh-rah)*
window	**la ventana** *(lah vehn-'tah-nah)*

Landscaping
La jardinería
(lah hahr-dee-neh-'ree-ah)

ant	**la hormiga** *(lah ohr-'mee-gah)*
ax	**el hacha** *(ehl 'ah-chah)*
bee	**la abeja** *(lah ah-'beh-hah)*
beetle	**el escarabajo** *(ehl ehs-kah-rah-'bah-hoh)*
blower	**la sopladora** *(lah soh-plah-'doh-rah)*
branches	**las ramas** *(lahs 'rah-mahs)*
broom	**la escoba** *(lah ehs-'koh-bah)*
bush	**el arbusto** *(ehl ahr-'boos-toh)*
butterfly	**la mariposa** *(lah mah-ree-'poh-sah)*
chainsaw	**la motosierra** *(lah moh-toh-see-'ehr-rah)*

channel	**el canal** *(ehl kah-'nahl)*
clippers	**las tijeras de podar** *(lahs tee-'heh-rahs deh poh-'dahr)*
cricket	**el grillo** *(ehl 'gree-yoh)*
ditch	**la zanja** *(lah 'sahn-hah)*
dragonfly	**la libébula** *(lah lee-'beh-boo-lah)*
drainage	**el drenaje** *(ehl dreh-'nah-heh)*
dumpster	**el basurero de hierro** *(ehl bah-soo-'reh-roh deh ee-'ehr-roh)*
dust	**el polvo** *(ehl 'pohl-voh)*
fence	**la cerca** *(lah 'sehr-kah)*
fertilizer	**el fertilizante** *(ehl fehr-tee-lee-'sahn-teh)*
flea	**la pulga** *(lah 'pool-gah)*
flower	**la flor** *(lah flohr)*
fly	**la mosca** *(lah 'mohs-kah)*
foliage	**el follaje** *(ehl foh-'yah-heh)*
gardener	**el jardinero/la jardinera** *(ehl hahr-dee-'neh-roh/lah hahr-dee-'neh-rah)*
grass	**el pasto** *(ehl 'pahs-toh)*
grasshopper	**el saltamontes** *(ehl sahl-tah-'mohn-tehs)*
gravel	**la grava** *(lah 'grah-vah)*
hoe	**el azadón** *(ehl ah-sah-'dohn)*
hole	**el hoyo** *(ehl 'oh-yoh)*
hornet	**el avispón** *(ehl ah-vees-'pohn)*
hose	**la manguera** *(lah mahn-'geh-rah)*
insect	**el insecto** *(ehl een-'sehk-toh)*
ladder	**la escalera** *(lah ehs-kah-'leh-rah)*
ladybug	**la mariquita** *(lah mah-ree-'kee-tah)*
land	**el terreno** *(ehl tehr-'reh-noh)*
lawn	**el césped** *(ehl 'sehs-pehd)*
lawnmower	**el cortacésped** *(ehl kohr-tah-'sehs-pehd)*
leaves	**las hojas** *(lahs 'oh-hahs)*
mosquito	**el zancudo** *(ehl sahn-'koo-doh)*
moth	**la polilla** *(lah poh-'lee-yah)*
mud	**el lodo** *(ehl 'loh-doh)*
path	**el camino** *(ehl kah-'mee-noh)*
pick	**el pico** *(ehl 'pee-koh)*
pipe	**el tubo** *(ehl 'too-boh)*
plant	**la planta** *(lah 'plahn-tah)*
poison	**el veneno** *(ehl veh-'neh-noh)*
post	**el poste** *(ehl 'pohs-teh)*
rake	**el rastrillo** *(ehl rahs-'tree-yoh)*
rock	**la piedra** *(lah pee-'eh-drah)*
sand	**la arena** *(lah ah-'reh-nah)*
seed	**la semilla** *(lah seh-'mee-yah)*

shovel	**la pala** *(lah 'pah-lah)*
slug	**la babosa** *(lah bah-'boh-sah)*
snail	**el caracol** *(ehl kah-rah-'kohl)*
soil	**la tierra** *(lah tee-'ehr-rah)*
spider	**la araña** *(lah ah-'rahn-yah)*
sprinklers	**las rociadoras** *(lahs roh-see-ah-'doh-rahs)*
trash bag	**la bolsa de basura** *(lah 'bohl-sah deh bah-'soo-rah)*
tree	**el árbol** *(ehl 'ahr-bohl)*
wasp	**la avispa** *(lah ah-'vees-pah)*
water	**el agua** *(ehl 'ah-gwah)*
weeds	**la mala hierba** *(lah 'mah-lah ee-'ehr-bah)*
wheelbarrow	**la carretilla** *(lah kahr-reh-'tee-yah)*
worm	**el gusano** *(ehl goo-'sah-noh)*

Tailoring and Dry-Cleaning
La sastrería y la tintorería
(lah sahs-treh-'ree-ah ee lah teen-toh-reh-'ree-ah)

belt	**el cinturón** *(ehl seen-too-'rohn)*
bleach	**el cloro** *(ehl 'kloh-roh)*
blouse	**la blusa** *(lah 'bloo-sah)*
boots	**las botas** *(lahs 'boh-tahs)*
bra	**el sostén** *(ehl sohs-'tehn)*
buckle	**la hebilla** *(lah eh-'bee-yah)*
button	**el botón** *(ehl boh-'tohn)*
cap	**la gorra** *(lah 'gohr-rah)*
chemicals	**los productos químicos** *(lohs proh-'dook-tohs 'kee-mee-kohs)*
clothing	**la ropa** *(lah 'roh-pah)*
collar	**el cuello** *(ehl 'kweh-yoh)*
cotton	**el algodón** *(ehl ahl-goh-'dohn)*
cuff	**el puño** *(ehl 'poon-yoh)*
detergent	**el detergente** *(ehl deh-tehr-'hehn-teh)*
dress	**el vestido** *(ehl vehs-'tee-doh)*
dryer	**la secadora** *(lah seh-kah-'doh-rah)*
fabric	**la tela** *(lah 'teh-lah)*
fashion	**la moda** *(lah 'moh-dah)*
girdle	**la faja** *(lah 'fah-hah)*
gloves	**los guantes** *(lohs 'gwahn-tehs)*
handkerchief	**el pañuelo** *(ehl pahn-yoo-'eh-loh)*
hanger	**el gancho** *(ehl 'gahn-choh)*
hat	**el sombrero** *(ehl sohm-'breh-roh)*
hem	**el dobladillo** *(ehl doh-blah-'dee-yoh)*
iron	**la plancha** *(lah 'plahn-chah)*

ironing board	la **tabla de planchar** *(lah 'tah-blah deh plahn-chahr)*
jacket	la **chaqueta** *(lah chah-'keh-tah)*
label	la **etiqueta** *(lah eh-tee-'keh-tah)*
leather	el **cuero** *(ehl 'kweh-roh)*
linen	el **lino** *(ehl 'lee-noh)*
mittens	los **mitones** *(lohs mee-'toh-nehs)*
necktie	la **corbata** *(lah kohr-'bah-tah)*
needle	la **aguja** *(lah ah-'goo-hah)*
overcoat	el **abrigo** *(ehl ah-'bree-goh)*
patch	el **remiendo** *(ehl reh-mee-'ehn-doh)*
pajamas	el **pijama** *(ehl pee-'hah-mah)*
panties	las **bragas** *(lahs 'brah-gahs)*
pants	los **pantalones** *(lohs pahn-tah-'loh-nehs)*
pattern	el **patrón** *(ehl pah-'trohn)*
pin	el **alfiler** *(ehl ahl-fee-'lehr)*
pleat	el **pliegue** *(ehl plee-'eh-geh)*
polyester	el **poliéster** *(ehl poh-lee-'ehs-tehr)*
raincoat	el **impermeable** *(ehl eem-pehr-meh-'ah-bleh)*
robe	la **bata** *(lah 'bah-tah)*
scarf	la **bufanda** *(lah boo-'fahn-dah)*
seam	la **costura** *(lah kohs-'too-rah)*
sewing machine	la **máquina de coser** *(lah 'mah-kee-nah deh koh-sehr)*
shirt	la **camisa** *(lah kah-'mee-sah)*
shorts	los **calzoncillos** *(lohs kahl-sohn-'see-yohs)*
size	la **talla** *(lah 'tah-yah)*
skirt	la **falda** *(lah 'fahl-dah)*
sleeve	la **manga** *(lah 'mahn-gah)*
slip	la **enagua** *(lah eh-'nah-gwah)*
slippers	las **zapatillas** *(lahs sah-pah-'tee-yahs)*
socks	los **calcetines** *(lohs kahl-seh-'tee-nehs)*
softener	el **suavizante** *(ehl swah-vee-'sahn-teh)*
spool	la **bobina** *(lah boh-'bee-nah)*
sportcoat	el **saco** *(ehl 'sah-koh)*
stain	la **mancha** *(lah 'mahn-chah)*
stockings	las **medias** *(lahs 'meh-dee-ahs)*
strap	la **correa** *(lah kohr-'reh-ah)*
style	el **estilo** *(ehl ehs-'tee-loh)*
suit	el **traje** *(ehl 'trah-heh)*
sweater	el **suéter** *(ehl 'sweh-tehr)*
sweatsuit	la **sudadera** *(lah soo-dah-'deh-rah)*
tennis shoes	los **tenis** *(lohs' teh-nees)*
thread	el **hilo** *(ehl 'ee-loh)*
T-shirt	la **camiseta** *(lah kah-mee-'seh-tah)*

umbrella	**el paraguas** *(ehl pah-'rah-gwahs)*
underpants	**los calzoncillos** *(lohs kahl-sohn-'see-yohs)*
underwear	**la ropa interior** *(lah 'roh-pah een-teh-ree-'ohr)*
vest	**el chaleco** *(ehl chah-'leh-koh)*
washing machine	**la lavadora** *(lah lah-vah-'doh-rah)*
wool	**la lana** *(lah 'lah-nah)*
zipper	**la bragueta** *(lah brah-'geh-tah)*

Vehicle Repair
La reparación de vehículos
(lah reh-pah-rah-see-'ohn deh veh-'ee-koo-lohs)

air	**el aire** *(ehl 'ah-ee-reh)*
alternator	**el alternador** *(ehl ahl-tehr-nah-'dohr)*
audio system	**el sistema de audio** *(ehl sees-'teh-mah deh 'aw-dee-oh)*
auto shop	**el taller de reparaciones** *(ehl tah-'yehr deh reh-pah-rah-see-'oh-nehs)*
axle	**el eje** *(ehl 'eh-heh)*
battery	**el acumulador** *(ehl ah-koo-moo-lah-'dohr)*
blinkers	**las luces intermitentes** *(lahs 'loo-sehs een-tehr-mee-'tehn-tehs)*
body	**la caja** *(lah 'kah-hah)*
bolt	**el perno** *(ehl 'pehr-noh)*
brake light	**la luz de freno** *(lah loos deh 'freh-noh)*
brakes	**los frenos** *(lohs 'freh-nohs)*
bulb	**la bombilla** *(lah bohm-'bee-yah)*
bumper	**el parachoques** *(ehl pah-rah-'choh-kehs)*
bus	**el autobús** *(ehl aw-toh-'boos)*
button	**el botón** *(ehl boh-'tohn)*
cab	**la cabina** *(lah kah-'bee-nah)*
cable	**el cable** *(ehl 'kah-bleh)*
car	**el carro** *(ehl 'kahr-roh)*
choke	**el ahogador** *(ehl ah-oh-gah-'dohr)*
circuit	**el circuito** *(ehl seer-koo-'ee-toh)*
computer	**la computadora** *(lah kohm-poo-tah-'doh-rah)*
connection	**la conexión** *(lah koh-nehk-see-'ohn)*
dashboard	**el tablero** *(ehl tah-'bleh-roh)*
dent	**la abolladura** *(lah ah-boh-yah-'doo-rah)*
door	**la puerta** *(lah 'pwehr-tah)*
drill bit	**la broca** *(lah 'broh-kah)*
drill	**el taladro** *(ehl tah-'lah-droh)*
engine	**el motor** *(ehl moh-'tohr)*
exhaust pipe	**el tubo de escape** *(ehl 'too-boh deh ehs-'kah-peh)*
fan	**el ventilador** *(ehl vehn-tee-lah-'dohr)*

fan belt	**la correa del ventilador** *(lah kohr-'reh-ah dehl vehn-tee-lah-'dohr)*
fender	**el guardabarro** *(ehl gwahr-dah-'bahr-roh)*
filter	**el filtro** *(ehl 'feel-troh)*
flat tire	**el neumático desinflado** *(ehl neh-oo-'mah-tee-koh dehs-een-'flah-doh)*
fluid	**el líquido** *(ehl 'lee-kee-doh)*
fuse	**el fusible** *(ehl foo-'see-bleh)*
garage	**el garaje** *(ehl gah-'rah-heh)*
gas	**la gasolina** *(lah gah-soh-'lee-nah)*
gas station	**la gasolinera** *(lah gah-soh-lee-'neh-rah)*
gasket	**la junta** *(lah 'hoon-tah)*
gauge	**el indicador** *(ehl een-dee-kah-'dohr)*
gears	**los cambios** *(lohs 'kahm-bee-ohs)*
glove compartment	**la guantera** *(lah gwahn-'teh-rah)*
grease	**la grasa** *(lah 'grah-sah)*
hex wrench	**la llave hexagonal** *(lah 'yah-veh ex-ah-goh-'nahl)*
hood	**la cubierta** *(lah koo-bee-'ehr-tah)*
horn	**la bocina** *(lah boh-'see-nah)*
horsepower	**el caballaje** *(ehl kah-bah-'yah-heh)*
hose	**la manguera** *(lah mahn-'geh-rah)*
hubcap	**el tapacubos** *(ehl tah-pah-'koo-bohs)*
jack	**la gata** *(lah 'gah-tah)*
jumper cables	**los cables de batería** *(lohs 'kah-blehs deh bah-teh-'ree-ah)*
lights	**las luces** *(lahs 'loo-sehs)*
lubrication	**el engrase** *(ehl ehn-'grah-seh)*
machine	**la máquina** *(lah 'mah-kee-nah)*
make	**la marca** *(lah 'mahr-kah)*
manifold	**el collector** *(ehl koh-lehk-'tohr)*
mechanic	**el mecánico/la mecánica** *(ehl meh-'kah-nee-koh/lah meh-'kah-nee-kah)*
mirror	**el espejo** *(ehl ehs-'peh-hoh)*
model	**el modelo** *(ehl moh-'deh-loh)*
motorcycle	**la motocicleta** *(lah moh-toh-see-'kleh-tah)*
muffler	**el silenciador** *(ehl see-lehn-see-ah-'dohr)*
nut	**la tuerca** *(lah 'twehr-kah)*
oil	**el aceite** *(ehl ah-'seh-ee-teh)*
oil change	**el cambio de aceite** *(ehl 'kahm-bee-oh deh ah-'seh-ee-teh)*
oil filter	**el filtro de aceite** *(ehl 'feel-troh deh ah-'seh-ee-teh)*
oil pressure	**la presión del aceite** *(lah preh-see-'ohn dehl ah-'seh-ee-teh)*
overhaul	**el ajuste completo** *(ehl ah-'hoos-teh kohm-'pleh-toh)*
part	**la pieza** *(lah pee-'eh-sah)*
pick-up	**la camioneta** *(lah kah-mee-oh-'neh-tah)*
plates	**las placas** *(lahs 'plah-kahs)*
pliers	**los alicates** *(lohs ah-lee-'kah-tehs)*

points	**los platinos** *(lohs plah-'tee-nohs)*
psi	**libras por pulgada cuadrada** *('lee-brahs pohr pool-'gah-dah kwah-'drah-dah)*
pump	**la bomba** *(lah 'bohm-bah)*
repairs	**las reparaciones** *(lahs reh-pah-rah-see-'oh-nehs)*
roof	**el techo** *(ehl 'teh-choh)*
RPM	**las revoluciones por minuto** *(lahs reh-voh-loo-see-'oh-nehs pohr mee-'noo-toh)*
scooter	**el escúter** *(ehl ehs-'koo-tehr)*
screw	**el tornillo** *(ehl tohr-'nee-yoh)*
screwdriver	**el destornillador** *(ehl dehs-tohr-nee-yah-'dohr)*
seat	**el asiento** *(ehl ah-see-'ehn-toh)*
serial number	**el número de serie** *(ehl 'noo-meh-roh deh 'seh-ree-eh)*
shock absorber	**el amortiguador** *(ehl ah-mohr-tee-gwah-'dohr)*
socket wrench	**la llave de cubo** *(lah 'yah-veh deh 'koo-boh)*
spare tire	**el neumático de repuesto** *(ehl neh-oo-'mah-tee-koh deh reh-'pwehs-toh)*
specifications	**las especificaciones** *(lahs ehs-peh-see-fee-kah-see-'oh-nehs)*
starter	**el motor de arranque** *(ehl moh-'tohr deh ahr-'rahn-keh)*
steering wheel	**el volante** *(ehl voh-'lahn-teh)*
SUV	**el vehículo deportivo utilitario** *(ehl veh-'ee-koo-loh deh-pohr-'tee-voh oo-tee-lee-'tah-ree-oh)*
switch	**el interruptor** *(ehl een-tehr-roop-'tohr)*
tachometer	**el tacómetro** *(ehl tah-'koh-meh-troh)*
throttle	**el estrangulador** *(ehl ehs-trahn-goo-lah-'dohr)*
tire	**el neumático** *(ehl neh-oo-'mah-tee-koh)*
trim	**el acabado interior** *(ehl ah-kah-'bah-doh een-teh-ree-'ohr)*
truck	**el camión** *(ehl kah-mee-'ohn)*
trunk	**la maletera** *(lah mah-leh-'teh-rah)*
tune-up	**la afinación** *(lah ah-fee-nah-see-'ohn)*
valve	**la válvula** *(lah 'vahl-voo-lah)*
van	**la furgoneta** *(lah foor-goh-'neh-tah)*
washer	**la arandela** *(lah ah-rahn-'deh-lah)*
windshield	**el parabrisas** *(ehl pah-rah-'bree-sahs)*
wire brush	**el cepillo de alambre** *(ehl seh-'pee-yoh deh ah-'lahm-breh)*
wirecutters	**los cortaalambres** *(lohs kohr-tah-ah-'lahm-brehs)*
wrench	**la llave inglesa** *(lah 'yah-veh een-'gleh-sah)*

Employer Commands

Advise	**Avise** *(ah-'vee-seh)*
Answer	**Conteste** *(kohn-'tehs-teh)*
Arrange	**Arregle** *(ahr-'reh-gleh)*
Arrive	**Llegue** *('yeh-geh)*
Ask for	**Pida** *('pee-dah)*
Begin	**Comience** *(koh-mee-'ehn-seh)*
Bend	**Doble** *('doh-bleh)*
Bring	**Traiga** *('trah-ee'gah)*
Buy	**Compre** *('kohm-preh)*
Call	**Llame** *('yah-meh)*
Calm down	**Cálmese** *('kahl-meh-seh)*
Carry	**Lleve** *('yeh-veh)*
Change	**Cambie** *('kahm-bee-eh)*
Charge	**Cargue** *('kahr-geh)*
Check	**Revise** *(reh-'vee-seh)*
Choose	**Escoja** *(ehs-'koh-hah)*
Clarify	**Aclare** *(ah-'klah-reh)*
Clean	**Limpie** *('leem-pee-eh)*
Climb	**Suba** *('soo-bah)*
Close	**Cierre** *(see-'ehr-reh)*
Come	**Venga** *('vehn-gah)*
Connect	**Conecte** *(koh'nehk-teh)*
Continue	**Siga** *('see-gah)*
Cut	**Corte** *('kohr-teh)*
Deliver	**Entregue** *(ehn-'treh-geh)*
Do	**Haga** *('ah-gah)*
Drive	**Maneje** *(mah-'neh-heh)*
Dry	**Seque** *('seh-keh)*
Eat	**Coma** *('koh-mah)*
Empty	**Vacíe** *(vah-'see-eh)*
Explain	**Explique** *(ex-'plee-keh)*
Fill	**Llene** *('yeh-neh)*
Finish	**Termine** *(tehr-'mee-neh)*
Fix	**Repare** *(reh-'pah-reh)*
Get down	**Baje** *('bah-heh)*
Get in	**Suba** *('soo-bah)*
Get	**Consiga** *(kohn-'see-gah)*
Give	**Dé** *(deh)*
Glue	**Pegue** *('peh-geh)*
Go	**Vaya** *('vah-yah)*

Have	**Tenga** *('tehn-gah)*
Help	**Ayude** *(ah-'yoo-deh)*
Hit	**Golpee** *(gohl-'peh-eh)*
Hold	**Sostenga** *(sohs-'tehn-gah)*
Hurry up	**Apúrese** *(ah-'poo-reh-seh)*
Install	**Instale** *(eens-'tah-leh)*
Learn	**Aprenda** *(ah-'prehn-dah)*
Leave	**Salga** *('sahl-gah)*
Let	**Deje** *('deh-heh)*
Listen	**Escuche** *(ehs-'koo-cheh)*
Load	**Cargue** *('kahr-geh)*
Look for	**Busque** *('boos-keh)*
Look	**Mire** *('mee-reh)*
Lower	**Baje** *('bah-heh)*
Make	**Haga** *('ah-gah)*
Measure	**Mida** *('mee-dah)*
Move	**Mueva** *('mweh-vah)*
Observe	**Observe** *(ohb-'sehr-veh)*
Open	**Abra** *('ah-brah)*
Park	**Estacione** *(ehs-tah-see-'oh-neh)*
Pass	**Pase** *('pah-seh)*
Pay	**Pague** *('pah-geh)*
Pick up	**Recoja** *(reh-'koh-hah)*
Plug in	**Enchufe** *(ehn-'choo-feh)*
Prepare	**Prepare** *(preh-'pah-reh)*
Press	**Oprima** *(oh-'pree-mah)*
Pull	**Jale** *('hah-leh)*
Push	**Empuje** *(ehm-'poo-heh)*
Put	**Ponga** *('pohn-gah)*
Put away	**Guarde** *('gwahr-deh)*
Put in	**Meta** *('meh-tah)*
Put it on	**Póngaselo** *('pohn-gah-seh-loh)*
Raise	**Levante** *(leh-'vahn-teh)*
Read	**Lea** *('leh-ah)*
Relax	**Relájese** *(reh-'lah-heh-seh)*
Remember	**Recuerde** *(reh-'kwehr-deh)*
Remove	**Saque** *('sah-keh)*
Rest	**Descanse** *(dehs-'kahn-seh)*
Return	**Regrese** *(reh-'greh-seh)*
Run	**Corra** *('kohr-rah)*
See	**Vea** *('veh-hah)*
Sell	**Venda** *('vehn-dah)*

Send	**Mande** *('mahn-deh)*
Shake	**Sacuda** *(sah-'koo-dah)*
Ship	**Envíe** *(ehn-'vee-eh)*
Show	**Muestre** *('mwehs-treh)*
Sign	**Firme** *('feer-meh)*
Sit down	**Siéntese** *(see-'ehn-teh-seh)*
Speak	**Hable** *('ah-bleh)*
Spray	**Rocíe** *(roh-'see-eh)*
Stand up	**Levántese** *(leh-'vahn-teh-seh)*
Stay	**Quédese** *('kwee-deh-seh)*
Stop	**Pare** *('pah-reh)*
Study	**Estudie** *(ehs-'too-dee-eh)*
Take away	**Quite** *('kee-teh)*
Take off	**Quítese** *('kee-teh-seh)*
Take	**Tome** *('toh-meh)*
Teach	**Enseñe** *(ehn-'sehn-yeh)*
Tell	**Diga** *('dee-gah)*
Throw out	**Tire** *('tee-reh)*
Tie	**Amarre** *(ah-'mahr-reh)*
Touch	**Toque** *('toh-keh)*
Translate	**Traduzca** *(trah-'doos-kah)*
Try	**Trate** *('trah-teh)*
Turn it off	**Apague** *(ah-'pah-geh)*
Turn it on	**Prenda** *('prehn-dah)*
Turn	**Voltée** *(vohl-'teh-eh)*
Unload	**Descargue** *(dehs-'kahr-geh)*
Unplug	**Desenchufe** *(dehs-ehn-'choo-feh)*
Use	**Use** *('oo-seh)*
Verify	**Verifique** *(veh-ree-'fee-keh)*
Wait	**Espere** *(ehs-'peh-reh)*
Walk	**Camine** *(kah-'mee-neh)*
Wash	**Lave** *('lah-veh)*
Weigh	**Pese** *('peh-seh)*
Work	**Trabaje** *(trah-'bah-heh)*
Write	**Escriba** *(ehs-'kree-bah)*

Answers to Let's Practice!

1:     television   tomorrow   vertical   donkey
       problem   favorite   friend   excellent

2:     1. *¿Cómo está?*   *Bien. ¿Y usted?*
       2. *Gracias.*   *De nada.*
       3. *¿Entiende?*   *No, lo siento.*
       4. *Hasta luego.*   *Adiós.*
       5. *¿Qué pasa?*   *Sin novedad.*

3:     A.
       1. *el libro*   book
       2. *la mesa*   table
       3. *el trabajo*   job, work
       B.
       1. *la casa*   *las casas*
       2. *el baño*   *los baños*
       3. *el papel*   *los papeles*

4:     A.
       1. *treinta, cuarenta, <u>cincuenta</u>, sesenta*
       2. *primero, segundo, tercero, <u>cuarto</u>*
       3. *<u>cuatro</u>, cinco, seis, siete*
       4. I'm eighth.   <u>*Soy el octavo.*</u>
       5. It's red.   <u>*Es rojo.*</u>
       B.
       1. *alto*   *bajo*
       2. *malo*   *bueno*
       3. *bonito*   *feo*
       4. *rico*   *pobre*
       5. *frío*   *caliente*
       6. *largo*   *corto*
       7. *grande*   *chico*

5:     1. *La silla amarilla.*   *Las sillas amarillas.*
       2. *Una señora alta.*   *Unas señoras altas.*
       3. *La oficina nueva.*   *Las oficinas nuevas.*
       4. *Un piso sucio.*   *Unos pisos sucios.*
       5. *El trabajo excelente.*   *Los trabajos excelentes.*

6: A.

    1. *Ella*   *su*

    2. *Yo*   *mi*

    3. *Nosotros*   *nuestro*

  B.

    1. *¿Cuántos años tiene usted?*   How old are you?

    2. *¿Quién es el presidente?*   Who is the President?

    3. *¿Cuándo es Thanksgiving?*   When is Thanksgiving?

7: A.

    1. *enero, <u>febrero</u>, marzo, <u>abril</u>, mayo, <u>junio</u>, julio, <u>agosto</u>*

    2. *<u>lunes</u>, martes, <u>miércoles</u>, jueves, <u>viernes</u>, sábado, <u>domingo</u>*

  B.

    1. *¿Qué hora es?*   *Son las tres y media.*

    2. *¿Listo?*   *Sí, en seguida.*

    3. *¿Qué tiempo hace?*   *Está lloviendo.*

    4. *¿Cuál es la fecha?*   *El diez de junio.*

    5. *¿Dónde está Paulo?*   *Está afuera.*

8: 1. *Yo <u>estoy</u> bien.*

    2. *El libro <u>está</u> en la mesa.*

    3. *Los libros <u>son</u> importantes.*

    4. *Nosotros <u>somos</u> amigos.*

    5. *La niña <u>es</u> americana.*

9: A.

    1. They are cold.   *<u>Tienen frío.</u>*

    2. I don't have the job.   *<u>No tengo el trabajo.</u>*

    3. We are hungry.   *<u>Tenemos hambre.</u>*

  B.

    1. *Favor de <u>manejar</u> el carro.*

    2. *No <u>leer</u> el libro aquí.*

    3. *Favor de <u>hablar</u> español.*

    4. *Favor de <u>comer</u> en el restaurante.*

    5. *No <u>escuchar</u> la música.*

10: 1. *trabajar*   *<u>trabajando</u>*   **(Sentences will vary.)**

     2. *hablar*   *<u>hablando</u>*   **(Sentences will vary.)**

     3. *consultar*   *<u>consultando</u>*   **(Sentences will vary.)**

11: A. **Answers will vary.**
   B.

We need...	*Necesitamos...*
1. carpenters	*carpinteros*
2. your signature	*su firma*
3. the job	*el trabajo*

   C.
   Pedro is the new boss.
   Who is the new manager?
   I am the company owner.
   D. **Answers will vary.**

12: A.

1. schedule	*el horario*	**(Answers will vary.)**
2. contract	*el contrato*	**(Answers will vary.)**
3. tools	*las herramientas*	**(Answers will vary.)**

   B-C-D-E: **Answers will vary.**

13: A.

1. Workman's Compensation	*la compensación laboral*
2. medical insurance	*el seguro médico*
3. overtime pay	*los pagos por horas extra*

   B.

1. *TRABAJAR* (to work)	*trabaja*	She works a lot.
2. *MANDAR* (to send)	*mandamos*	We send the money.
3. *REGRESAR* (to return)	*regresan*	They return late.
4. *ESCRIBIR* (to write)	*escribo*	I write the information
5. *USAR* (to use)	*usa*	He uses the pen.

   C.
   1. *Conteste* la pregunta.
   2. *Firme* su nombre.
   3. *Traiga* la silla.
   D.

1. *hablar*	*escuchar*
2. *contestar*	*preguntar*
3. *escribir*	*leer*
4. *despedir*	*contratar*
5. *recibir*	*dar*

14: A.

tercero

cuarto

quinto

sexto

séptimo

octavo

noveno

décimo

B.

Translate these useful terms:

1. warehouse	*el almacén*
2. factory	*la fábrica*
3. shopping center	*el centro comercial*
4. business	*el negocio*
5. sales department	*el departamento de ventas*
6. office	*la oficina*

C.

1. *estudiante*	*universidad*
2. *dinero*	*banco*
3. *medicina*	*hospital*
4. *hamburguesa*	*restaurante*
5. *tigre*	*zoológico*
6. *carro*	*gasolinera*

15: A.

1. *escalones, escaleras, ascensor*

2. *horario, calendario, planificador*

3. *archivo, armario, gabinete*

4. *copiadora, computadora, impresora*

5. *lata, botella, caja*

6. *sofá, silla, asiento*

7. *borrador, lapicero, lápiz*

B. **Answers will vary.**

16: A.
  1. Press the button!   *¡Oprima el botón!*
  2. Fill the box!   *¡Llene la caja!*
  3. Check the meter!   *¡Revise el medidor!*
  B.
  1. *máquina*   *motor*
  2. *barrera*   *divisor*
  3. *balde*   *tina*
  4. *cable*   *alambre*
  5. *cierre*   *broche*
  6. *palo*   *estaca*

17: A.
  1. technical   *técnico*
  2. mechanical   *mecánico*
  3. electrical   *eléctrico*
  B.
  1. *el estéreo*   stereo
  2. *la fotocopiadora*   photocopier
  3. *el escáner*   scanner
  4. *el micrófono*   microphone
  5. *la cámara*   camera
  C. **Answers will vary.**

18: A.
  1. *gasolina*   *combustible*
  2. *soga*   *cordón*
  3. *hierro*   *acero*
  4. *lana*   *algodón*
  5. *brocha*   *pintura*
  6. *grava*   *arena*
  7. *taladro*   *broca*
  B.
  1. *el destornillador*
  2. *la motosierra*
  3. *el trapeador*

19: A.
  1. *desenchufar*   *enchufar*   **(Answers will vary)**
  2. *vaciar*   *llenar*   **(Answers will vary)**
  3. *jalar*   *empujar*   **(Answers will vary)**

4. *apagar*   <u>*prender, encender*</u>   **(Answers will vary)**

5. *cargar*   <u>*descargar*</u>   **(Answers will vary)**

B. **Answers will vary.**

20: A.

1. Pay attention!   <u>*¡Preste atención!*</u>

2. This is what I want.   <u>*Esto es lo que quiero.*</u>

3. That's it!   <u>*¡Eso es!*</u>

B. Join these opposites:

1. *algo*   *nada*

2. *alguién*   *nadie*

3. *mismo*   *diferente*

C. **Answers will vary.**

21: A.

1. *el modelo, el patrón, <u>el diseño</u>*

2. *el documento, la página, <u>la hoja</u>*

3. *el reglamento, la regla, <u>la ley</u>*

B.

1. *Tratamos de proveer servicio excelente.*

2. *Use la contraseña autorizada.*

3. *Vamos a practicar y repasar.*

22: **Answers will vary.**

23: A.

1. ¼   *un cuarto*

2. 7 mi.   *siete millas*

3. 100°   *cien grados*

4. 5 oz.   *cinco onzas*

5. ½   *una mitad*

6. 25%   *veinticinco por ciento*

7. 3 lbs.   *tres libras*

8. 12 in.   *doce pulgadas*

B.

1. *el balde*

2. *la jarra*

3. *la botella*

4. *quince*

5. *cuatro*

6. *siete*

C. **Answers will vary.**

24: A.

1. *Asegúrese de apagar la máquina.*
2. *Dígales que hay un problema.*
3. *Favor de no estacionar allí.*
4. *Puede traer los lentes de sol.*
5. *Póngase la camisa de manga larga.*
6. *Al principio la compañía era chica.*

B. **Answers will vary.**

25: A.

1. It's dangerous to touch the machine.
2. I can mix the two materials.
3. It's important to lock the door.
4. You should review the lesson.
5. I want to learn more Spanish.

B.

1. *¿Trató usted?*	*Sí, yo traté.*
2. *¿Comió usted?*	*Sí, yo comí.*
1. *¿Estudió usted?*	*Sí, yo estudié.*
2. *¿Subió usted?*	*Sí, yo subí.*
3. *¿Taladró usted?*	*Sí, yo taladré.*
4. *¿Aprendió usted?*	*Sí, yo aprendí.*
5. *¿Fue usted?*	*Sí, yo fui.*

26: A.

1. *la fuerza*	*la potencia*
2. *el perno*	*la tuerca*
3. *el rasgón*	*la rotura*
4. *el ruído*	*el sonido*
5. *el jabón*	*el detergente*
6. *la chispa*	*la llama*
7. *el tamaño*	*la medida*
8. *el polvo*	*la tierra*

B.

1. *desconectar*	disconnect	*conectar*
2. *desactivar*	disactivate	*activar*
3. *desenchufar*	unplug	*enchufar*

27:   A. **Answers will vary.**
      B.
      1. *incompleto*
      2. *irresponsable*
      3. *incapaz*
      4. *deshonesto*
      5. *irrespetuoso*
      C.
      1. *el lenguaje sucio*
      2. *la arma de fuego*
      3. *la orden de corte*

28:   A.
      1. priority
      2. correction
      3. punctual
      4. limitation
      5. apathetic
      6. diarrhea
      7. ambulance
      8. nausea
      B. *relajarse, <u>blasfemar</u>, reconocer, <u>chismear</u>, repasar, <u>mentir</u>, compartir*
      C. **Answers will vary.**
      D.
      1. *¡Todos tienen que trabajar juntos!*
      2. *Hay buen esfuerzo.*
      3. *Creo que debe buscar ayuda.*

29:   A. **Answers will vary.**
      B.
      1. *torcido*
      2. *cadena*
      3. *celoso*
      C. **Answers will vary.**

30: A.
1. to come (*venir*) *Venga*
2. to throw away (*tirar*) *Tire*
3. to drink (*beber*) *Beba*
4. to bring (*traer*) *Traiga*
5. to help (*ayudar*) *Ayude*

B.
1. *Lleve la caja, por favor.* Please carry the box.
2. *Haga el trabajo, por favor.* Please do the job.
3. *Prenda la máquina, por favor.* Please turn on the machine.

C.
1. Give *Dé*
2. Send *Mande*
3. Follow *Siga*
4. Look for *Busque*
5. Tell *Diga*
6. Call *Llame*

D.
1. *contestar* (to answer) in Spanish *Contestaba en español.*
2. *desenchufar* (to unplug) computer *Desenchufaba la computadora.*
3. *ir* (to go) to work late *Iba al trabajo tarde.*
4. *aprender* (to learn) a lot *Aprendía mucho.*
5. *obedecer* (to obey) the boss *Obedecía el jefe.*

31: A.
1. *suma* *cantidad*
2. *etiqueta* *marca*
3. *dueño* *gerente*
4. *flete* *carga*
5. *factura* *recibo*

B.
1. *¿Venden Uds.?* *Sí, vendemos.*
2. *¿Instalan Uds.?* *Sí, instalamos.*
3. *¿Compran Uds.?* *Sí, compramos.*
4. *¿Construyen Uds.?* *Sí, construímos.*
5. *¿Invierten Uds.?* *Sí, invertimos.*

32: 1. *principio, propósito, razón*
2. *efectivo, crédito, cheque*
3. *correo, entrega, envío*
4. *pagado, gratuito, incluído*
5. *consumidora, compradora, cliente*
6. *revista, periódico, artículo*

33: A.
> *¿Aló, está Antonio? Es muy urgente.*
< *No, lo siento. ¿Quiere dejar un mensaje?*
> *Sí, gracias. Me llamo Sr. Miller, y estoy llamando sobre un problema en la oficina.*
B.
1. *Lea el <u>informe</u>, por favor.*
2. *No creo que es <u>peor</u>.*
3. *¡Venga a la <u>cena</u>!*
4. *Ella no <u>trabaja</u> aquí.*
5. *Voy a <u>explicar</u> todo.*
C.
1. *Han visto las ganancias.*
2. *Miramos al promedio en la cuenta.*
3. *Tiene una llamada de la clienta.*

34: **Answers will vary.**

35: **Answers will vary.**

36: A.
1. *<u>¿Los está vendiendo Ud.?</u>*
2. *<u>¿La ha vendido Ud.?</u>*
3. *<u>¿Lo venderá Ud.?</u>*
4. *<u>¿Las vende Ud.?</u>*
5. *<u>¿La vendía Ud.?</u>*
B.

1. *Ella quiere saber.*	*<u>Díga**le**</u>.*
2. *Ellos quieren saber.*	*<u>Díga**les**</u>.*
3. *Nosotros queremos saber.*	*<u>Díga**nos**</u>.*

C.

1. <u>to spend</u>	***<u>gastar</u>***
I'm spending	*Estoy gastando*
I spend	*Gasto*
I will spend	*Gastaré*
I spent	*Gasté*
I have spent	*He gastado*
2. <u>to save</u>	***<u>ahorrar</u>***
I'm saving	*Estoy ahorrando*
I save	*Ahorro*
I will save	*Ahorraré*
I saved	*Ahorré*
I used to save	*Ahorraba*
I have saved	*He ahorrado*

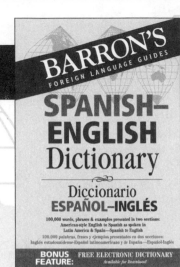

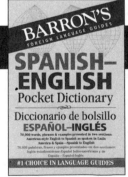